IMAGES of America

CIVIL RIGHTS IN ST. LOUIS

On the Cover: Pictured here is a 1963 Jefferson Bank demonstration. (Courtesy of the St. Louis Mercantile Library, University of Missouri–St. Louis.)

IMAGES
of America

CIVIL RIGHTS IN ST. LOUIS

Dr. John A. Wright Sr., Dr. John A. Wright Jr.,
and Dr. Curtis A. Wright Sr.,
Foreword by Gwen Moore

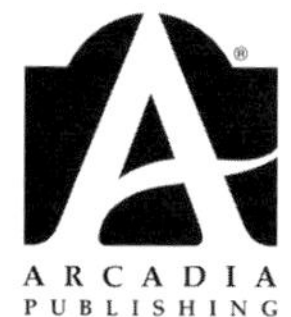

ISBN 978-1-4671-0719-8

Published by Arcadia Publishing
Charleston, South Carolina

Printed in the United States of America

Library of Congress Control Number: 2021935796

For all general information, please contact Arcadia Publishing:
Telephone 843-853-2070
Fax 843-853-0044
E-mail sales@arcadiapublishing.com
For customer service and orders:
Toll-Free 1-888-313-2665

Visit us on the Internet at www.arcadiapublishing.com

This book is dedicated to the children of the Wright family—John Wright III, Anastasia Wright, Chloi Wright, Haley Landre, Clayton Wright, Curtis Wright Jr., Caleb Wright, Ezana Wright, and Isabella Wright—with the hope they will live to see our community achieve the true meaning of brotherhood and sisterhood.

Contents

Foreword

As a curator at the Missouri Historical Society, I have a long-standing acquaintance with and admiration for the prolific work of Dr. John A. Wright. The dean of historians of the local African American experience, his wide-ranging histories are a starting point for anyone seeking to know more about the black past. The many books he has penned over several decades have informed my own work and substantially added to my knowledge of the diverse stories that comprise the trials and triumphs of African American St. Louis. I can safely say that Dr. Wright has done more to popularize our understanding of our common regional past than any other single author. From his early study of the desegregation of all-black schools to his groundbreaking *Discovering African-American St. Louis: A Guide to Historic Sites* followed by his community histories of Kinloch, the Ville, Carondelet, and Florissant, he has unearthed valuable stories and heightened our appreciation of the jewels in our midst.

Civil Rights in St. Louis promises to add to his solid body of work and his equally solid reputation. With his co-authors John A. Wright Jr. and Curtis Wright Sr., we are provided with a comprehensive guide to the roles of black St. Louisans in the fight for citizenship rights. Beginning in 1821 and progressing to the present, the authors delve deep, chronicling 200 years of the many achievements of African Americans as they forged a path toward equality. This wide swath of history is an essential introduction to the freedom movement, bringing to light little-known facts and providing fresh insights into the better known. There is much in this richly detailed book, but it is digestible due to the Wrights' easy writing style that will appeal to the serious scholar as well as the general reader.

Civil Rights in St. Louis is a welcome addition to the literature on civil rights, highlighting the people, places, and events that comprise the long struggle for racial justice. It is a valuable reference that deserves a place on everyone's bookshelf. It will certainly be on mine.

Gwen Moore
Curator of Urban Landscapes and Community Identity

Acknowledgments

Special thanks go to Charles Brown and the St. Louis Mercantile Library for their support and assistance, without which this project would not have gotten off the ground. A special thank-you goes to Angel Prohaska, title manager at Arcadia Publishing, for her expert guidance when requested and prodding when needed.

We want to thank the following individuals and institutions that provided assistance enabling the authors to accomplish this project: Jacqueline Ervin Creighton, Arnold Parks, Tishaura Jones, Art McCoy, Shirly Brown, Ella Brown, Zaki Baruti, Hazel Erby, Robert Tabscott, Andrew Thersing, Richard Hudlin, Michael Willis, James Vincent, Carondelet Historical Society, First Baptist Church of Kinloch, Archdiocese of St. Louis, St. Louis Public Schools, Central Baptist Church, Missouri Historical Society, St. Louis Landmarks Association, Washington University Archives, City of St. Louis, Urban League of Metropolitan St. Louis, Ferguson-Florissant School District, St. Louis University Archives, Elijah P. Lovejoy Society, City of Creve Coeur, St. Louis Argus, 1984 Kinloch History Project, St. Louis Public Library, National Archives, Murphy-Blair Housing Project, Lincoln University Archives, National Baseball Hall of Fame, and the Western Manuscript Collection, University of Missouri–St. Louis (UMSL).

The authors are also deeply grateful to the following individuals who are no longer with us for providing and making a great deal of the information and material presented in this book available for this project: Margaret Bush Wilson, Frankie Freeman, Billie Crumpton, Doris Westley, Georgia Rusan, Vivian Dreer, Betty Wheeler, Tim Person, Fr. Patrick Malloy, Geraldine Johnson, Samella Woodson, and Nathan Young.

Introduction

The idea for this book was conceived during the protest that erupted with the killing of Michael Brown. The national attention the protest drew to the St. Louis area sparked interest in how such an event could take place. So great was the interest that a federal investigation took place to learn why so many were so upset. For many, the struggle within the African American community went unnoticed. The history of black people fighting for justice in St. Louis had been unknown to many. Sadly, many people are unaware of the omitted American history of St. Louis and the civil rights movement.

With so much material to cover, it would be an impossible task to place everything into one book. This is simply an attempt to introduce readers to the ongoing struggle of African Americans who are in pursuit of America's promise. The writers are well aware that a great deal of very important information was written with limitations. We hope that the reader will be inspired to continue on and further their knowledge with additional research.

Since the city of St. Louis's founding, black people have struggled for freedom and equality. The settling of the St. Louis region by colonial European powers has ties to the American Civil Rights Movement. When Missouri was petitioning for statehood, free people of color fought language proposed in the state constitution that would have banned them from living in the state. The ongoing fight for equality remained on many fronts thereafter, which included freedom from slavery, equal protection under the law, and equality in housing, education, healthcare, and employment.

Black people did not fight alone in their struggle for equality. People of several ethnic groups stood with African Americans in their pursuit of justice. Men like Elijah Lovejoy, Roswell Fields, Henry Blow, Arnold Krekel, and Rev. William Elliot are just a few of the unsung figures who helped advance the cause of civil rights for black people in St. Louis

African Americans have played a vital role in shaping the history of St. Louis and the United States. Litigation like the Dred Scott decision, the Lloyd Gaines suit for education, *Shelly* v. *Kraemer*, *Jones* v. *Mayer*, *Arnold* v. *St. Louis Housing Authority*, *United States of America* v. *City of Blackjack* for housing, and *Green* v. *McDonnel Douglas* for employment discrimination are just a few examples.

The fight has not been without costs. Lives have been lost, properties have been destroyed, and neighborhoods have suffered from neglect and abandonment, yet advancements continue. We have the city's first black female mayor. Several black men and women have been elected to public office in both St. Louis City and the surrounding areas of St. Louis County. Despite these changes, systemic racism remains a problem that continues to spark unrest. St. Louis has one of the highest rates of police violence against its citizens nationally. Healthcare in heavily black populated areas is lacking. Many areas heavily populated by people of color are considered food deserts because of the lack of access to supermarkets and fresh fruits and vegetables. Housing conditions for many people of color are poor and inadequate. Neighborhood schools are closing at an alarming rate. Unemployment remains disproportionately higher in the black community. With all these factors in motion, it is hard to imagine the area maintaining its present course without an eruption born out of frustration.

For societal change to occur, society must educate its people. With true education, an understanding develops that will bring about the changes needed to move forward. We hope this book will provide some insight, knowledge, and a desire for meaningful change. If it does, our efforts will have been rewarded.

One

The Peculiar Institution

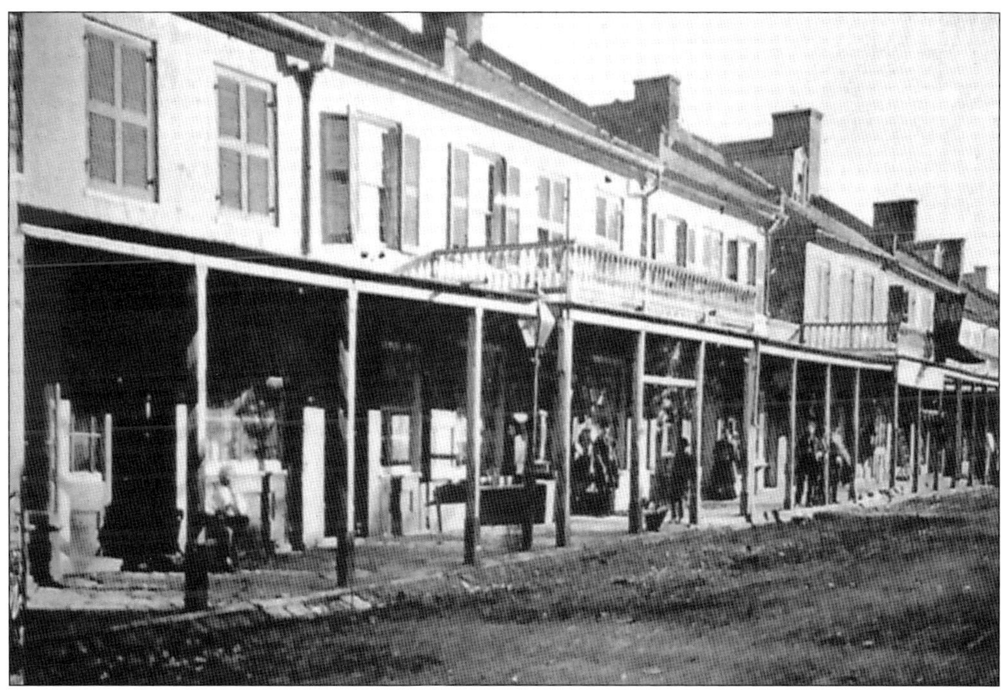

In 1821, Missouri's Second Compromise was signed in the state's first capital, St. Charles. The first constitution submitted to the US Congress for approval forbade the immigration of free blacks into the state. Congress objected strongly to this provision, as did protesting free blacks and their white supporters. A second constitution was adopted, prohibiting Missouri from depriving citizens of other states (such as free blacks) of their rights. (Courtesy of the St. Charles Historical Society.)

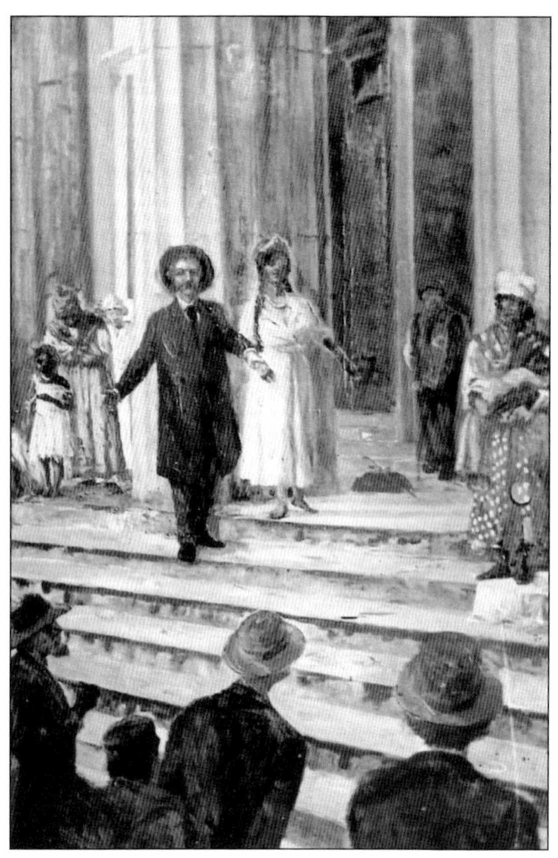

The Old Court House served as the site for civil court proceedings until 1930. Numerous public gatherings took place there, including public auctions. In addition to other property being auctioned, human beings were traded as slaves on the steps of the courthouse until 1861. At that time, antislavery demonstrations created such a disruption, it was believed to have been the last year slave auctions took place. (Left, courtesy of the St. Louis Mercantile Library, UMSL; below, courtesy of the Missouri Historical Society.)

SHERIFF'S SALE.

John Warburton and others, vs. Robert Taylor.

Attachment in the St. Louis Circuit Court.

Whereas, on the 14th day of April, 1845, an order was made in the above entitled cause, by the Hon. John M. Krum, Judge of the 8th Judicial Circuit of the State of Missouri, ordering and directing the undersigned, Sheriff of the County of St. Louis, to sell the property attached by virtue of the writ of attachment in this case, in the manner prescribed by law, which said property is described as follows, to wit:

1 Negro woman, named AMERICA, aged about 25 years, and her child, aged about 18 months.

Also, twin negro boys, aged about 5 years, named FRANK and WILLEY.

Now, therefore, I, the said Sheriff, will, on *Monday*, the 25th day of August, inst., between the hours of nine and five o'clock, of that day, at the east front door of the Court house, in the City and County of St. Louis, State of Missouri, sell the said attached property above described, to the highest bidder, for cash, in pursuance of said order.

WILLIAM MILBURN, Sheriff.

St. Louis, Aug. 13, 1845.

REPORTER PRESS, ST. LOUIS.

B. M. LYNCH.

NO. 100 Locust street, between Fourth and Fifth, St. Louis, Mo. Being permanently located for the purchase of negroes, will always pay the highest market value.

He will also buy and sell on commission, having a suitable yard for their accommodation.

☞ Particular attention paid to the selecting of homes for favorite servants.

☞ Negroes for sale at all times. oct19—d&w

The 1858 St. Louis directory listed two slave traders: Corbin Thompson at 3 South Sixth Street and Bernard Lynch at 100 Locast Street. In his advertising, Thompson claimed his slave pens had "a high and healthy location with ample room." Lynch engaged in the slave trade for many years. When he outgrew an earlier facility at Fifth and Myrtle Streets, he purchased the Locust Street site. (Courtesy of St. Louis Public Library.)

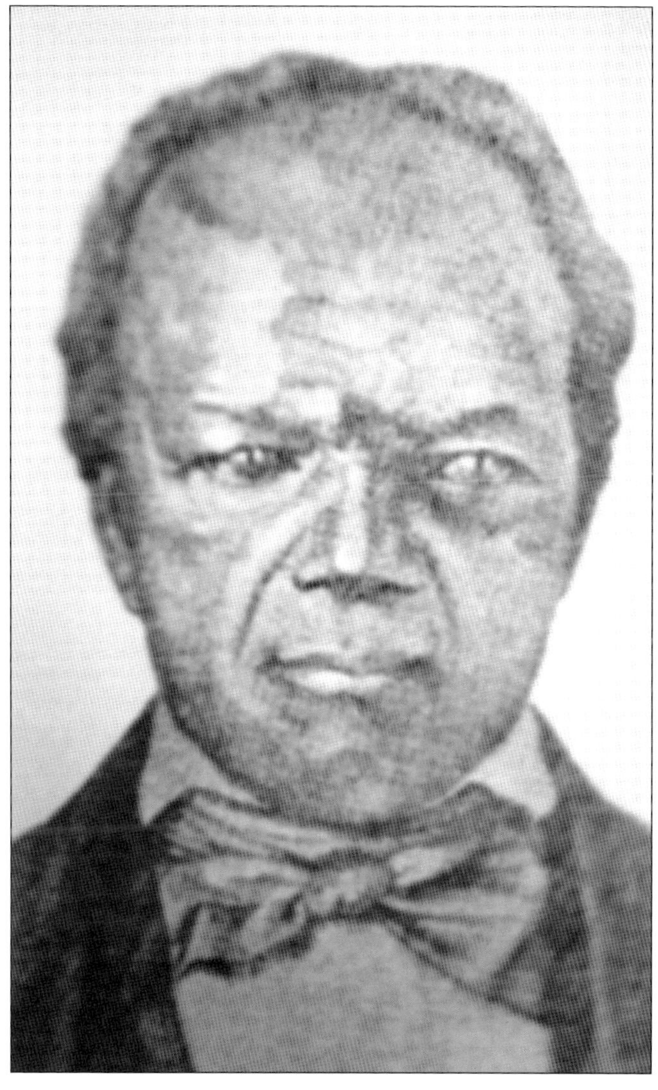

There were many famous African Americans in St. Louis before the Civil War. One was John Berry Meachum, founder of First Baptist Church. He owned a barrow factory where 20 slaves were employed. After purchasing slaves, Meachum would allow them to work to pay him back. Both he and his wife were supporters of the Underground Railroad. (Courtesy of Central Baptist Church.)

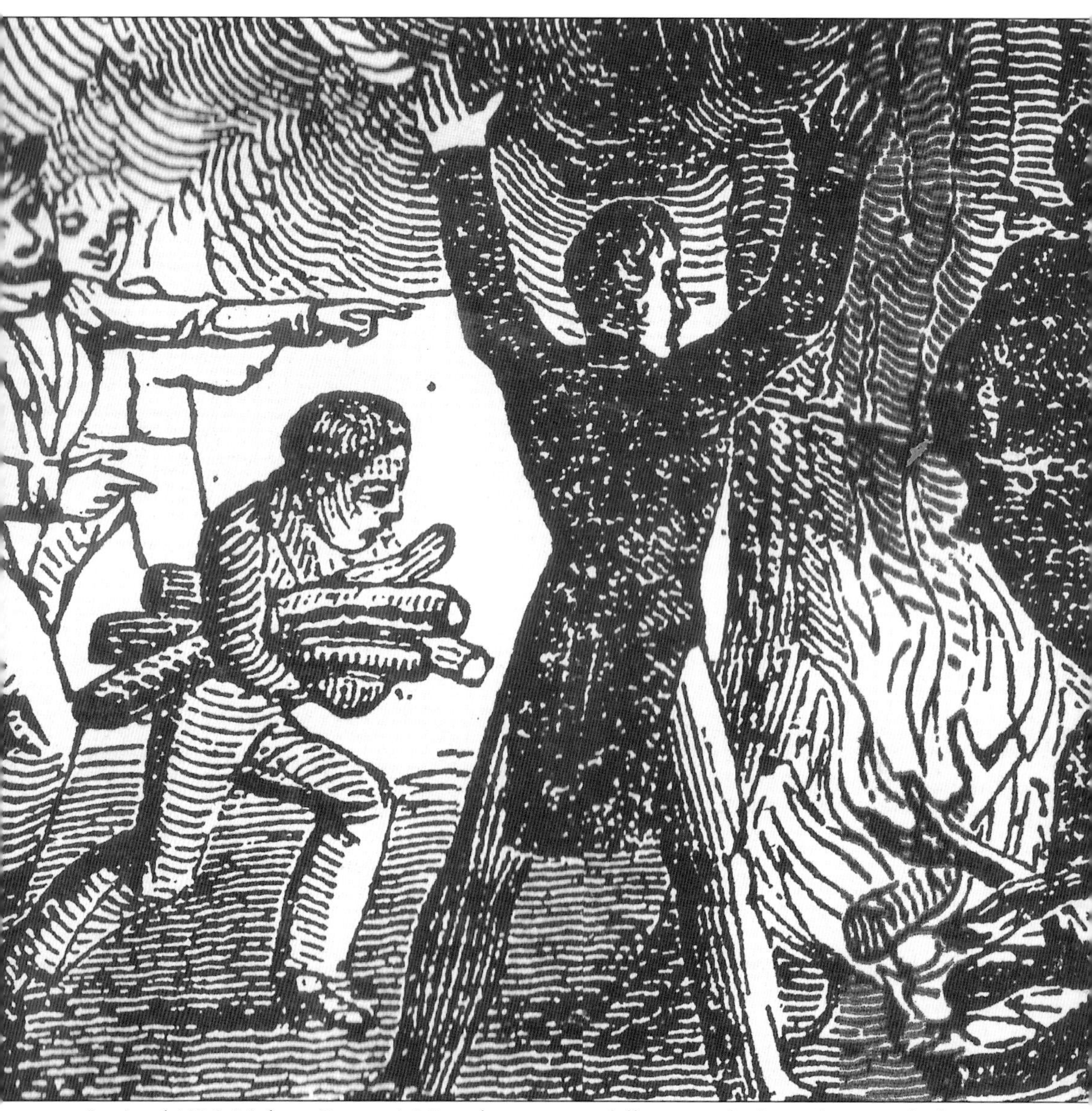

In April 1836, Mulatto Francis McIntosh was wrongfully accused of interfering with the arrest of two boatmen. After being taken into custody, McIntosh was told he would serve five years in prison. McIntosh panicked, stabbed one officer to death, and seriously injured another. He was

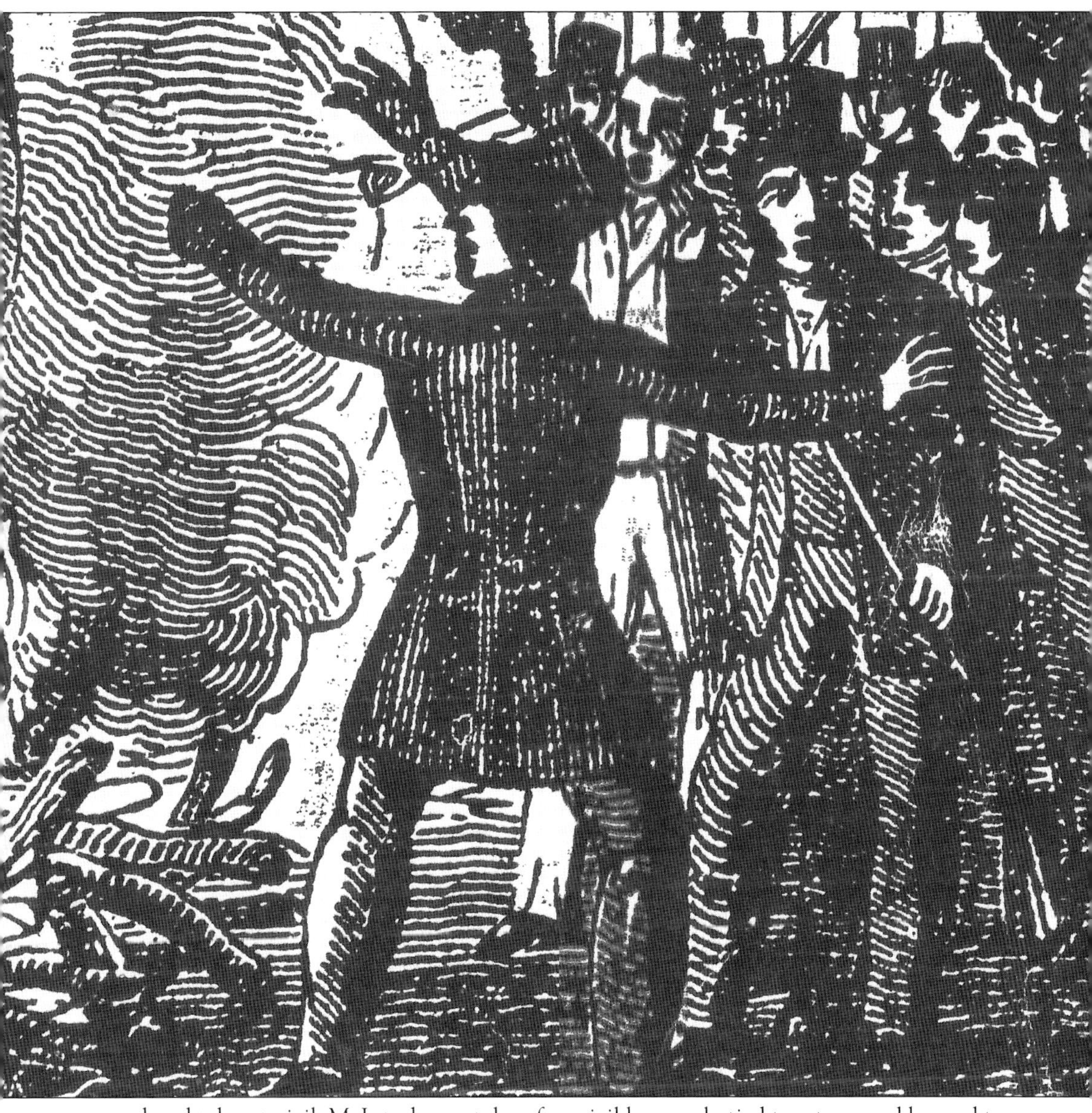

captured and taken to jail. McIntosh was taken from jail by a mob, tied to a tree, and burned to death. (Courtesy of Robert Tabscott.)

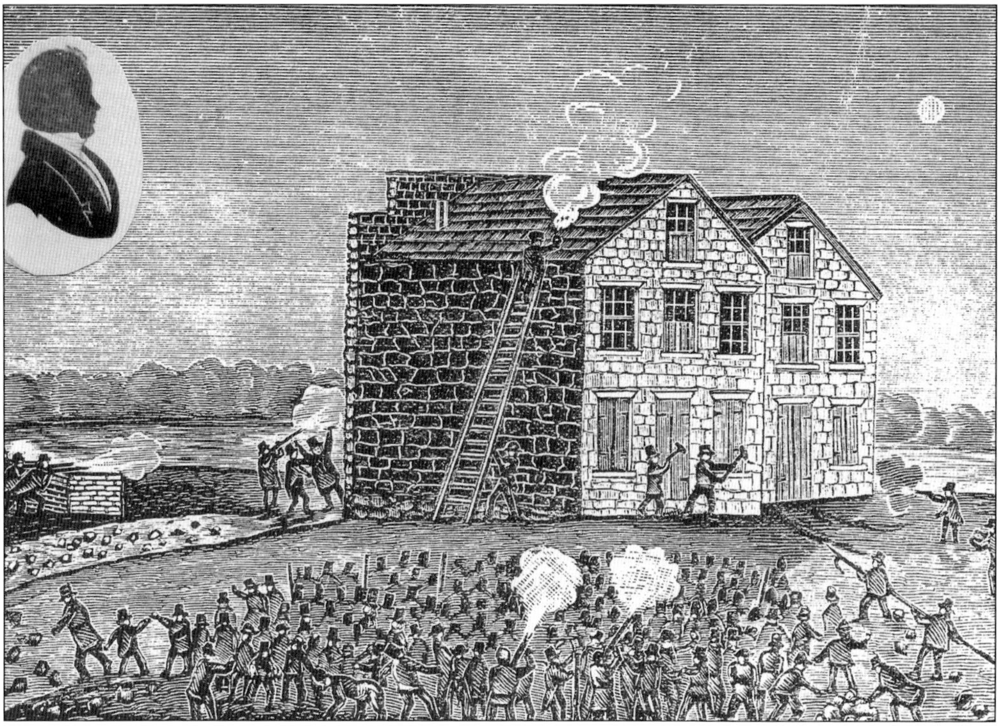

One of the strong opponents of slavery was the Rev. Elijah Parish Lovejoy, editor of the Presbyterian newspaper the *St. Louis Observer.* Lovejoy used his newspaper to publish a detailed account of the Francis McIntosh tragedy. He was forced to move to Alton, Illinois, where he was later killed in this warehouse, becoming "Freedom's First Martyr." (Courtesy of Central Baptist Church.)

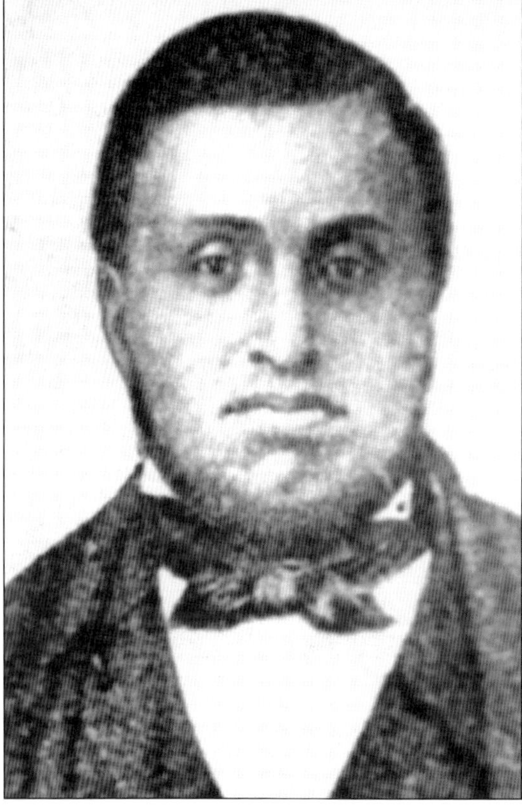

John Anderson was present the night of November 7, 1837, when Rev. Elijah Lovejoy was killed by a pro-slave mob in Alton. Anderson was a typesetter for Lovejoy, and many felt his experience with Lovejoy prepared him for his work as pastor of the Second Baptist Church. Before the Civil War, Anderson spoke out against slavery and drew crowds of whites to hear him preach. (Courtesy of Central Baptist Church.)

Pictured with his daughter is Peter Hudlin, a conductor of the underground railroad. In his home on the 1400 block of Thirteenth Street, Hudlin housed and fed runaway slaves, providing them a place to rest in his basement until nightfall. He would then crate the runaways and take them across the river to another underground station near Alton, Illinois. (Courtesy of Richard A. Hudlin.)

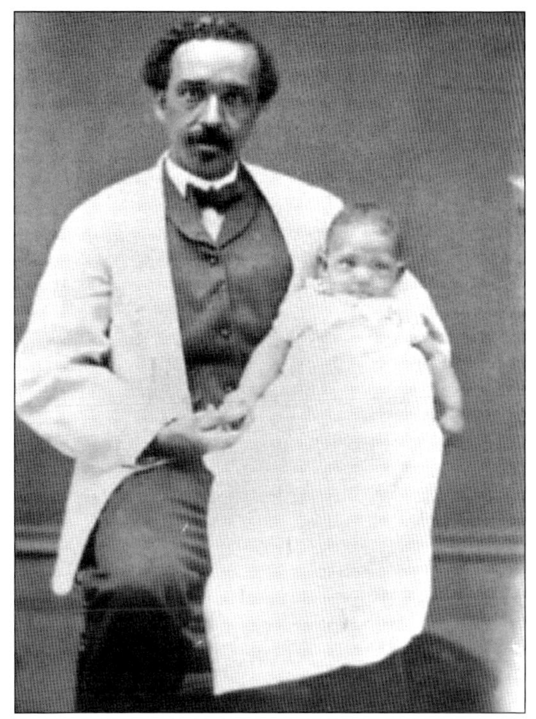

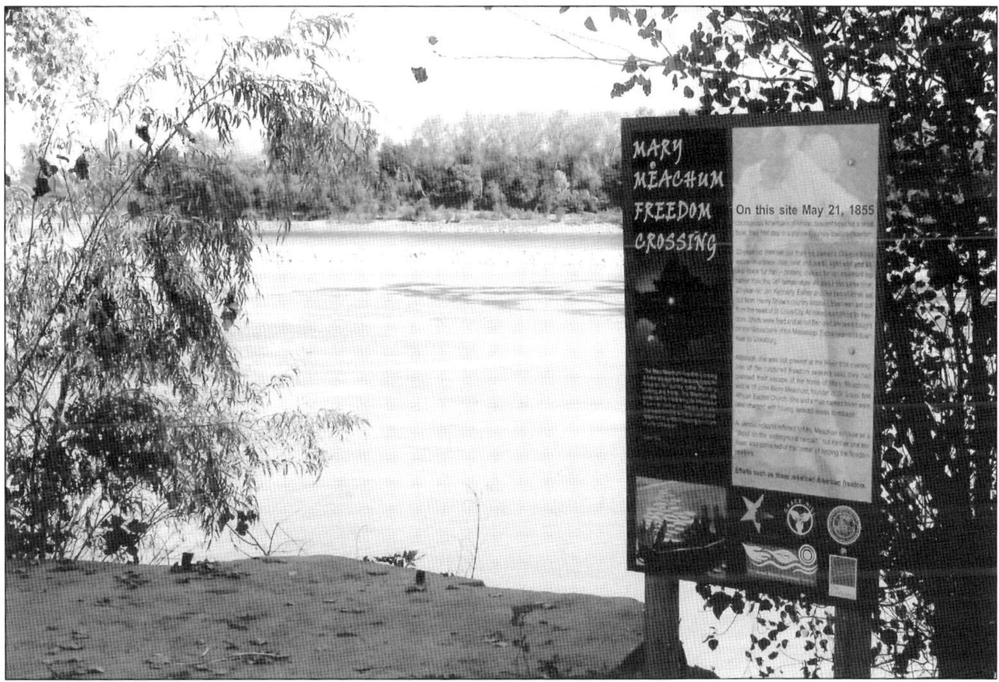

On November 1, 2001, Mary Meachum Freedom Crossing became the first site in Missouri to be accepted in the National Underground Railroad Network to Freedom. Located on the banks of the Mississippi River, the site can be found 500 feet north of the Merchants Bridge. On this site, courageous African Americans boarded a small boat to escape to freedom on May 21, 1855. (Photograph by John A. Wright Sr.)

25 DOLLARS REWARD.

Ranaway from Franklinville Farm, on the 23d Inst. a negro boy, called Frederick Sams, born in the state of Georgia: he is about 17 years old, five feet high, short wool, black complexion, knock-kneed, he has a small scar on the forehead, and an other on his chin near the lip, and some marks of the whip on his back.—He had on and took with him one Buffaloe robe marked in the centre, Fred. Bissells—one *Blanket, an old hat,* short brown great coat, blue roundabout with red coller and cuffs which likely he will tear off—three pair of old trowsers, one leather, one brown and one gray twilled kersey, two pair old socks, one blue the other white, a pair of course shoes, red flannel shirt, his apperance is slovenly.

It is expected he is lurking about the neighborhood of Florisant or St. Louis. Whoever will take up said boy and lodge him in St. Louis goal, or deliver him at my farm 8 miles north of St. Louis, shall receive the above reward and reasonable expences.

DAN'L. BISSELL.

Franklinville Farm Jan. 7.

There were always slaves who refused to accept their status and ran away. These slaves deprived their masters of their investment and the economic gain they could expect from it. To make matters worse and add insult to injury, the runaway slave usually carried away some of his owner's property. Owners often placed advertisements in the paper that carried a description of their runaway slaves. (Courtesy of Andrew Theising.)

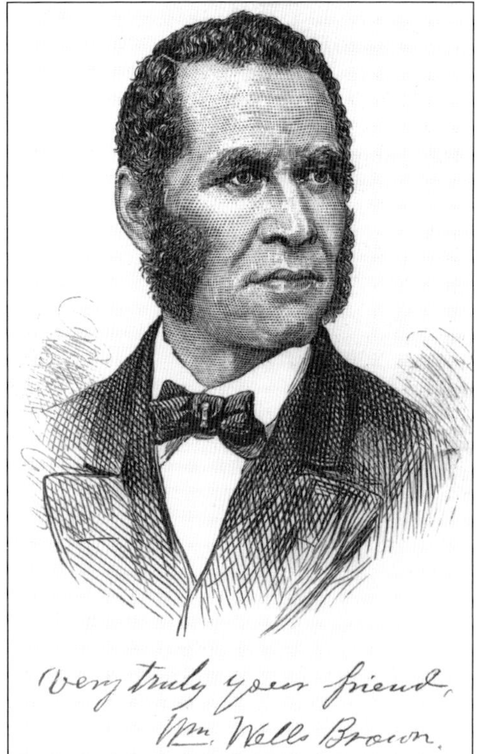

William Wells Brown was born a slave in Kentucky in 1817. He moved to the St. Louis area with his master's family. Brown was hired out to at least 10 different employers. Employer James Walker gave Brown the task of preparing slaves for sale to the "negro pens" of New Orleans. Brown later escaped and became a conductor on the Underground Railroad. He later became one of America's first black authors. (Courtesy of the St. Louis Mercantile Library, UMSL.)

FOR SAINT LOUIS!

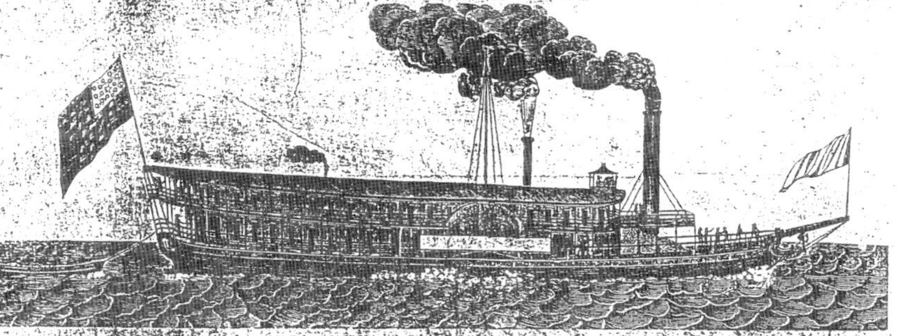

The Regular Steam Packet

EAGLE!

THE undersigned, having chartered the above Steam-boat, for the purpose of accommodating all the citizens of ALTON, and the vicinity, who may wish to see the

Four Negroes Executed,

At St. Louis, on *FRIDAY NEXT*, would inform the public that the Boat will leave this place at SEVEN o'clock, A. M., and St. Louis at about FOUR, P. M., so as to reach home the same evening.

The Boat will be repaired and fitted up for the occasion, and every attention will be paid to the comfort of Passengers.

FARE FOR THE TRIP TO ST. LOUIS & BACK

ONLY $1 50!!!

The Negroes are to be hung on the point of *Duncan's Island*, just below St. Louis. The Boat will drop alongside, so that ALL CAN SEE WITHOUT DIFFICULTY.

For Passage, apply to

W. A. Wentworth,
P. M. Pinckard.

ALTON, JULY 7, 1841

On July 9, 1841, approximately 75 percent of St. Louis came out to watch the execution of four black men. They were charged with the murder of two white bank tellers, bank robbery, and arson. None testified in their defense. Despite their attorney's objections, they all were found guilty and hanged. Their decapitated heads were placed on display in Corse's Drug Store. (Courtesy of the Elijah P. Lovejoy Society.)

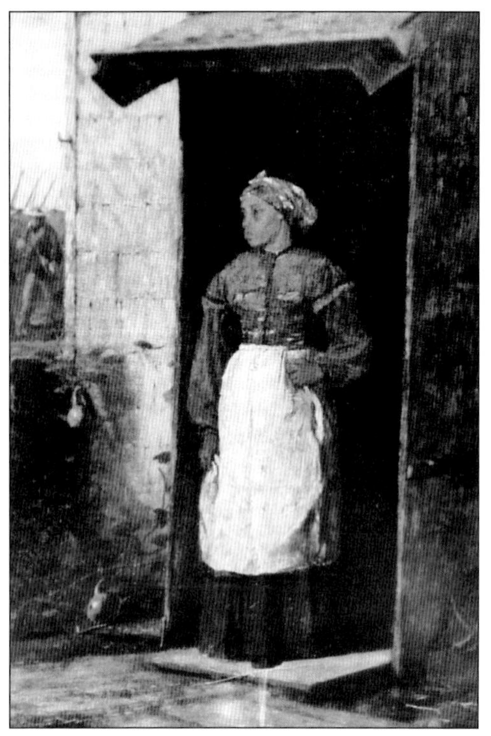

In 1850, fourteen-year-old Celia was purchased by Robert Newsom, a Missouri farmer. For the next five years, she was repeatedly and cruelly molested by Newsom and bore him two children. In 1853, Celia fought back and killed Newsom. She soon found herself on trial and sentenced to be hanged by the Missouri Supreme Court after she gave birth to her baby. This unrelated later painting by Winslow Homer is sometimes called *At the Cabin Door*. (Courtesy of John A. Wright Sr.)

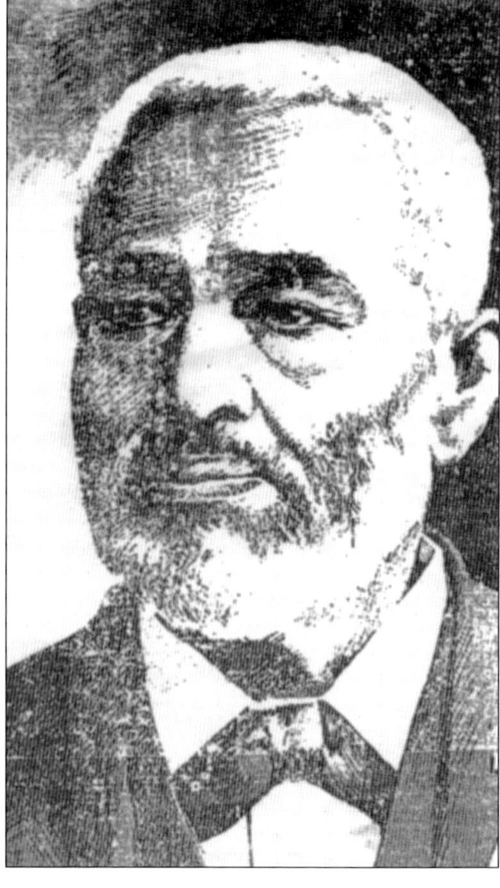

Moses Dickson was one of the men who created the secret organization Knights of Liberty. The Knights sought to enlist a slave army for an insurrection to end slavery. When the Civil War began, the men suspended their plans and agreed to organize and fight with the Union forces. They also agreed to support the Underground Railroad. (Courtesy of John A. Wright Sr.)

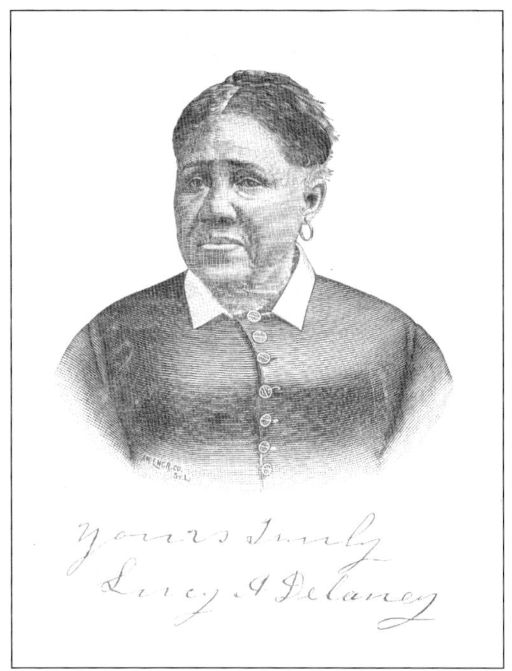

In her autobiography, *From the Darkness Cometh the Light or Struggles for Freedom*, Lucy Delaney describes her life in bondage and her mother's successful legal action to win her freedom. Her prominent St. Louis attorney Edward Bates successfully won the case for Delaney's freedom, based on evidence that she was the legitimate daughter of a free woman of color. Delaney became a skilled seamstress. (Courtesy of the St. Louis Mercantile Library, UMSL.)

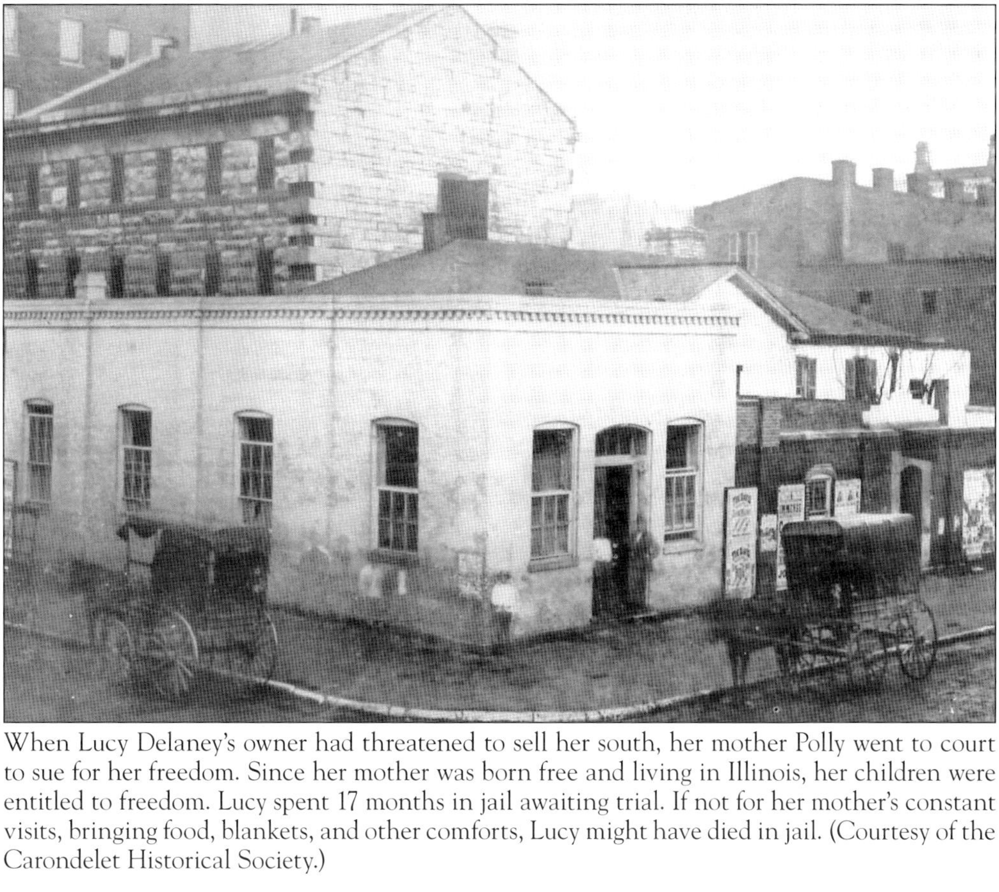

When Lucy Delaney's owner had threatened to sell her south, her mother Polly went to court to sue for her freedom. Since her mother was born free and living in Illinois, her children were entitled to freedom. Lucy spent 17 months in jail awaiting trial. If not for her mother's constant visits, bringing food, blankets, and other comforts, Lucy might have died in jail. (Courtesy of the Carondelet Historical Society.)

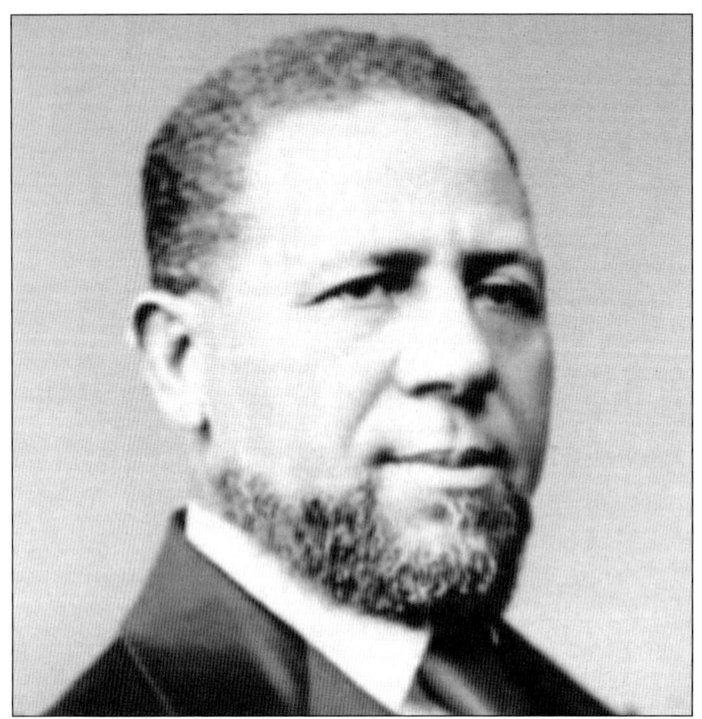

While serving as pastor of the AME Church on Seventh Street and Washington Avenue in 1852, Hiram Revels created a clandestine school to teach reading and writing to slaves and free blacks. During Reconstruction, Revels moved south to Mississippi, becoming the first African American to serve in the US Congress. He was selected by the Mississippi legislature to fill the seat that had been occupied by Jefferson Davis. (Courtesy of the National Archives.)

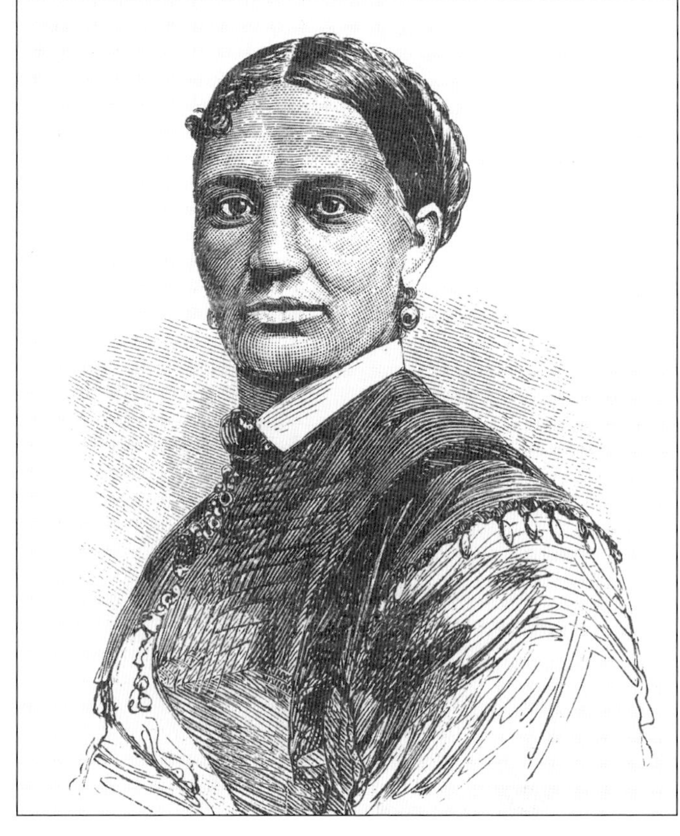

Elizabeth Keckley, who worked in the White House, was born in slavery. She came to St. Louis, where she was hired out to assist the family as a seamstress. With the help of some of her patrons, she was able to purchase her freedom. She became active at First Baptist Church, where she taught children to read and write under the guise of teaching sewing. (Courtesy of the St. Louis Mercantile Library, UMSL.)

Several individuals of mixed ancestry were able to have a great deal of success at the founding of the city. The whiter an individual looked, the greater their possibilities. John Audubon, the naturalist and artist who spent time in St. Louis in 1843, was accepted without question. Jacques Clamorgan, a businessman, was able to move about with great ease. Clamorgan held the title to a considerable amount of land in Missouri and Arkansas, where he established a rope factory. He bought slaves, and one became his mistress. He had children with several women. In his will, he placed his mistress Esther in charge of their welfare. (Right, courtesy of James Vincent; below, courtesy of the St. Louis Mercantile Library, UMSL.)

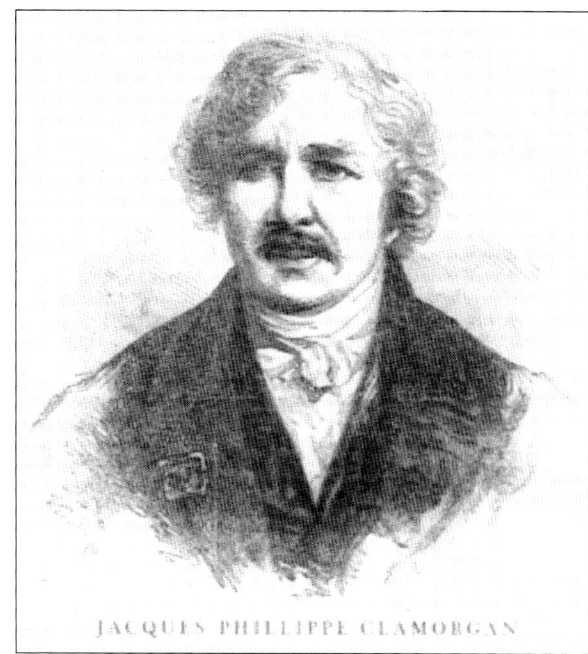

JACQUES PHILLIPPE CLAMORGAN

TITLE PAPERS

OF

THE CLAMORGAN GRANT,

OF

536,904 ARPENS OF ALLUVIAL LANDS

IN

MISSOURI AND ARKANSAS.

NEW-YORK:
PRINTED BY T. SNOWDEN, 58 WALL STREET.

1837.

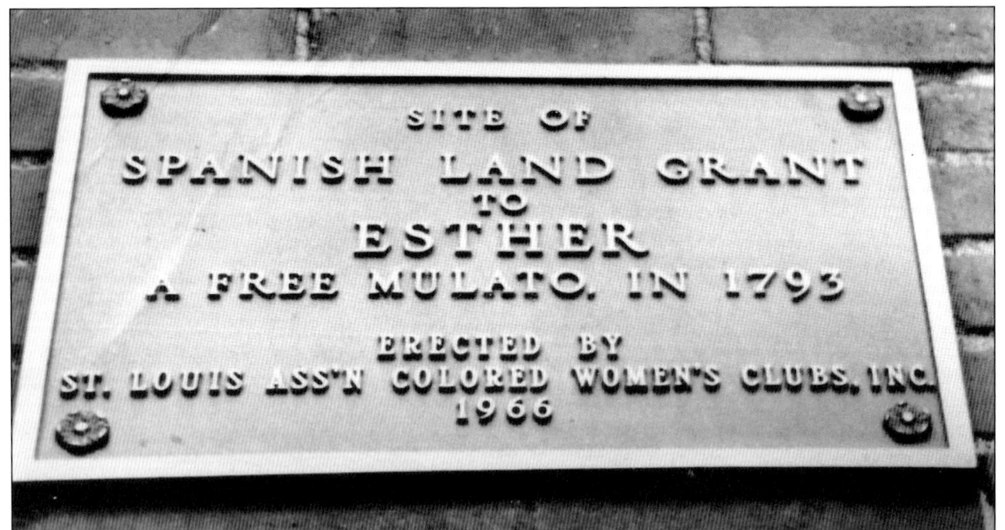

Several blacks owned land and property in the village's early beginning. The exact number is unknown. Esther, a former slave of Clamorgan, petitioned Spain in 1793 and received a land grant at 725 North Second Street. Another black woman, Jeanette Forchet, owned property on Church Street. She and her husband received one of the original lots in the common fields of St. Louis. (Courtesy of John A. Wright Sr.)

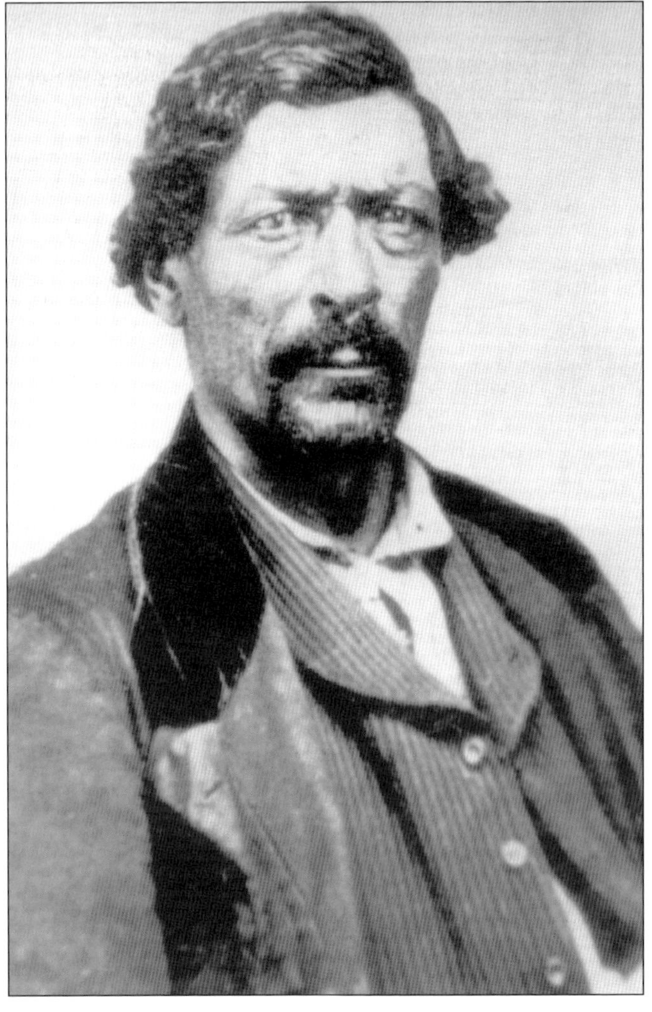

Several free blacks, such as James Beckwourth, made history. Beckwourth joined Gen. William Ashley's fur trapping expedition, which took him up the Mississippi River and to the Rocky Mountains. During his travels, he was adopted by the Crow Indians, and in time assumed the role of chief. In April 1850, he discovered an important passage through the Sierra Nevada range that now bears his name. (Courtesy of the St. Louis Mercantile Library, UMSL.)

Dred Scott was a slave who lived in St. Louis. He was taken to live in free territories. Upon his return to St. Louis, he sued for freedom for himself and his family. He took his case to the US Supreme Court without success. After the trial was over, ownership was transferred to his original owner, who set him free. This drawing is from *Frank Leslie's Illustrated Newspaper*, June 27, 1857. (Courtesy of John A. Wright Sr.)

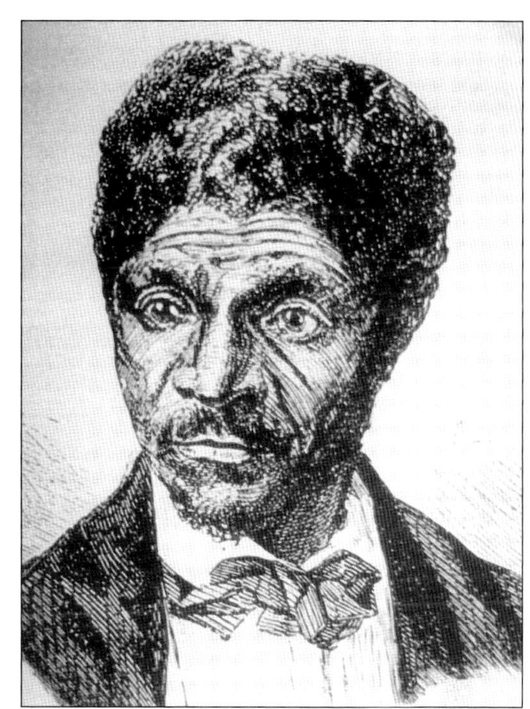

The Scotts had two daughters, Lizzie and Eliza. Eliza was born in 1838 on a steamboat in the Mississippi River on free waters in northern territory. Lizzie was born in 1845 in Jefferson Barracks, Missouri. The courts maintained that if an enslaved person were transported to a free state or territory, that person became free, even if they returned to a slave state. This drawing is from *Frank Leslie's Illustrated Newspaper*, June 27, 1857. (Courtesy of John A. Wright Sr.)

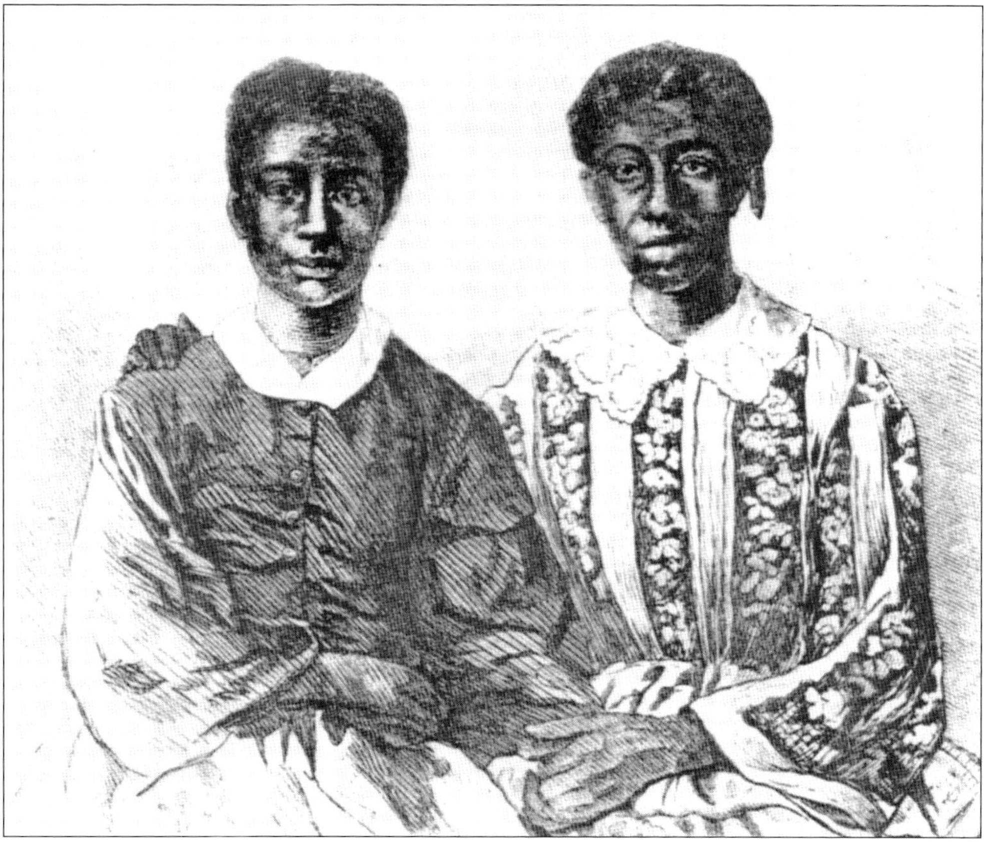

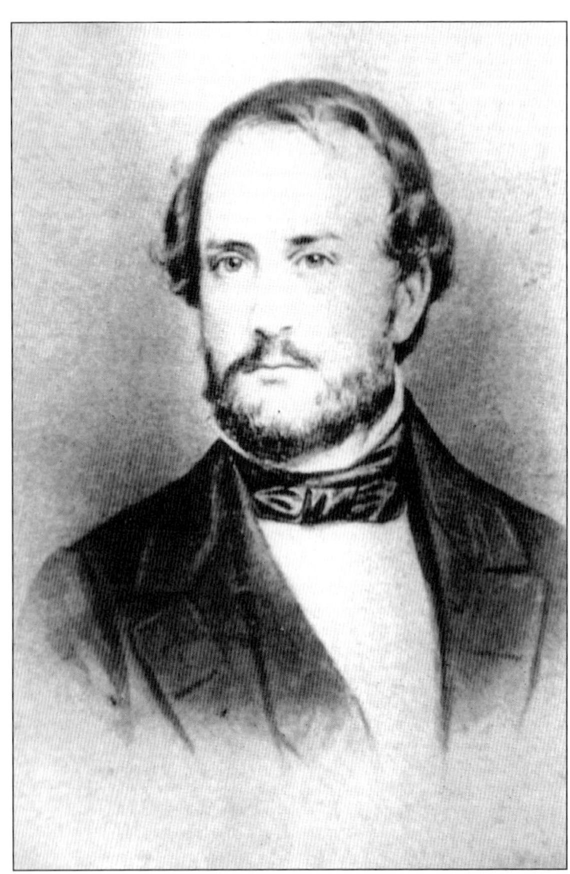

After the Missouri lower court ruled against the Scotts, St. Louis attorney Roswell Fields brought a suit on their behalf in federal court. Fields accused John Sanford of illegally assaulting, holding, and imprisoning Dred Scott, a citizen of Missouri. As anticipated, the case was lost, then taken to the US Supreme Court, where the Scotts again lost. (Courtesy of the Eugene Field House and St. Louis Toy Museum.)

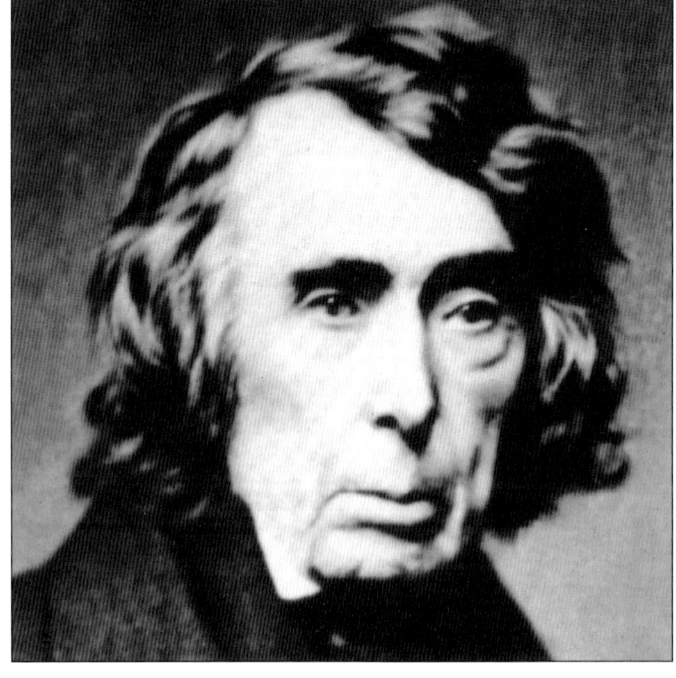

In 1851, the Supreme Court declared that a slave was not a citizen and dismissed the Scott case. Speaking for the majority, Justice Roger B. Taney wrote, "slaves had no rights which white men are bound to, and that the Negro might justly and lawfully be reduced to slavery for his benefit." This decision was a contributing factor to the Civil War. (Courtesy of the National Archives.)

Two

THE CIVIL WAR AND RECONSTRUCTION

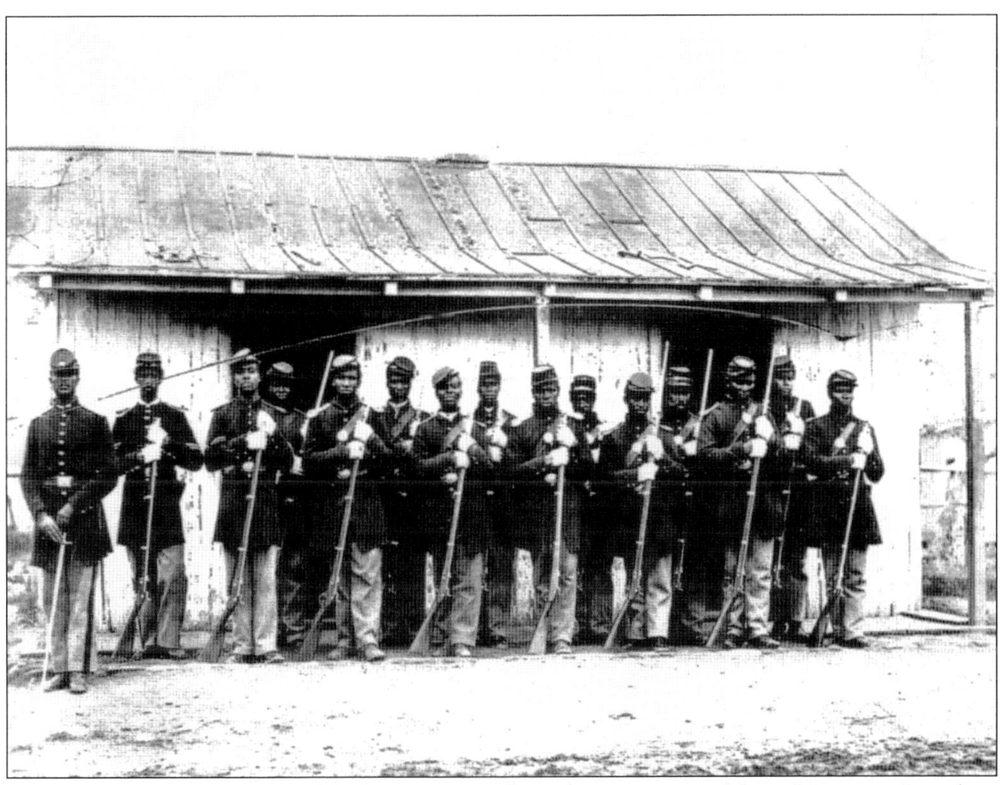

When the Civil War began, blacks were not allowed to serve as soldiers. However, President Lincoln realized they were needed to save the Union. On March 26, 1863, Lincoln wrote to Andrew Jackson, his successor, "To not avail ourselves of this force is very important if not indispensable." The Union army began recruiting its first black Missouri regiment in June 1863 at Schofield Barracks in St. Louis. (Courtesy of the National Archives.)

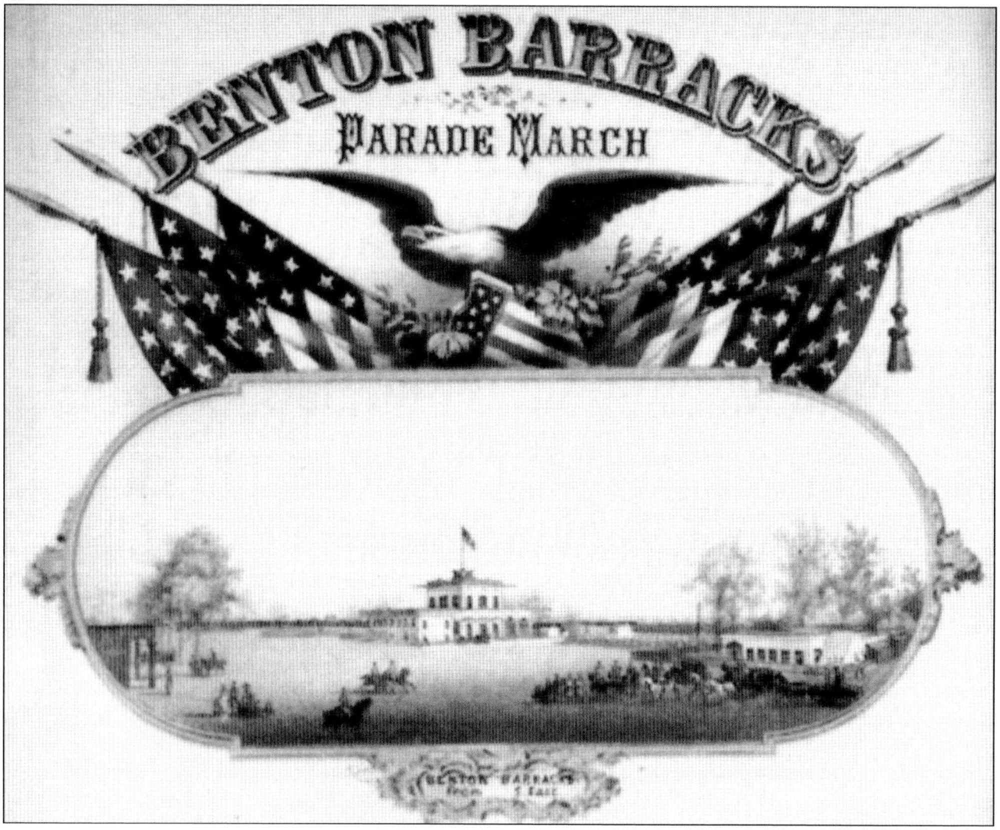

BENTON BARRACKS

PARADE MARCH

The first black soldiers during the Civil War were mustered in at Benton Barracks in December 1863. Benton Barracks was more than a military encampment. Schools were organized by the Christian Commission to teach reading and spelling skills formerly denied by law to slaves. The barracks also served as a camp for refugee slaves. (Courtesy of the St. Louis Mercantile Library, UMSL.)

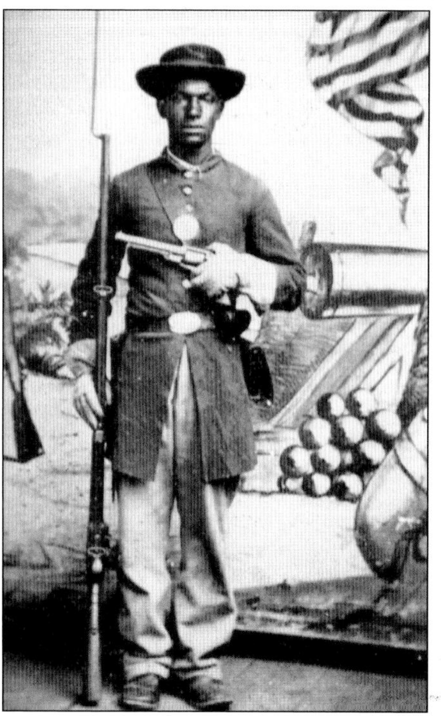

The black soldiers slowly gained the respect of at least some white St. Louisans. On January 17, 1864, a conductor objected to a black soldier riding on board rather than on the platform. The conductor insisted that he move or leave the car. Rather than leave their comrade, all the soldiers left the car in a group. The civilians applauded their collective action. (Courtesy of the National Archives.)

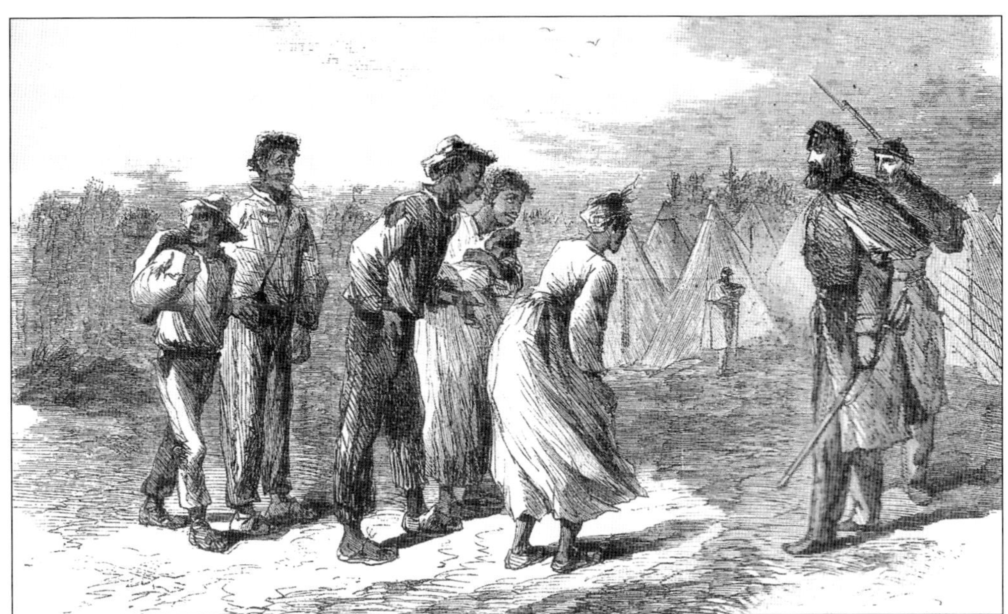

Not all troops at Benton Barracks experienced good treatment from the government. It was reported that over 100 men died at the barracks. Many had been recruited throughout the state during an inclement season. They were thinly clad, hatless, shoeless, and without food. A number suffered amputations because of frozen feet and hands. Some died of exposure. (Courtesy of the National Archives.)

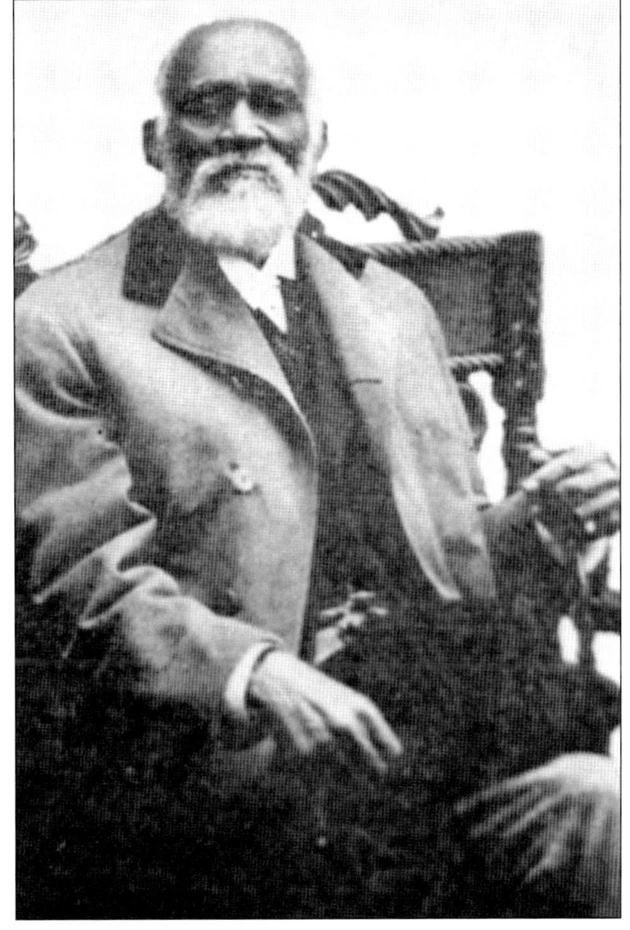

Charlton Tandy was one of the first volunteers to answer the governor's call when General Price and Confederate soldiers invaded the state. Tandy enlisted in Company B of the state militia as a private. Tandy became a captain of Tandy's St. Louis Guard, a state militia composed of black volunteers recruited by him. He held this position until the end of the war. (Courtesy of John A. Wright Sr.)

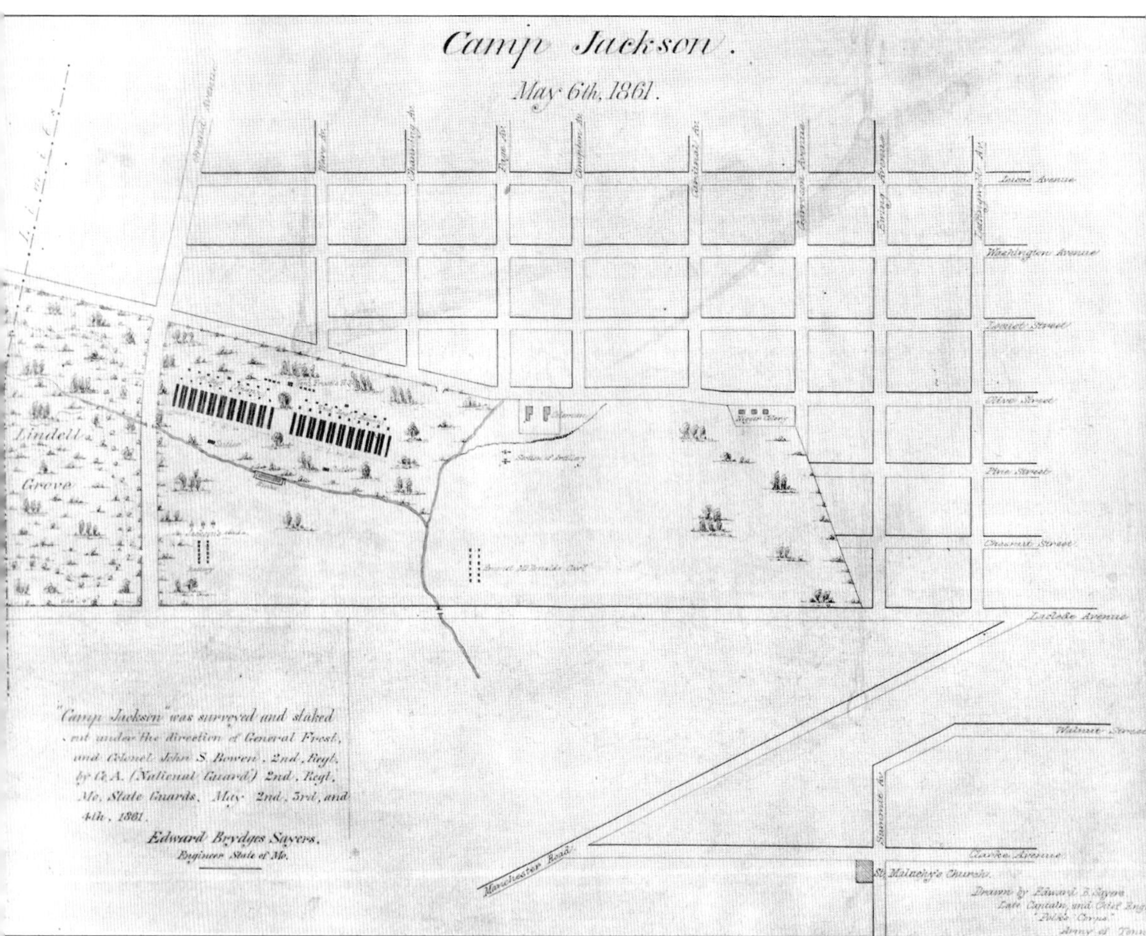

During the Civil War, Missouri remained a slave state loyal to the Union. Camp Jackson, pictured here, was bounded roughly by Garrison Avenue on the east, Olive Street on the north, Grand Avenue on the west, and Laclede Avenue. It was considered pro-Confederate. The small parcel of land in the northeast corner of the camp was called "Nigger Colony" and was used to house African Americans. The camp was named for pro-Confederate governor Claiborne Fox Jackson. In May 1861, in anticipation of possible disturbance or antislavery agitation, the police board, composed of Southern sympathizers, prohibited blacks from holding evening church services or meetings without a policeman present and set a 10:00 p.m. curfew. Free blacks were ordered to leave the city by April 24, 1861. The capture of Camp Jackson was considered by many a turning point in the Civil War. (Courtesy of the St. Louis Mercantile Library, UMSL.)

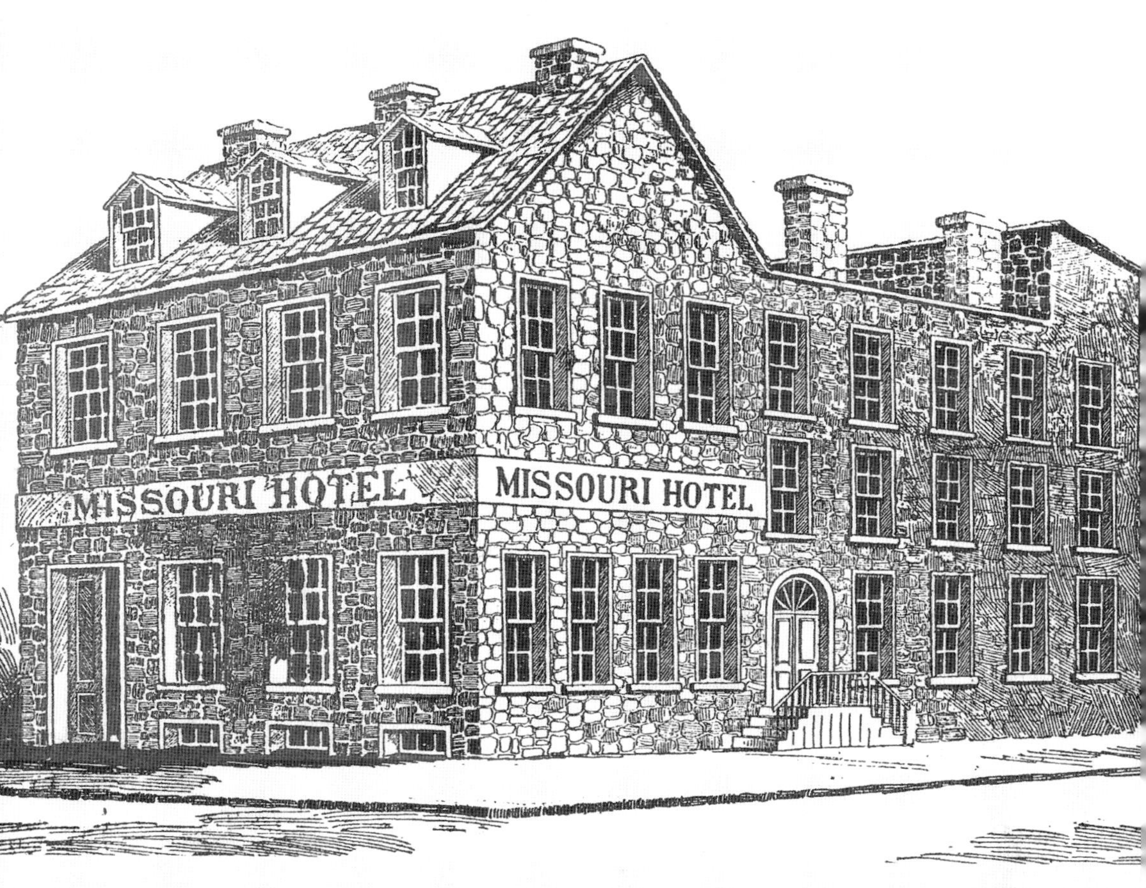

The congregation of thousands of blacks during the Civil War on the St. Louis riverfront became known as "Camp Ethiopia." The vacant Missouri Hotel at Main and Morgan Streets was acquired for the thousands of refugees. The hotel was the site of the framing of the state's first constitution in 1820. Thousands of slaves simply abandoned their owners when Union troops were nearby. Many carried with them as many of their owners' possessions as they could. While many came to St. Louis, others sought the free states of Illinois, Iowa, and Michigan. (Courtesy of Billy Crumpton.)

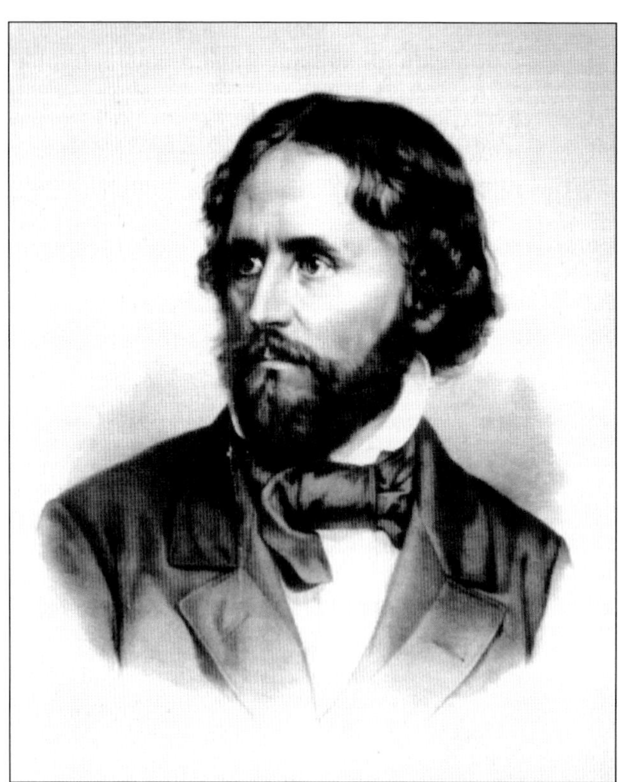

In 1861, President Lincoln appointed Maj. Gen. John Fremont commander of the Union army's headquarters. Throughout the night of August 29, Freemont worked at his desk, and in the morning, he read to his wife an emancipation proclamation in which he placed the state under martial law. All anti-Union Missouri citizens would have their property confiscated and their slaves freed. Those found with arms in the northern part of the state would be court-martialed. If found guilty, they would be executed. Upon hearing of Freemont's plan, Lincoln immediately rescinded the order and relieved Freemont of his command. (Left, courtesy of the National Archives; below, courtesy of the Missouri Historical Society.)

PROCLAMATION

Head Quarters Western Department,

ST. LOUIS, MO., August 14, 1861.

I hereby declare and establish

Martial Law

In the City and County of St. Louis.

Major J. McKINSTRY, U. S. Army, is appointed Provost Marshal. All orders and regulations issued by him will be respected and obeyed.

J. C. FREMONT,

Major General Commanding.

On the evening of June 10, 1861, Archer Alexander, a slave and overseer, learned that rebel sympathizers had sawed the timbers of a railroad bridge near St. Louis. He walked five miles to warn Union forces. The bridge was repaired. Suspected of being the informer, Alexander decided to go for freedom and ran away. He was befriended by Rev. William Elliot, who later became the founder of Washington University. (Courtesy of Washington University Archives.)

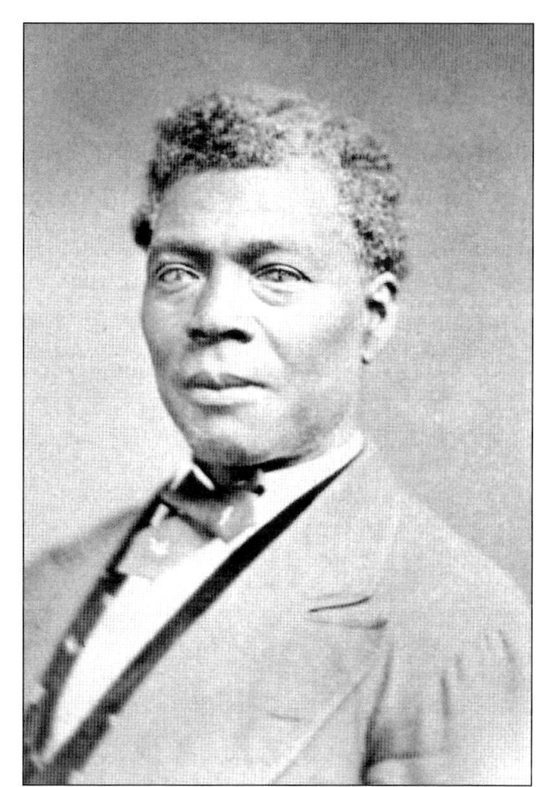

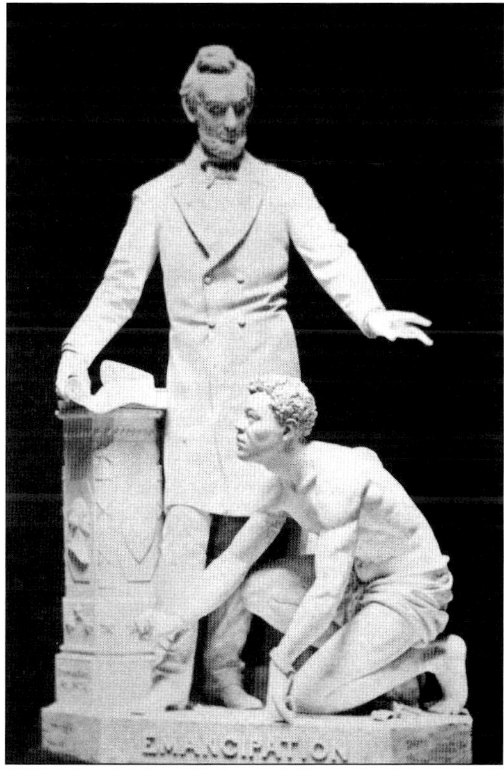

Alexander's deed went unsung until he received a small measure of immorality when he served as the model of the famous emancipation statute in Washington, DC. In 1938, the monument was pictured on a 3¢ stamp commemorating the 75th anniversary of emancipation. (Courtesy of Washington University Archives.)

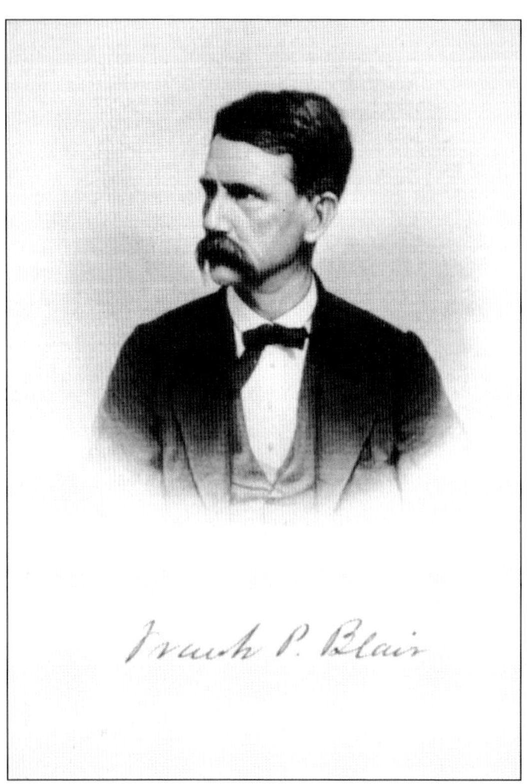

After the war ended, a strong debate took place at the St. Louis Mercantile Library. Gen. Francis P. Blair gave a blistering speech on September 26, 1863, challenging the growing emancipationist sentiment among his fellow Unionists. Blair had been a key player in saving the city and the state for the Union and believed that freeing the slaves would split the cause. (Courtesy of the St. Louis Mercantile Library, UMSL.)

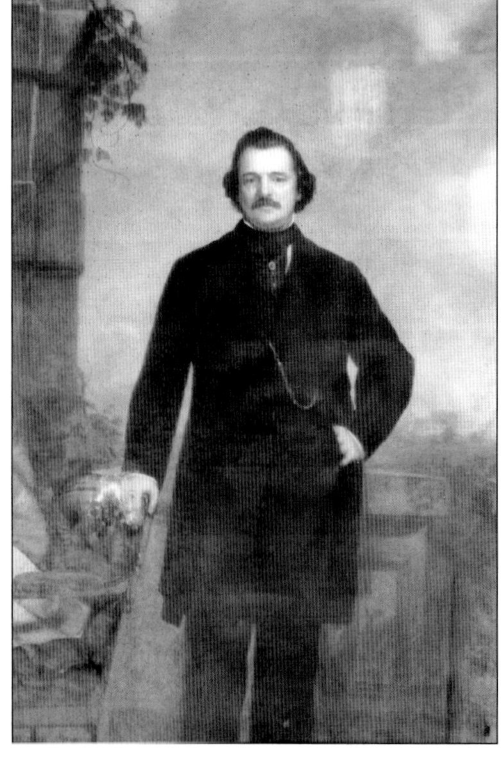

US representative Henry Blow gave a radical response to Blair's speech five days later in the Mercantile Library. Blow said he was proud to be for emancipation and that the war had cost too many lives to allow slavery to continue. Blow's family had once owned and freed Harriet and Dred Scott. He donated land for Carondelet's first black school. (Courtesy of the Carondelet Historical Society.)

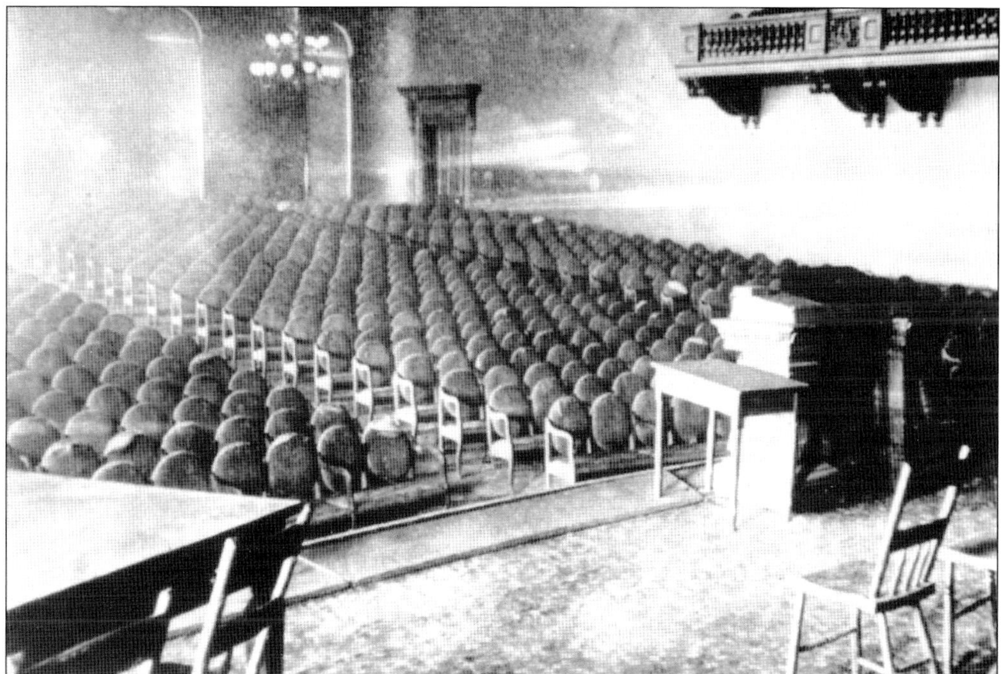

On January 1, 1863, President Lincoln's Emancipation Proclamation came into effect, freeing slaves in all Confederate-held territory. This did not include Missouri, Kentucky, Tennessee, and Maryland. Legal freedom for African American slaves in Missouri came by the action of a state convention held in the Mercantile Hall in St. Louis, pictured here. German immigrant Judge Arnold Krekel served as president. Radical Republicans comprised two-thirds of the convention seats. The vote on the emancipation ordinance passed overwhelmingly, 60-4, on January 11, 1865. (Both, courtesy of the St. Louis Mercantile Library, UMSL.)

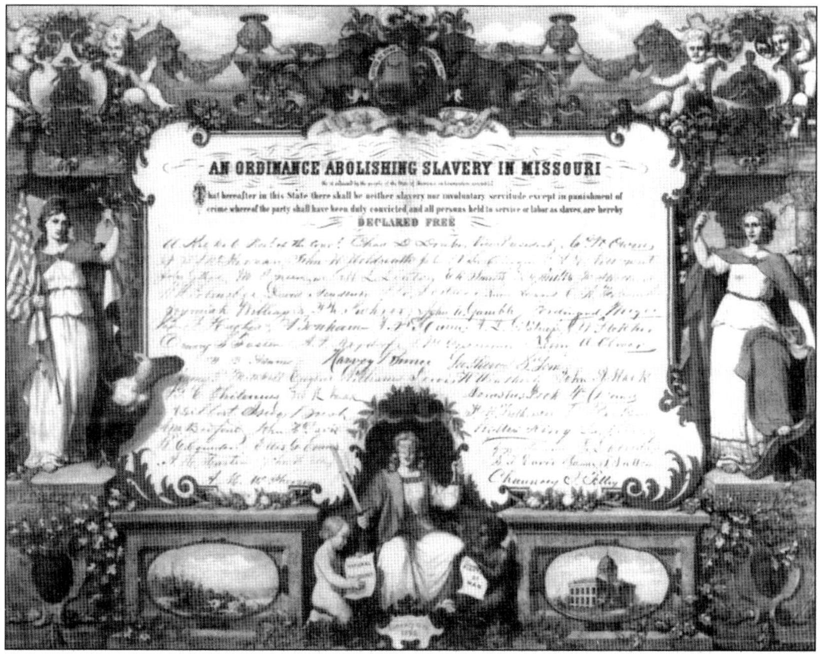

AN ORDINANCE ABOLISHING SLAVERY IN MISSOURI

That hereafter in this State there shall be neither slavery nor involuntary servitude except in punishment of crime whereof the party shall have been duly convicted, and all persons held to service or labor as slaves, are hereby

DECLARED FREE

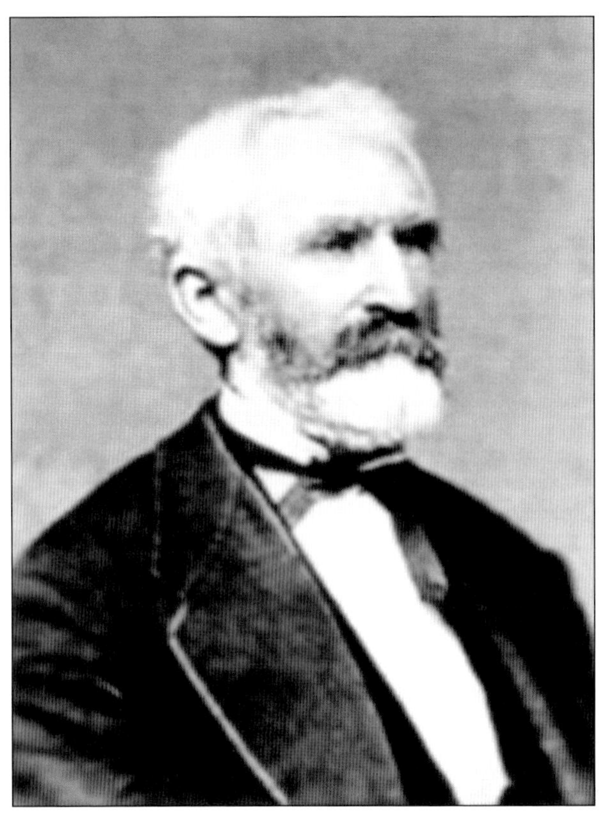

Judge Krekel, in addition to working for black suffrage, played an important role in ensuring that African Americans would have access to quality education. African American soldiers dreamed of a school for African Americans and Krekel traveled to the east coast to secure funds from Northern supporters and civil rights activists and educators. These efforts ended in the establishment of the Lincoln Institute. (Courtesy of Dorris Keeven-Franke.)

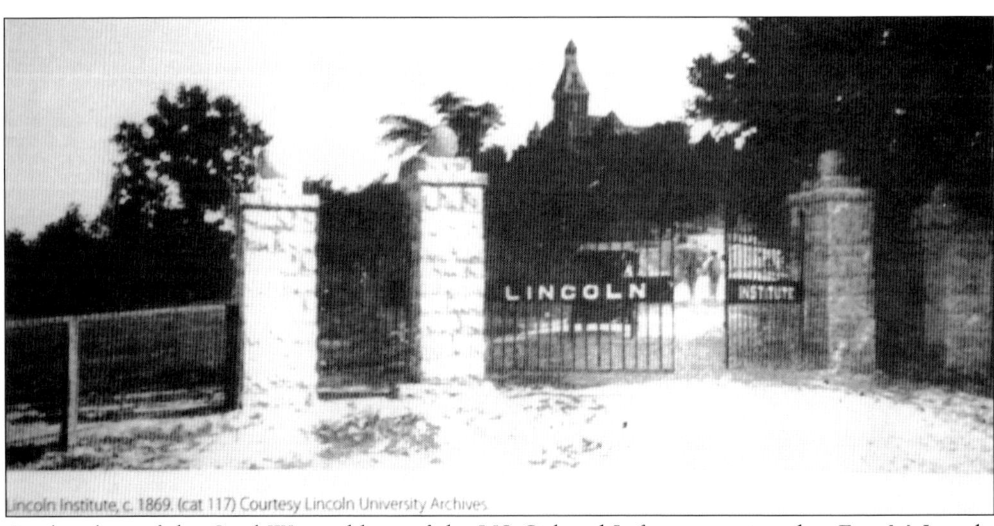

At the close of the Civil War, soldiers of the US Colored Infantry stationed at Fort McIntosh, Texas, decided they wanted to establish an educational institution in Missouri. The soldiers had learned to read and write around a campfire. Despite their low pay of $13 a month, they were able to raise $6,000 toward the establishment of Lincoln Institute. One soldier gave $100. (Courtesy of Arnold Parks.)

After the Civil War, the Missouri legislature adopted a new constitution that provided for black children to be educated just as whites in free, tax-supported public schools. To achieve this goal, James Milton Turner was appointed to the position of assistant superintendent of schools in charge of postwar black schools. He joined Judge Arnold Krekel and Rev. Moses Dickson in securing money for the Lincoln Institute. (Courtesy of the St. Louis Mercantile Library, UMSL.)

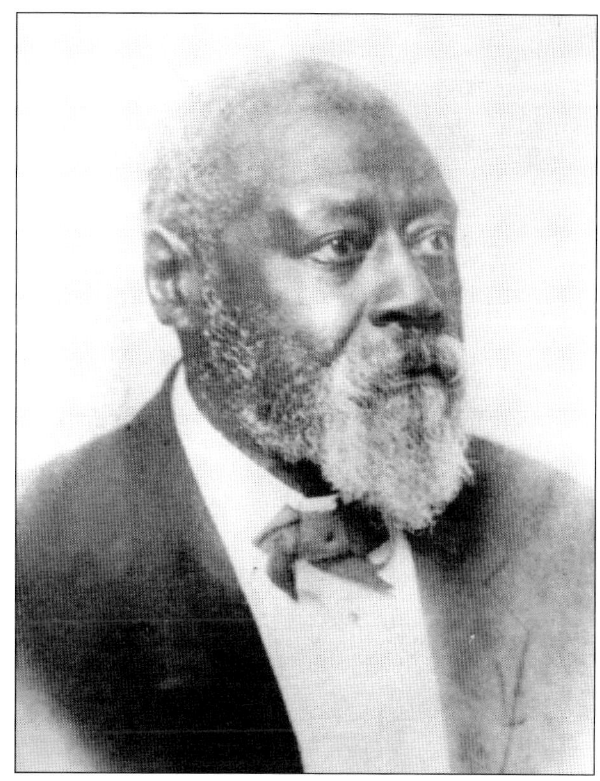

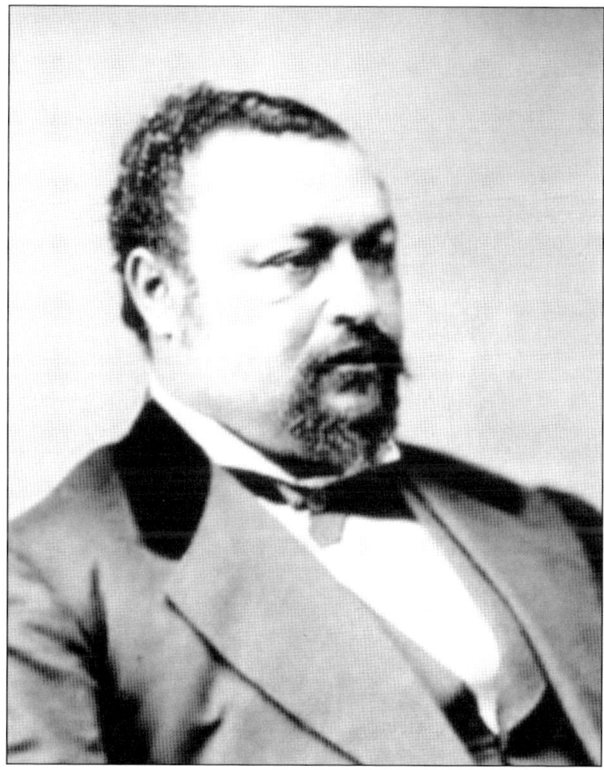

Blanche Bruce later became the first African American to serve a full term in the US Senate and the first to preside over a Senate session. Bruce worked and lived in St. Louis before and after the Civil War. He was profoundly disappointed about being rejected by the Union army. After the war, he established the first school for blacks in Hannibal, Missouri. (Courtesy of the Library of Congress.)

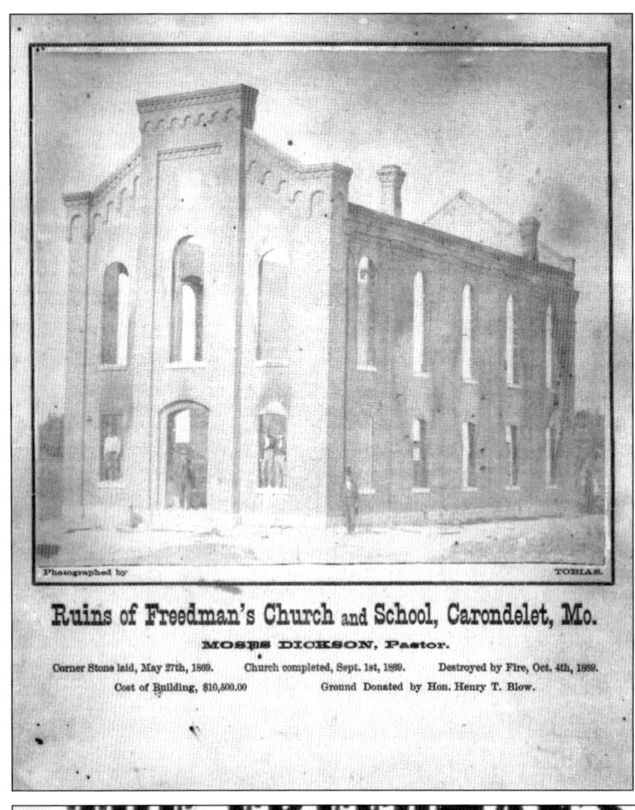

The Freedmen's Bureau and white benevolent associations such as the Western Sanitary Commission and the American Missionary Association (AMA) worked to establish schools for African Americans. This Freedman's School was completed on September 1, 1869, and destroyed by fire a month later. Earlier, a school established by the AMA in 1863 was destroyed by fire three days after it opened. (Left, courtesy of James Brown; below, courtesy of the National Archives.)

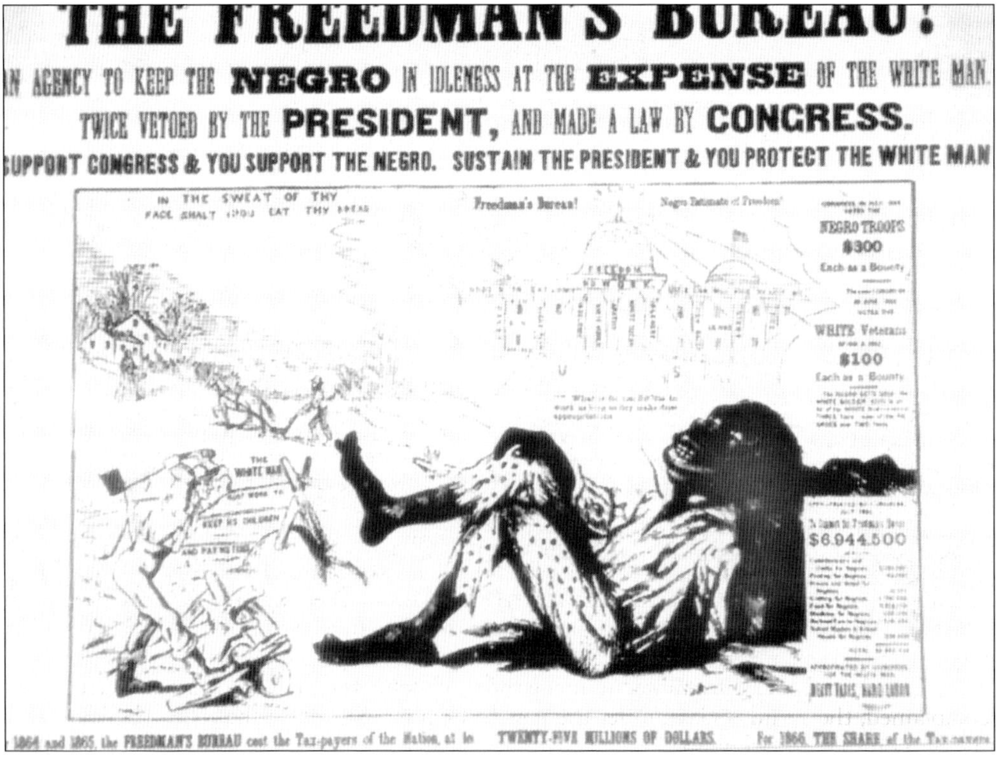

THE FREEDMAN'S BUREAU!

AN AGENCY TO KEEP THE NEGRO IN IDLENESS AT THE EXPENSE OF THE WHITE MAN.

TWICE VETOED BY THE PRESIDENT, AND MADE A LAW BY CONGRESS.

SUPPORT CONGRESS & YOU SUPPORT THE NEGRO. SUSTAIN THE PRESIDENT & YOU PROTECT THE WHITE MAN

IN THE SWEAT OF THY FACE SHALT THOU EAT THY BREAD

Freedman's Bureau!

NEGRO TROOPS $300 Each as a Bounty

WHITE Veterans $100 Each as a Bounty

THE WHITE MAN

$6,944,500

1864 and 1865, the FREEDMAN'S BUREAU cost the Tax-payers of the Nation, at least TWENTY-FIVE MILLIONS OF DOLLARS. For 1866, THE SHARE of the Tax-payers

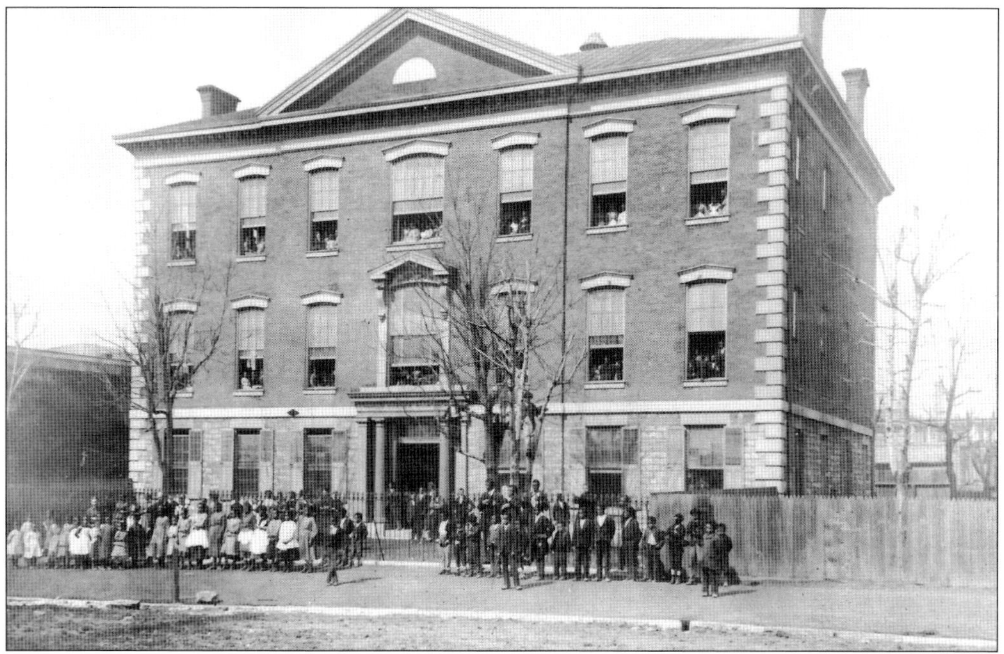

In 1875, after African American parents in St. Louis complained about inadequate educational buildings for their children, the state legislature directed the city's school board to provide a high school for black children. The board designated a formerly all-white elementary school the high school for "colored" students. Charles Sumner became the first high school west of the Mississippi River for African Americans. (Courtesy of the St. Louis Public Schools.)

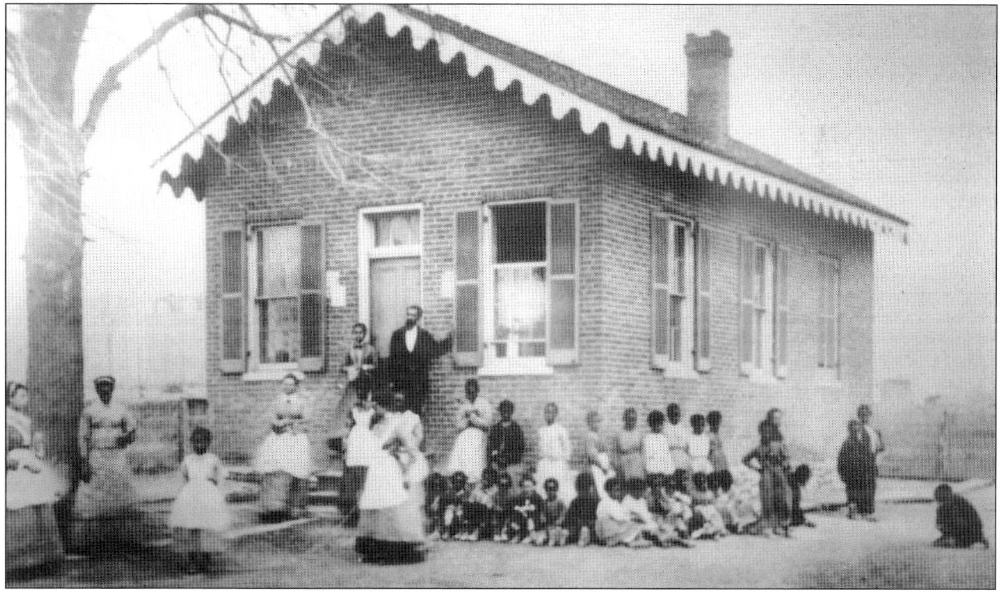

When schools first opened for black children, they were given numbers instead of names. Wheatley Elementary School, pictured here, opened in 1866 and was originally called Colored School No. 7. At first, the school board wanted to name the black schools for famous whites. When parents complained, the board decided to let the new black principals name the schools. (Courtesy of the St. Louis Public Schools.)

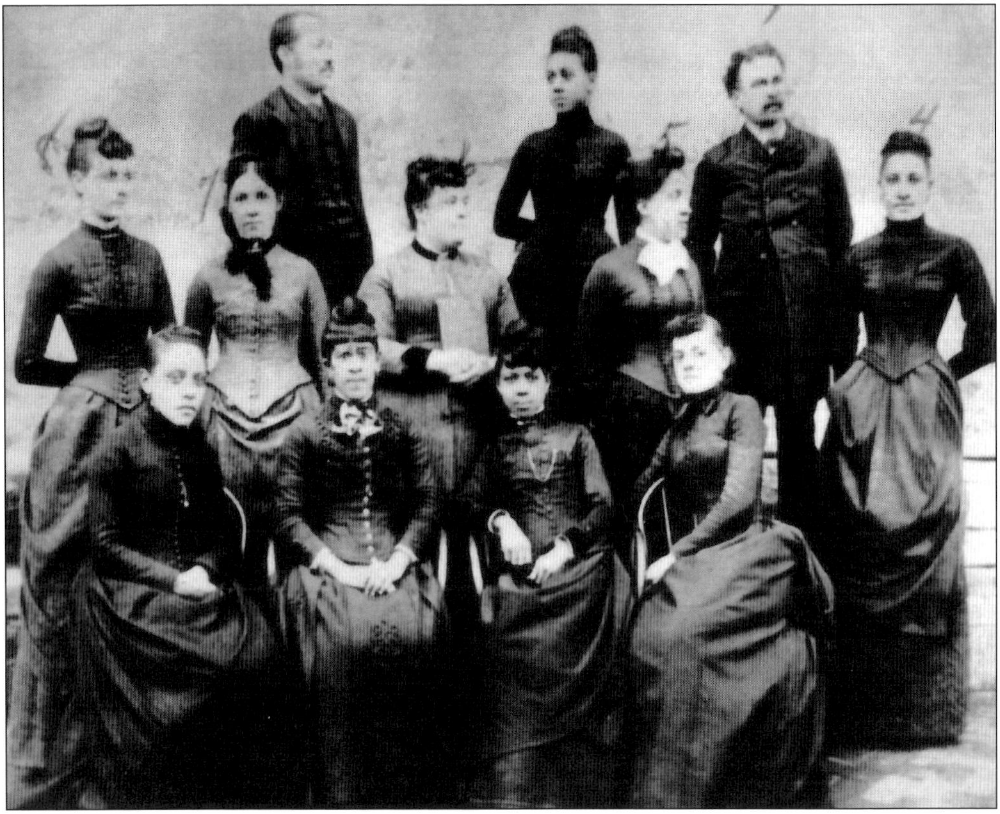

In 1877, black teachers were employed to teach in the black school. The Colored Education Council had petitioned the Board of Education, explaining that black teachers were better equipped, and it was more desirable that black teachers should teach black students because they were free from unfavorable social surroundings that breed prejudice. Pictured are early teachers and administrators. (Both, courtesy of the St. Louis Public School Archives.)

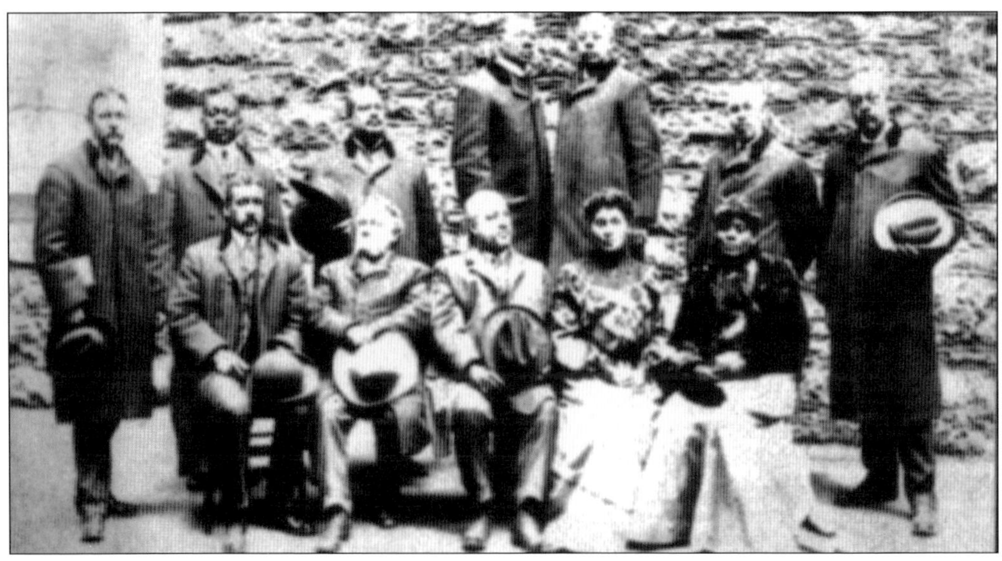

Three

Reaction and Renewal

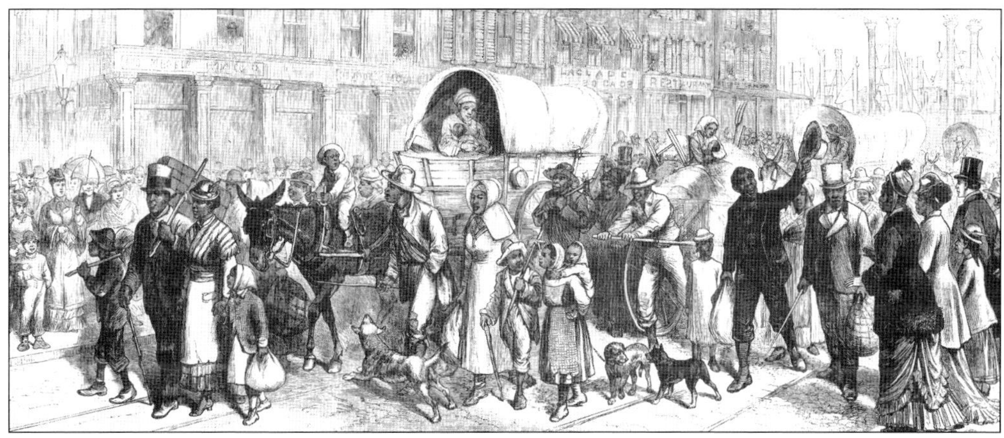

In 1879, thousands of penniless black men, women, and children, known as the "Exodusters," passed through St. Louis on their way to Kansas and other midwestern and western states where they hoped to find a better life. They had suffered harsh political, social, and economic oppression at the hands of former slave masters. The end of slavery and Reconstruction marked a new beginning for blacks. This image appeared in *Frank Leslie's Illustrated Newspaper* on April 19, 1879. (Courtesy of John A. Wright Sr.)

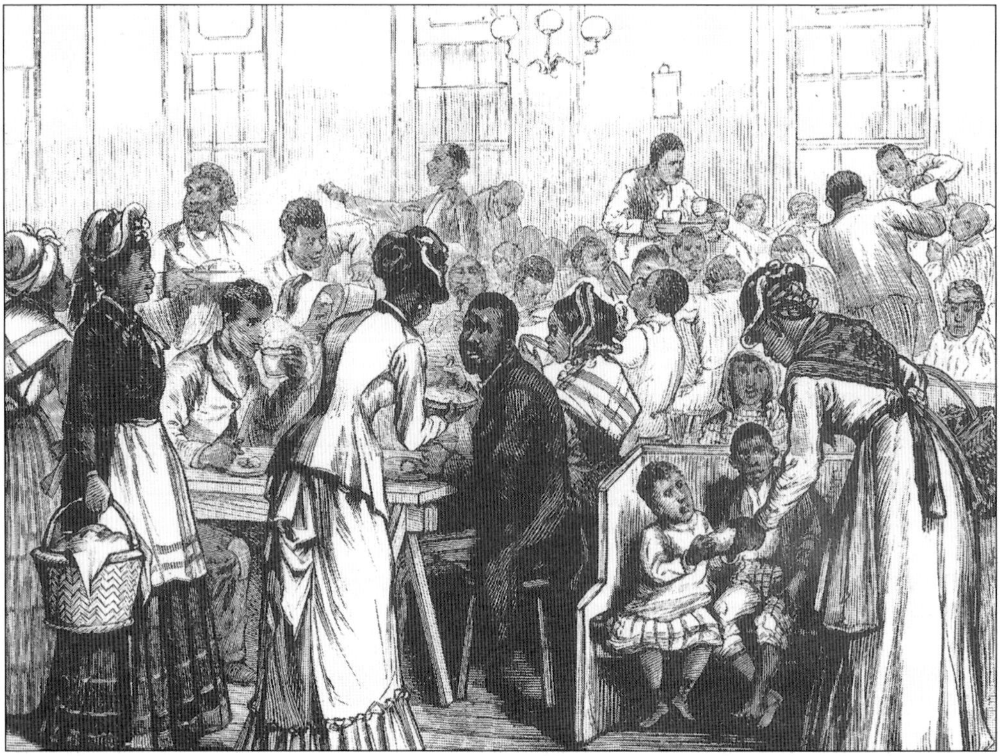

Prominent African Americans in St. Louis organized to feed, house, and supply transportation for the impoverished Exodusters as they reached the city. As their numbers increased, they were sheltered at St. Paul's African Methodist Church and the First Baptist Church and in the homes of African Americans in the community. They were dependent almost entirely on the black community. This image is also from *Frank Leslie's Illustrated Newspaper*, April 19, 1879. (Courtesy of John A. Wright Sr.)

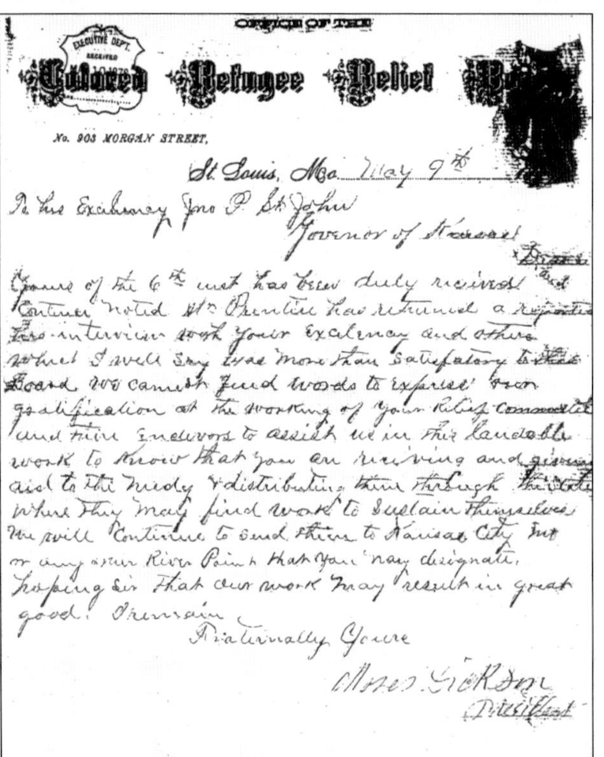

OFFICE OF THE
Colored Refugee Relief Board

No. 903 MORGAN STREET,

St. Louis, Mo. May 9th

To his Excellency Jno P. St. John
Governor of Kansas
Dear Sir

Yours of the 6th inst has been duly received and contents noted Mr Prentice has returned a report of his interview with your Excellency and others which I will say was more than satisfactory to this Board we cannot find words to express our gratification at the working of your Relief Committee and their endeavors to assist us in this laudable work to know that you are receiving and giving aid to the needy & distributing them through the state where they may find work to sustain themselves we will continue to send them to Kansas City Mo or any other River Point that you may designate. hoping sir that our work may result in great good! I remain

Fraternally Yours

Moses Dickson
President

A committee of 25 organized as the Colored Refugee Relief Board, headed by Moses Dickson, to assist the Exodusters as they moved west. Dickson, in this letter, is requesting assistance for the travelers when they reached Kansas. (Courtesy of James Vincent.)

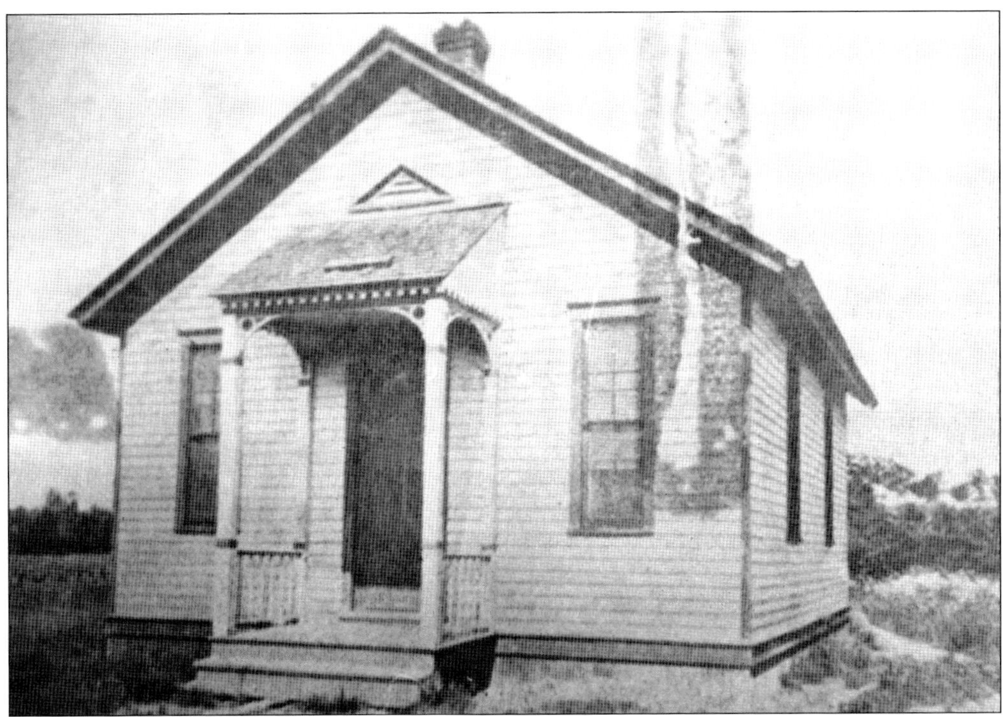

The state's new constitution provided for segregated schools for black children when their number exceeded 20. It stipulated that when the number of students in attendance dropped below 12 in any month, the school could be closed for a maximum of six months. Because of the small black population in Ferguson, the Vernon school closed often and students had to travel by train to Normandy. (Courtesy of the Ferguson-Florissant School District.)

Proceedings of the Board of Directors.

Office of Mr Fred Marget Oct 31st 1892 Regular Meeting - present Messrs. Marget and [illegible]

The Reports of Teachers for the month beginning Oct. 3rd 1892 and ending Oct. 28th 1892, were received, examined and approved and warrants ordered drawn to pay salaries -

Miss Eva M White Principal, and Teacher Room No. 1 - $100.00
" Carrie E Scott " " 4 60.00
" Margaret Stark " " 3 50.00
" Belle G Page " " 2 40.00
Mrs. Katie Rector (colored) " " 5 25.00

Warrants were also ordered drawn to pay the Janitors for services ending Oct. 31st 1892.

W. J. Applebee, one Mo. from Oct 1st to 31st (inclusive) 1892 - $25.00
R. Shoby (colored school) " " " 1 - 31 " " 1892 - 4.00

The following Bills were read and allowed, and warrants ordered drawn to pay the amounts. Viz: -

Woodward and Tiernan Printg. Co. School supplies as per bills - $32.70
J. W. Holtsclaw - furnishing Material and Carpentering - - - 165.49
P. K. Wagner Paying Ex. Chgs. and furnishing supplies &c - - - [illegible]

Nothing further appearing the Board adjourned -

Attest
P. K. Wagner
Dist. Clerk.

Fred Marget
President

As seen in this ledger, black teachers were not always paid the same as their white colleagues. This pay disparity lasted in the state until the Negro Teachers Association filed a lawsuit in the early 1940s. Teachers in schools with low enrollment were never secure in their employment. When the school enrollment dropped below the required number, it was closed. (Courtesy of the Ferguson-Florissant School District.)

THE SHAME OF AMERICA

Do you know that the United States is the Only Land on Earth where human beings are BURNED AT THE STAKE?

In Four Years, 1918-1921, Twenty-Eight People Were Publicly BURNED BY AMERICAN MOBS

3436 People Lynched 1889 to 1922

For What Crimes Have Mobs Nullified Government and Inflicted the Death Penalty?

Is Rape the "Cause" of Lynching?

83 WOMEN HAVE BEEN LYNCHED IN THE UNITED STATES

AND THE LYNCHERS GO UNPUNISHED

THE REMEDY

The Dyer Anti-Lynching Bill Is Now Before the United States Senate

THE DYER ANTI-LYNCHING BILL IS NOW BEFORE THE SENATE
TELEGRAPH YOUR SENATORS TODAY YOU WANT IT ENACTED

NATIONAL ASSOCIATION FOR THE ADVANCEMENT OF COLORED PEOPLE

THIS ADVERTISEMENT IS PAID FOR IN PART BY THE ANTI-LYNCHING CRUSADERS

After Reconstruction, lynching increased across America and in Missouri. St. Louis County, in 1894, became a part of the statistics with the lynching of John Buckner in Valley Park. Buckner was accused of assaulting an elderly black woman and her daughter. He was taken from his home by men described by the newspaper as the "best citizens" in the county. This NAACP advertisement appeared in the St. Louis *Argus*. (Courtesy of the National Archives.)

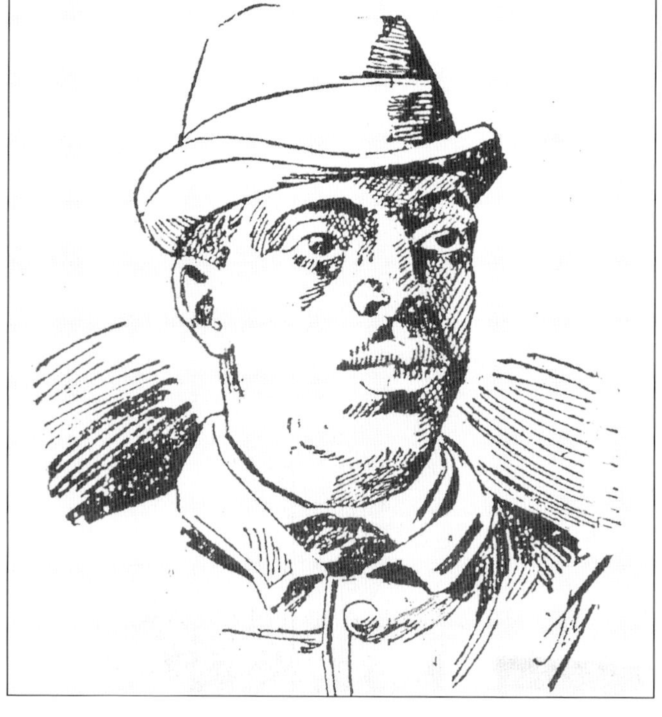

In 1894, William Harrison Duncan was hanged at the St. Louis County Courthouse for the murder of police officer James Brady at Charles Stark's saloon at 715 North Eleventh Street. Duncan maintained his innocence but was found guilty. During the trial and after, tensions in the city ran high. Stark later admitted to the murder. Duncan's hanging was memorialized in the folk ballad "Brady and Duncan." (Courtesy of John A. Wright Sr.)

Capt. Charlton Tandy led the movement to end segregated public streetcars in the 1880s. He worked to enforce an 1867 court order allowing blacks to ride inside public transportation. In 1902, before his wife could safely disembark a transit vehicle, it pulled away, causing her to be severely injured. Tandy sued in the Missouri Supreme Court for $2,500 but was awarded only $600. (Courtesy of John A. Wright Sr.)

IN THE

Supreme Court of Missouri

DIVISION No. 1.

OCTOBER TERM, 1902.

CHARLTON H. TANDY,
(Plaintiff) Respondent,
vs.
ST. LOUIS TRANSIT COMPANY,
(Defendant) Appellant.

No. 10,746.

APPEAL FROM THE CIRCUIT COURT OF THE CITY OF ST. LOUIS, COURT ROOM NO. 5, HON. D. D. FISHER, JUDGE.

Statement and Brief for Appellant.

STATEMENT.

The petition in this case was filed in the Circuit Court on October 27, 1900, and was in substance as follows:

That on or about the 10th day of August, 1900, Annie E. Tandy, lawful wife of the plaintiff, was a passenger on a Page Avenue car owned and operated by the defendant corporation. That "while she was in the act of alighting from said car, after it had stopped on the west side of Walton avenue, at its intersection

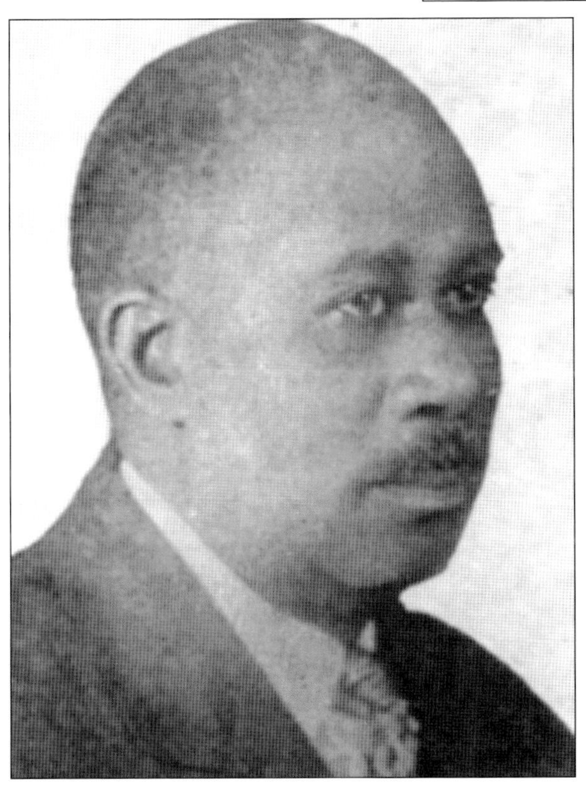

Joseph Everett Mitchell, founder of the *St. Louis Argus* newspaper in 1912, was instrumental in organizing and founding the Citizens' Liberty League, whose goal was to elect blacks to public office. The organization was successful in electing Charles Turbin as a constable, the first black elected to public office in Missouri, and Walthall M. Moore, the first black elected to the Missouri General Assembly. (Courtesy of John A. Wright Sr.)

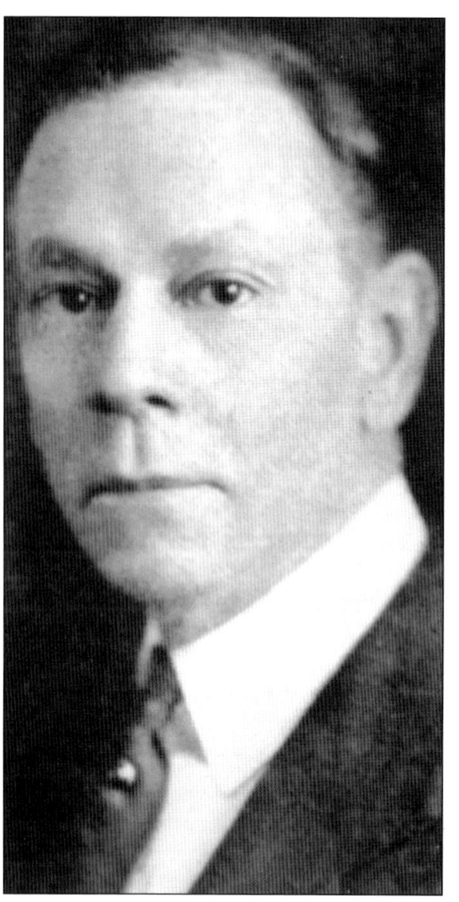

In 1910, Charles Turbin became the first black elected to public office in Missouri when he won the race for constable in St. Louis. The daily papers declared him defeated. However, knowing there were some irregularities, he requested a recount. After going to the court and receiving permission for the recount, it was determined that he had won by more than two to one. (Photograph by Nathan Young.)

The St. Louis American newspaper was founded in 1928. The *St. Louis American's* first edition sold out of its 2,000 copies with the headline "Pullman Porter's May Strike." Since its first edition, the paper has aligned itself with the struggle for equal rights for black citizens and diligently covered the political and civil rights issues of the city. (Courtesy of the *St. Louis American*.)

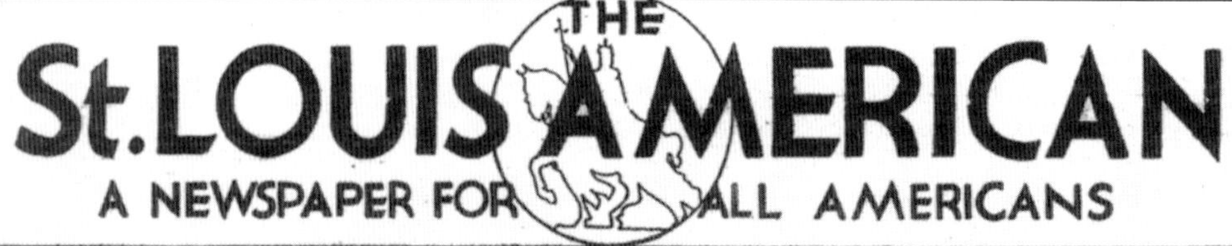

THE St. LOUIS AMERICAN

A NEWSPAPER FOR ALL AMERICANS

VOL. 22—NO. 22 ST. LOUIS, MISSOURI, THURSDAY, SEPTEMBER 8, 1949 SEVEN CENTS

TRAIN STRIKE AFFECTS HUNDREDS HERE

EAST SIDE SCHOOL COMPROMISE BLACKEYE TO CIVIL RIGHTS

"Fear of Mob Violence, Fear of No Police Protection" Given As Excuse For Making Compromise To Lay Off Jimcrow

(Continued on page 16)

BETWEEN 500 AND 1000 CAR PORTERS AND DINING CAR EMPLOYEES AFFECTED

The strike of three operating brotherhoods on the Missouri Pacific Railroad will affect hundreds of Negro trainmen in the St. Louis area according to officials of the dining car union and the Brotherhood of Sleeping Car Porters. James Matthews of the AFL Dining Car Union and E. T. Bradley of the Sleeping Car Brotherhood, estimate that approximately 300-500 members of their locals are affected in the layoffs as a result of the strike which began Friday morning.

(Continued on page 16)

BEAUTY AND BRAINS RETURN TO COLLEGE

ST. LOUIS WINS TRAPSHOOT

(See Page Four)

At the turn of the 20th century, many in the community went to great lengths to dehumanize blacks. In 1900, the American Book and Bible House at 209–213 North Seventh Street published *The Negro: A Beast or, In the Image of God* by Charles Carroll, which purported to show that African Americans were inhuman. In chapter four, pictured here, a comparison of brain weight is discussed. (Courtesy of the St. Louis Public Library.)

Chapter IV.

Convincing Biblical and Scientific Evidence that the Negro is not of the Human Family.

The following measurements of brain weights collected by Sanford B. Hunt, in the Federal army during the late war in the United States, demonstrates that the White blood is the lever which elevates; and that the Negro blood is the lever which lowers the mental grade of individuals, tribes, nations, continents, and the world at large.

	Weight of brain Grammes.
" 24 Whites	1424
25 Three parts white	1390
47 Half-white, or mulattoes	1334
51 One-quarter white	1319
95 One-eighth white	1308
22 A sixteenth white	1280
141 Pure negroes	1331"

[*Topinard's Anthropology*, p. 312.]

(105)

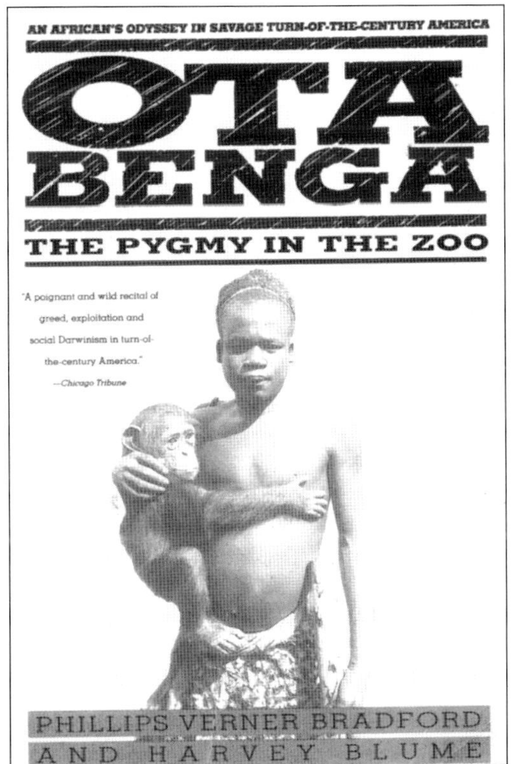

In 1904, a pigmy by the name of Ota Binga was brought to the World's Fair from Africa and placed on display. After leaving St. Louis, he was taken to the Bronx Zoo in New York, where he was forced to sleep in the primate house. After receiving his freedom, he committed suicide when he found he would never return to Africa. (Courtesy of John A. Wright Sr.)

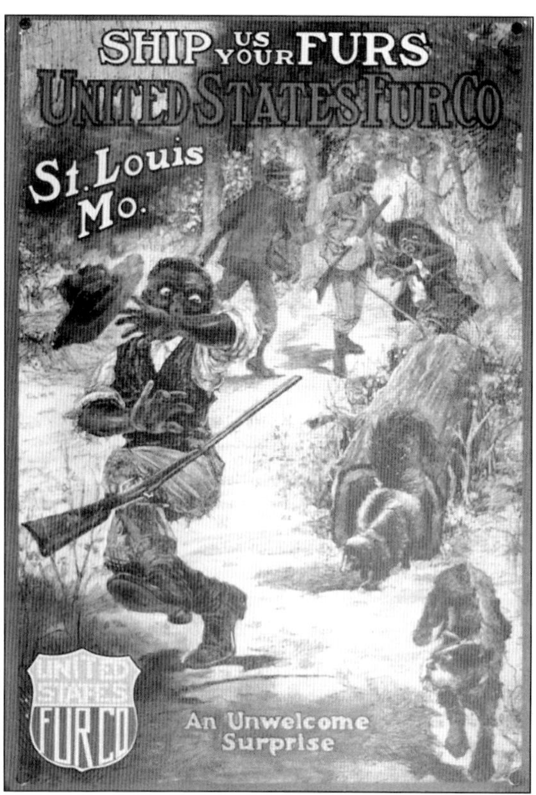

During the early 1900s, many St. Louisans put forth a large number of dehumanizing activities to justify racism and the treatment of blacks through movies like *Birth of a Nation* and widespread negative images in advertisements and minstrel shows. (Courtesy of Chauncey Trawick.)

THE LEGAL SEGREGATION OF NEGROES IN SAINT LOUIS

JANUARY 1913

THE LEGAL SEGREGATION OF NEGROES

THE COLORED POPULATION TODAY

There are approximately [illegible] colored people in St. Louis, slightly less than 7 per cent of the total population.

A map prepared from accurate sources showing the movement of the colored population in St. Louis within the last five years, shows a natural extension of the districts in which colored people have long lived. Those districts occur in practically every part of the city, from the river to the west end, from Carondelet to Baden.

One of the chief centers of population is Morgan street and adjacent streets, just north of the business section, extending from Eighth street, particularly along Morgan street to Ewing avenue. There the district joins the Market and Pine street district, which runs west from about Twelfth street to Cardinal and Compton. A large settlement follows the Mill Creek Valley from Union Station west as far as Kingshighway. The largest settlement, known as Elleardsville, begins at Vandeventer avenue on the east and extends west to Taylor, south to Easton avenue, and north to the Fair Grounds. Only four blocks south of Elleardsville, is a rapidly growing district, which may be termed the Finney avenue district. There is also a large settlement in Carondelet.

The other districts are scattered. A few blocks here and there are occupied by negroes, and there are instances of one colored family living among white in parts of the city where there are no other negroes. Such cases, however, are rare, colored people generally preferring to live in their own neighborhoods.

It is significant that all three of the segregated vice districts are surrounded by negroes. This is due, not to the negroes' preference to live near vice districts, but to the fact, first, that the police located these vice districts in negro neighborhoods, and second, that real estate men offer them homes in such places, knowing that they will take good houses at almost any sacrifice.

Movements of Population.

The map prepared by the Committee shows clearly the movement of population during the last five years, and demonstrates that colored people move almost exclusively only into blocks adjacent to those already inhabited by colored people. In other words, the colored districts in St. Louis are extending their boundaries through natural growth.

This process of growth often gives rise to feeling and serious friction, for whenever colored people move into an adjacent white block, property values immediately depreciate, the property is thrown on the market at a low value and is usually sold to negroes. The block then becomes chiefly a colored

In 1913, A white committee in the city of St. Louis placed on a ballot an issue for "the Legal Segregation of Negroes in St. Louis." The committee conducted a study and stated it found that blacks mostly moved into streets already inhabited by other blacks and that when they moved into an adjacent white block, the whites' property value went down. (Courtesy of the St. Louis Public Library.)

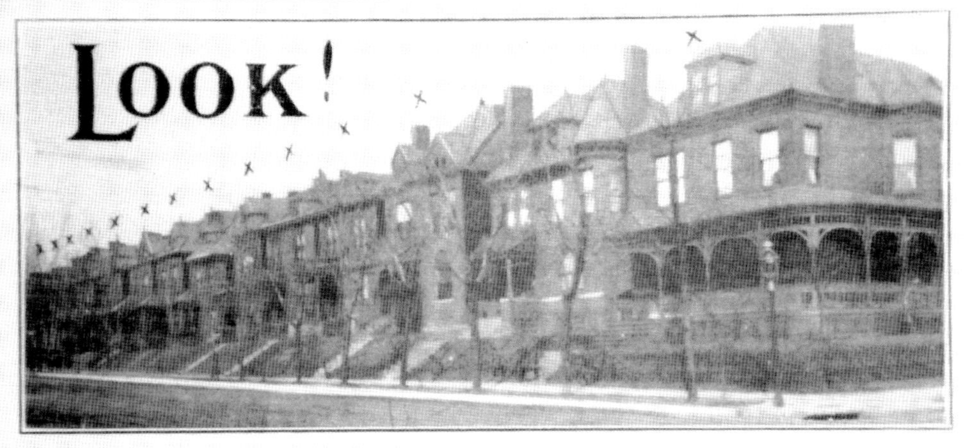

To promote the need for the ordinance, the committee used a lot of scare tactics, like the one shown here regarding housing. (Courtesy of the Missouri Historical Society.)

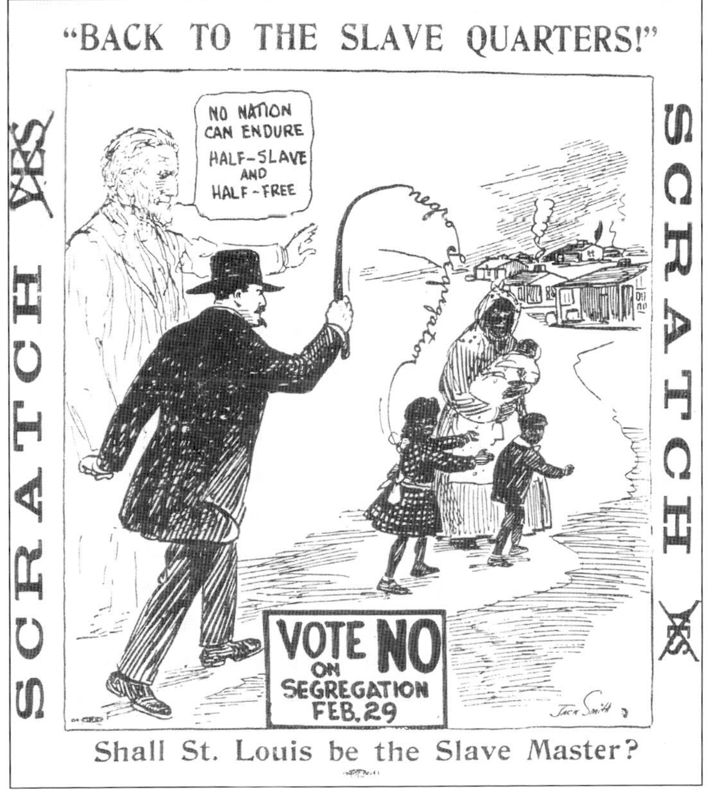

Although many organizations such as the NAACP opposed the 1916 ordinance, it was passed by a 2-1 majority. This decision increased the use of race-restrictive covenants to prohibit white property owners from selling to minorities. This practice lasted until 1948, when the Supreme Court ruled it unconstitutional. (Courtesy of the St. Louis Public Library.)

ST. LOUIS POST-DISPATCH WEDNESDAY EVENING, JANUARY 24, 1917.

LOTS WHITE MEN BUY DOUBLED IN PRICE TO NEGROES

Realty Company Engages to Re-sell Sites in New South Kinloch Park Subdvision.

WANTS NEGOTIABLE NOTES

Unable to Use Negro Purchasers' Paper as Collateral—Company Officers Explain Plan.

While segregation of negroes in St. Louis is restrained by a temporary injunction in the United States District Court and the question is pending in the United States Supreme Court, it is being exploited in St. Louis County by a real estate company which is selling lots to negroes in South Kinloch Park at double the price quoted to white investors.

The Olive Street Terrace Realty Co. is selling 25-foot lots in the subdivision at an average of $150 to white persons and reselling them at an average of $300 to negroes, and is doing so well it has just moved from the Merchants-Laclede Building to larger quarters in the Boatmen's Bank Building.

Negro Subdivision Laid Out.

The company first placed on the market the Kinloch Park subdivision. Negroes applied for lots there, but the restrictions prevented sales being made to them. That suggested, officers of the company say, the plan of laying out a subdivision exclusively for negroes. Property adjoining the Kinloch Park subdivision, restricted to whites, was purchased, and South Kinloch Park subdivision, restricted to negroes, was put on the market.

Negroes bought readily on the terms of $5 down and $5 a month, but difficulty was encountered when the company wished to use the negroes' notes as collateral for bank loans. To get around that difficulty the plan of selling to whites and reselling to negroes was adopted.

This plan, as explained by officers of the company, is to sell a lot or group of lots to a white person, who makes a small cash payment and gives a note to cover deferred payments at $2.50 per month on each lot.

White Men's Notes as Collateral.

The notes of the white purchasers are accepted as collateral at the bank and are discounted by the company, which then undertakes to resell the lots at double the price, charging 10 per cent for its services. If a resale is made the white investor receives monthly payments from the negroes in double the amount of the white person's payments.

After a [illegible] of the company had [illegible] ...ive investor that

Map Showing Kinloch Park's New Negro Subdivision and Its Relation to St. Louis

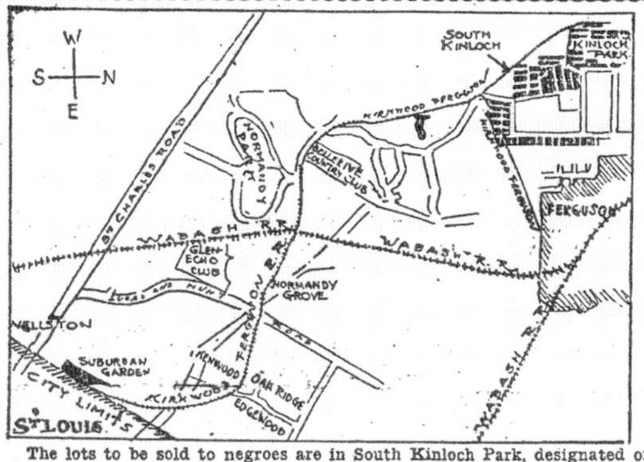

The lots to be sold to negroes are in South Kinloch Park, designated on the map by an arrow.

From THE ARGUS

This announcement has been running in St. Louis' principal negro newspaper.

White people who have bought more than one thousand lots in old Kinloch Park have been paying the same prices on the same terms as the colored people who have bought in South Kinloch Park. If there is any difference, the colored people have been getting the best of it, because South Kinloch Park is nearer the city and has better street car service.

The good colored people of South Kinloch Park have built themselves a little city of which they have a right to be proud.

More than a hundred homes, three churches, and a splendid public school have been built in the last few years.

And now we have something new that is going to mean a bigger and better South Kinloch Park.

We have been able to induce a number of white people of good standing to come in with us and co-operate with us—to help with their money, their influence and their good will to make South Kinloch Park a bigger and better place for the self-respecting negro to live and make his home.

We have given these people a big share of our profits in order to get their help because we believe it is for the benefit of everybody concerned.

We have always been ready to give land to the churches at a nominal price—because we believe they would help South Kinloch Park.

We have always been ready to give land to schools and public institutions at a nominal price—because we believed they would help South Kinloch Park.

And now we are giving land to a certain number of white people of good standing at a nominal price because we believe their money, their influence and their good will are going to help South Kinloch Park.

If you have any friends who have been thinking of buying, urge them to come out now, because there are bigger and better things in store for South Kinloch Park.

Olive Street Terrace Realty Company

No one knows for sure when the first blacks moved to Kinloch. This January 24, 1917, article in the *Post-Dispatch* describes whites purchasing home lots in the Kinloch Park subdivision and selling them to blacks for twice the price. Some say blacks moved in large numbers into the community after the 1917 East St. Louis Race Riot. Kinloch later became Missouri's first black city. (Courtesy of the 1984 Kinloch History Committee.)

ACTUAL EXPERIENCES

February 23, 1917.

Olive Street Terrace Realty Co.,
1403 Boatmen's Bank Bldg.,
City.

Gentlemen:

I have just received check for the first payment made to me by the negro who bought two of my lots. These lots cost me $325.00 and were sold inside of ninety days at a price that will net me over $600.00.

I am well pleased with the investment.

Yours truly,

(Signed) W. B. CRAWFORD,
1601 Locust St

February 19, 1917.

Olive Street Terrace Realty Co.,
Boatmen's Bank Bldg.,
City.

Dear Sirs:

I am very glad that you advised me to purchase lots in your South Kinloch Park Subdivision. Since making this investment a little over sixty days ago, two of my lots have been sold for just double what they cost me.

Your proposition is conservative and safe, as I consider these lots at one-half the market price, ample security.

Sincerely,

(Signed) MRS. IDA E. GLADDING,
6012 Waterman Ave.

February 23rd, 1917.

TO WHOM IT MAY CONCERN:

Fortunately for me, I was given the opportunity to buy some lots in the negro subdivision of South Kinloch Park. Looked like would surely make money, if I had to hold them indefinitely.

Two of my lots were sold for me last week at double the price I paid.

Very truly,

(Signed) M. M. SEUFERT,
810 N. Fourth St.

February 19, 1917

To Whom it May Concern:

On December 6th, 1916, I bought lots six, seven, eight and nine (6, 7, 8 and 9) block two (2) of South Kinloch Park.

These lots cost me $550.00, and were sold for me by the Olive Street Terrace Realty Co. on Feb. 17th, 1917, for $1100.00, or just double what I paid.

The Company has made good their promises and I appreciate their service.

Yours truly,

(Signed) LURA M. GOCHENOUR
1715 Pierce Bldg.

WE HAVE MANY SUCH LETTERS

Miss Lura Gochenour felt like she wanted a larger income - there are so many additional comforts, pleasures and luxuries one can buy with a little extra money.

She heard of several people who had been making a great deal of money in something quite unusual in the way of a very profitable land deal.

So she tried it herself.

She paid $50.00 cash - giving her note for a small amount additional.

In less than 90 days she made a profit of $550.00 on a cash investment of $50.00

Read her letter on the back of this sheet - read the letters from others who had the same experience read the article from the Post-Dispatch.

Let us show you how it is possible to invest $50.00 cash and make a legitimate profit of $500.00 or $1,000.00 in a few months and at the same time help these people to get homes who need them and want them.

Give our representative a few minutes to explain the details of this unique plan.

Just sign and mail the card.

Yours very truly,

W C Ferris

President.

These are some testimonies from whites who purchased lots in Kinloch regarding profitable returns on investments. (Courtesy of the 1984 Kinloch History Committee.)

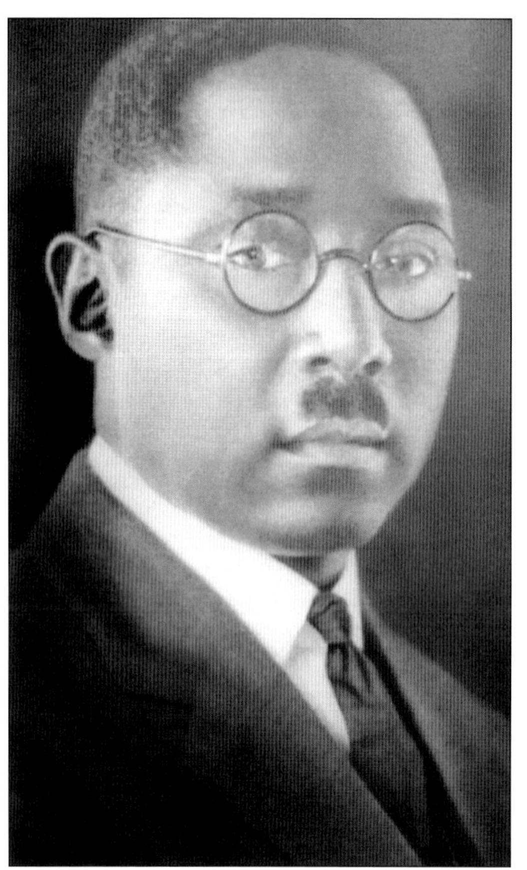

Enough blacks moved into Kinloch to elect Rev. Walter Johnson to the school board, becoming the first black school board member in the state. He immediately began pushing for equal treatment for black students. After blacks elected another member to the school board, whites feared black control and voted to incorporate their section into the City of Berkeley, forming a white school district. (Courtesy of First Baptist Church of Kinloch.)

In 1917, East St. Louis was the scene of one of the bloodiest race riots in American history. Rioting erupted on July 2, 1917, when white mobs pulled innocent black citizens off streetcars and clubbed or stoned them. Later, mob leaders murdered black victims who lay wounded in the streets. Whites set fire to homes owned by blacks and then shot black residents as they tried to escape. (Courtesy of the Missouri Historical Society.)

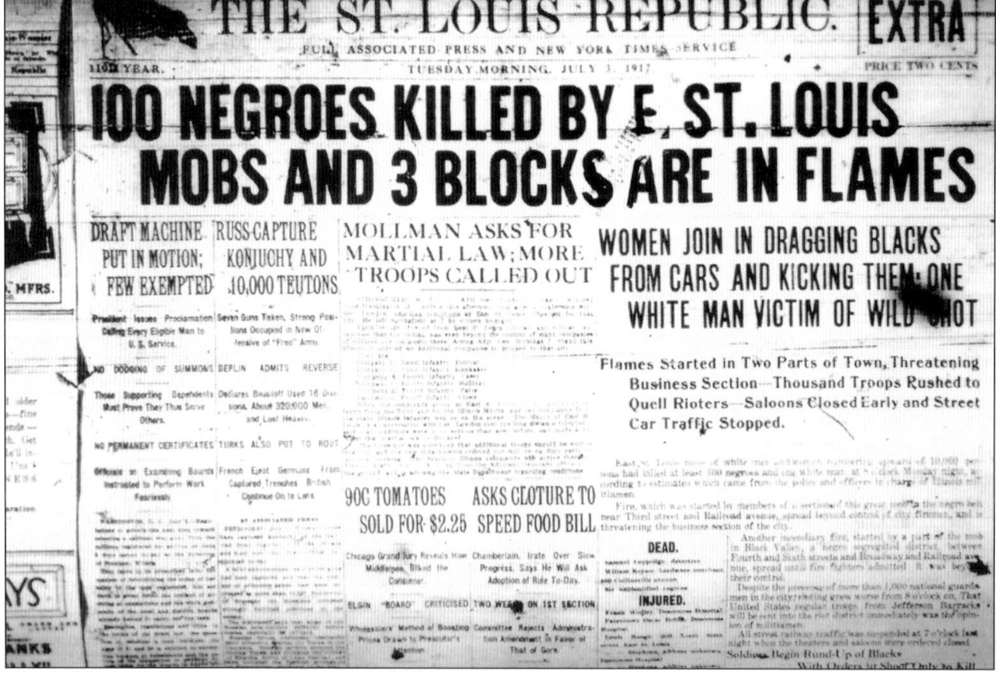

THE ST. LOUIS REPUBLIC. EXTRA

FULL ASSOCIATED PRESS AND NEW YORK TIMES SERVICE

TUESDAY MORNING, JULY 3, 1917

PRICE TWO CENTS

100 NEGROES KILLED BY E. ST. LOUIS MOBS AND 3 BLOCKS ARE IN FLAMES

DRAFT MACHINE PUT IN MOTION; FEW EXEMPTED

President Issues Proclamation Calling Every Eligible Man to U. S. Service.

NO DODGING OF SUMMONS

Those Supporting Dependents Must Prove They Thus Serve Others.

NO PERMANENT CERTIFICATES

Officials on Examining Boards Instructed to Perform Work Fearlessly.

RUSS CAPTURE KONJUCHY AND 10,000 TEUTONS

Seven Guns Taken, Strong Positions Occupied in New Offensive of "Free" Army.

BERLIN ADMITS REVERSE

Declares Brusiloff Used 16 Divisions, About 320,000 Men, and Lost Heavily.

TURKS ALSO PUT TO ROUT

French Eject Germans From Captured Trenches. British Continue On to Lens.

MOLLMAN ASKS FOR MARTIAL LAW; MORE TROOPS CALLED OUT

90C TOMATOES SOLD FOR $2.25

Chicago Grand Jury Reveals How Middlemen Bilked the Consumer.

ELGIN "BOARD" CRITICISED

Wholesalers' Method of Boosting Prices Drawn to Prosecutor's Attention.

ASKS CLOTURE TO SPEED FOOD BILL

Chamberlain, Irate Over Slow Progress, Says He Will Ask Adoption of Rule To-Day.

TWO WEEKS ON 1ST SECTION

Committee Rejects Administration Amendment in Favor of That of Gore.

WOMEN JOIN IN DRAGGING BLACKS FROM CARS AND KICKING THEM; ONE WHITE MAN VICTIM OF WILD SHOT

Flames Started in Two Parts of Town, Threatening Business Section—Thousand Troops Rushed to Quell Rioters—Saloons Closed Early and Street Car Traffic Stopped.

DEAD.

INJURED.

Soldiers Begin Rund-Up of Blacks

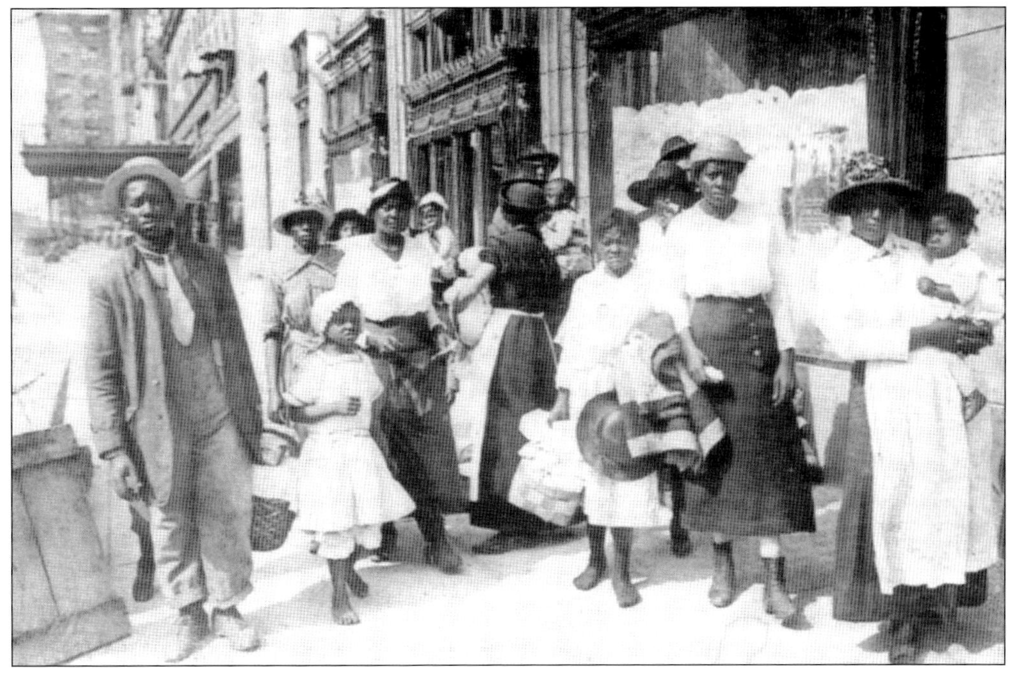

Many of the blacks who were able to escape the riot found themselves on the streets of St. Louis homeless and without resources. A number had come to East St. Louis in search of employment in the stockyards and packing plants. Animosities were aggravated when some companies hired black employees to take the place of white workers striking for better working conditions. (Both, courtesy of the University of Massachusetts Special Collection Archives.)

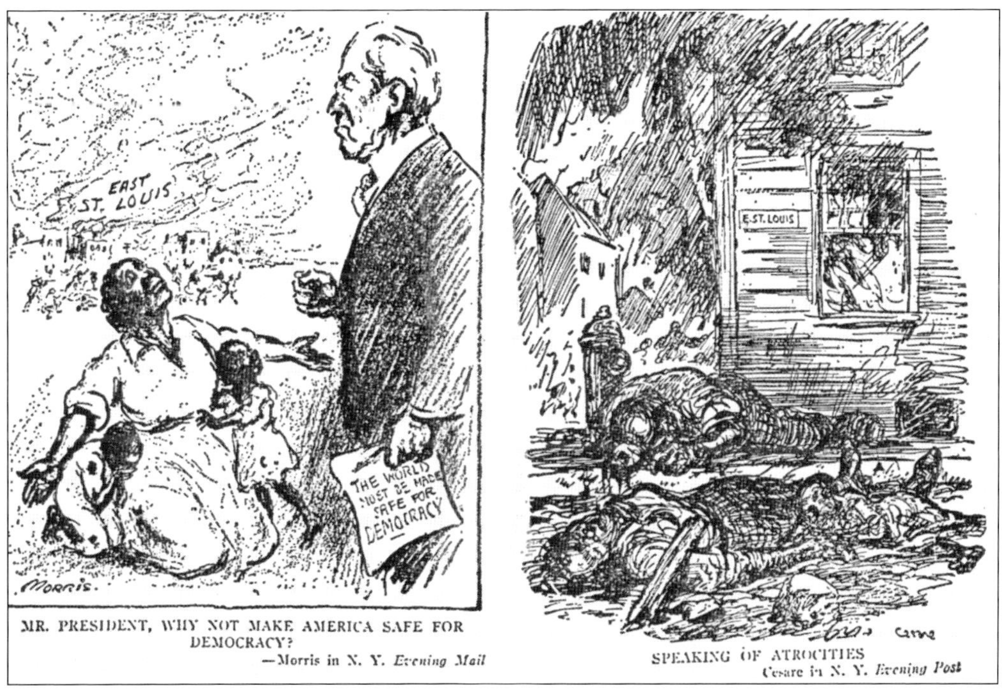

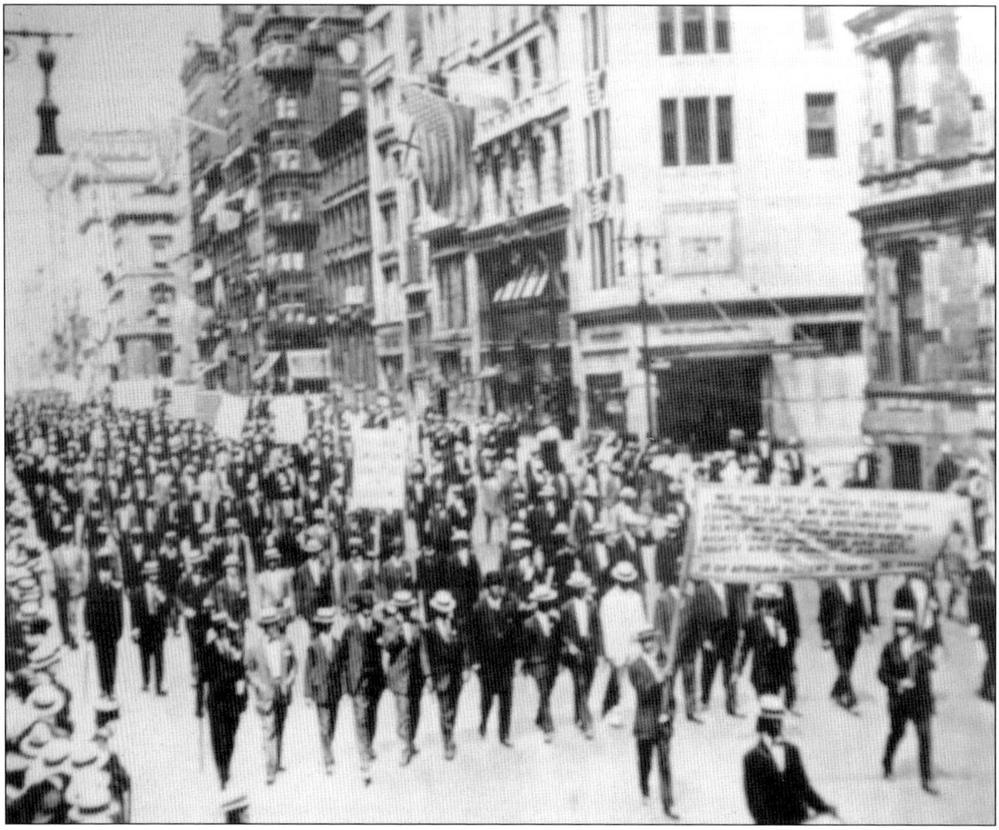

On July 28, 1917, an estimated 8,000 to 15,000 African Americans marched in silent protest of lynchings in Waro, Memphis, and especially the East St. Louis riot. Protesters carried signs that highlighted their discontent. Some signs and banners appealed directly to Pres. Woodrow Wilson. The organizers felt that it was important that only black people participate because they were the main victims of the violence. (Courtesy of the National Archives.)

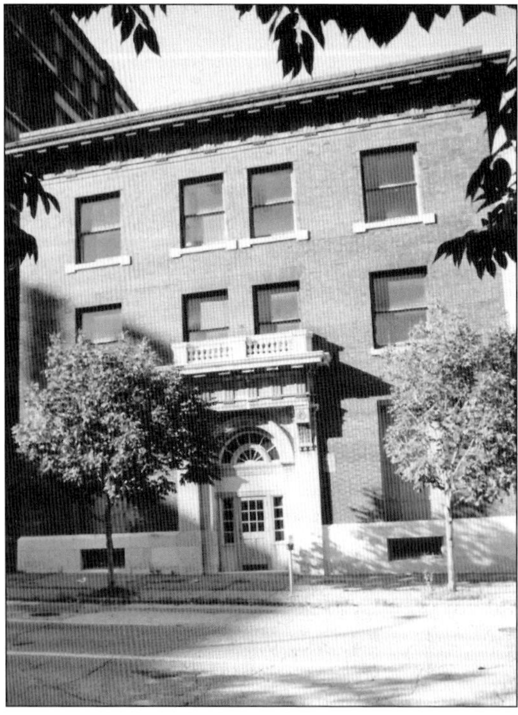

The Urban League of St. Louis was created in 1918 in reaction to the East St Louis Race Riot. It also had to deal with the number of blacks coming from the South pouring into overcrowded black areas of the city. Blacks were faced with a horrible environment and experienced a multitude of problems including health, unemployment, limited municipal services, segregation, and discrimination. (Photograph by John A. Wright Sr.)

Frank Williams, principal of Sumner High School, was instrumental in the founding of New Age Federal Savings and Loan in 1915 to assist blacks in securing loans when they were denied financing by other institutions. The company closed in 1991 because of a change in federal regulations. It was the oldest minority-owned financial institution in the state and among the oldest in the nation. (Courtesy of John A. Wright Sr.)

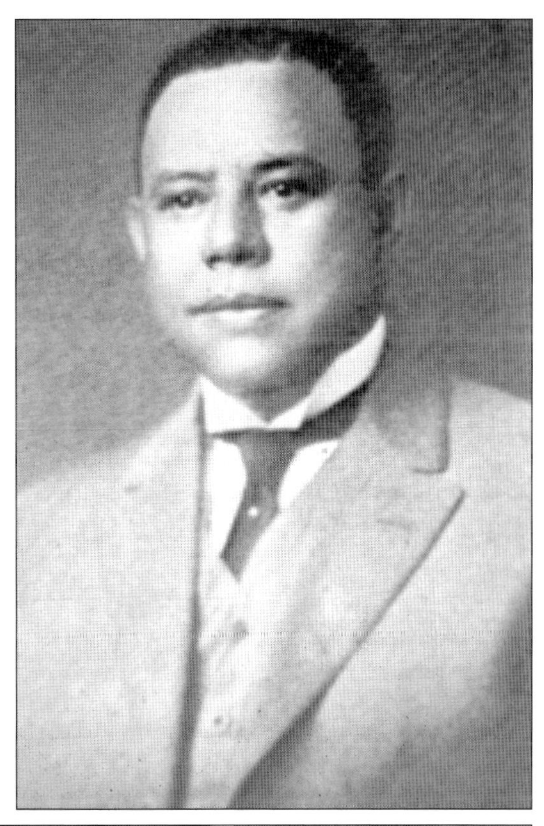

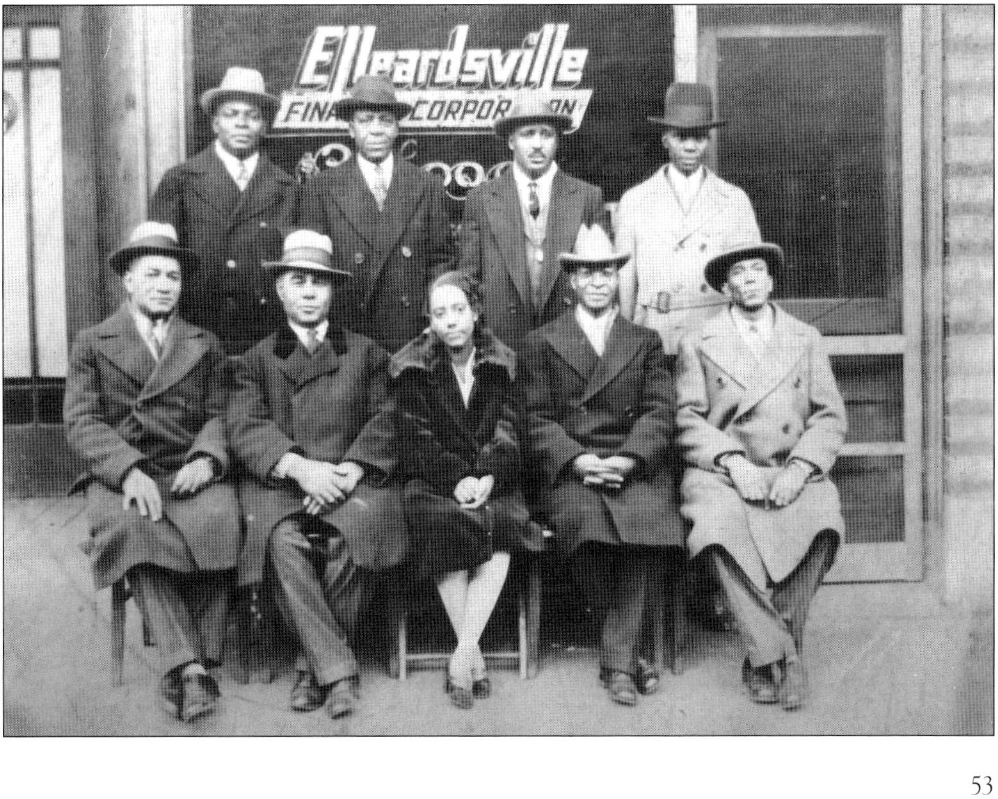

Herman Dreer, seated second from right, an administrator at Sumner High School, was instrumental in the establishment of the Elleardsville Finance Corporation in 1926 to meet the needs of new residents moving into the community for construction of new homes and the repair of existing ones. The organizers put up $15,000 of their assets to form the corporation. (Courtesy of Vivian Dreer.)

If Every Wife Knew What Every Widow Knows
Every Husband Would Be A Member Of

The Knights of Pythias

Headquarters:

Grand Lodge Knights of Pythias of Missouri

3137 PINE BOULEVARD ST. LOUIS, MO.

JEfferson 4469

W. T. ANCELL, G. K. R. & S **A. W. LLOYD, Grand Chancell**

Assets Over $200,000.00

We have placed $75,000.00 in assisting our people in the purchase of home
We care for the sick. We bury the dead. We pay the widows and orphans.

Our large, conveniently located Auditorium can be rented at reduced rates for Conventions and Entertainments. Call JEfferson 4469 for particulars.

Publisher's Note:—The Grand Lodge Knights of Pythias of Missouri has its general headquarters housed in its own building at 3137 Pine Boulevard. The offices of Grand Chancellor A. W. Lloyd and Grand Keeper of Records and Seal W. T. Ancell, are located on the second floor of the building and remain open for business each day during business hours. Grand Chancellor Lloyd at the last Grand Lodge Session, which was held at Moberly, Mo., the past July, was re-elected for the twenty-eighth consecutive year.

With the absence of government assistance for blacks, the Knights of Pythias and other social and fraternal organizations took on the responsibility of assisting with loans for the purchasing of a home, burial assistance, and assistance for widows, orphans, and the sick. The Knights of Pythias were very involved in civic activities and offered their hall for community gatherings. (Courtesy of Central Baptist Church.)

ANCIENT UNITED KNIGHTS & DAUGHTERS OF AFRICA

Incorporated Under The Laws of Missouri and Registered at Washington, District of Columbia

1. The principles are so sublime that the white people cannot claim one word is from their brain.
2. It not only takes care of the sick and buries the dead, but protects its members in every way.
3. It pays endowment at death.
4. It helps its members improve their condition, morally, financially and intellectually while they are living.
5. It protects its business and profesional men by urging its members to spend their money with them in preference to any other.
6. It is the champion of manhood and womanhood rights in this country, and promises to secure for its members their constitutinal rights by agitation and through their legal representatives.
7. The work of this society is recognized by all races of the country, and thereby will eliminate race prejudice and promote the principles of brotherhood and sisterhood

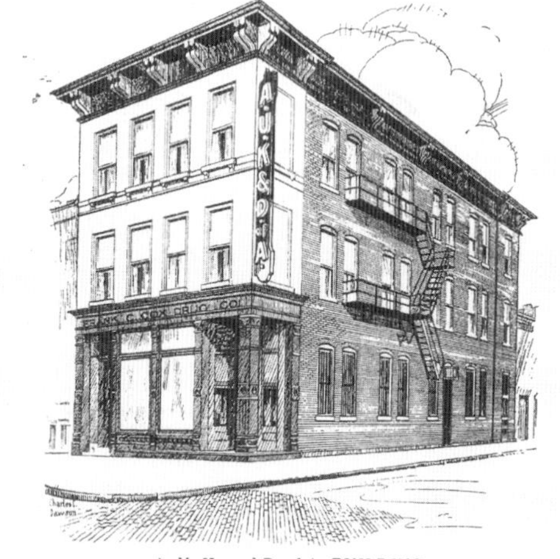

A. U. K. and D. of A. BUILDING
Northwest corner Lucas and Compton Avenues
The offices of the National Grand Master are located on Second Floor

The Ancient United Knights and Daughters of Africa, another fraternal group, was on the northwest corner of Lucas and Compton Avenues. Like the Knights of Pythias, the organization provided for the welfare of its members. (Courtesy of Central Baptist Church.)

In 1919, Christopher K. Robinson, owner of a printing company and publisher of the *Clarion* newspaper, convinced the city to purchase the vacant Barnes Medical College as a health care center for black city residents and doctors. It was one of five institutions in the United States offering training for black doctors. (Courtesy of Jacqueline Irvin Creighton and Ella Brown.)

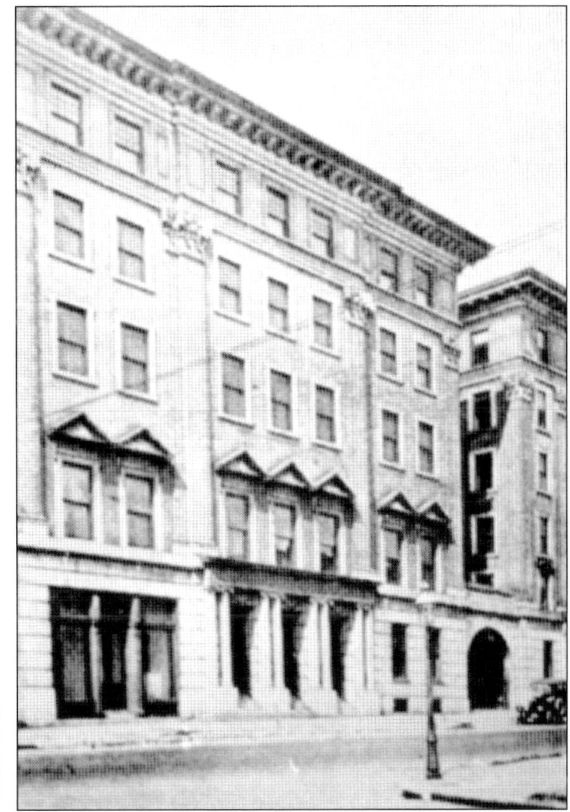

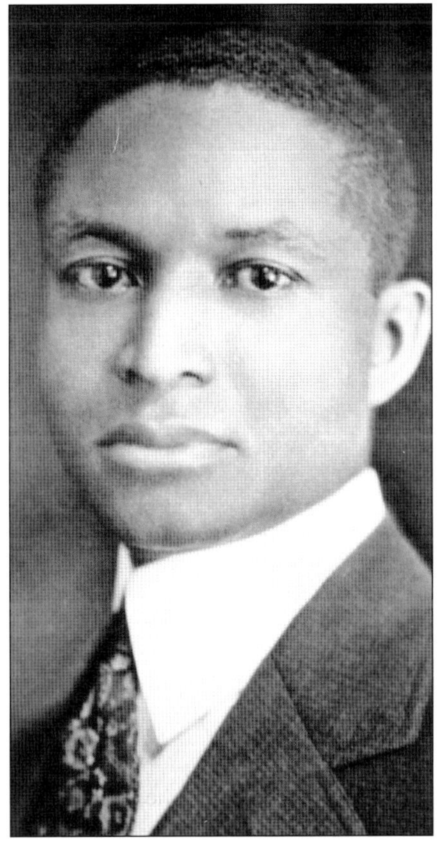

The former Barnes building, which became known as City Hospital No. 2, was soon found inadequate as a medical facility. Through the efforts of attorney Homer G. Phillips, a bond issue was passed in 1925 by the citizens of St. Louis with the understanding that some funds would be used to construct a new hospital for African Americans. (Courtesy of the Western Manuscript Collection, UMSL.)

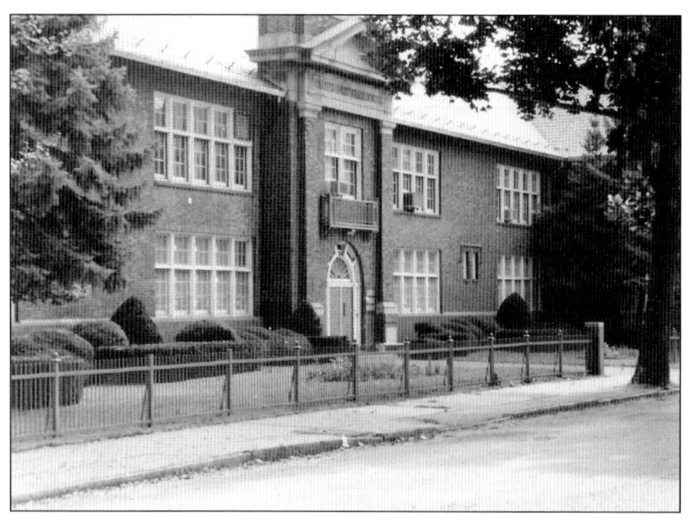

During the early part of the 1900s, tuberculosis was killing more young children in St. Louis than all other infectious diseases combined. It was five times as high among blacks as whites among those suffering from poor nutrition and living in crowded and unsanitary conditions. The Urban League, under Dr. Charles Turner, led the construction of a school for handicapped black children. (Courtesy of John A. Wright Sr.)

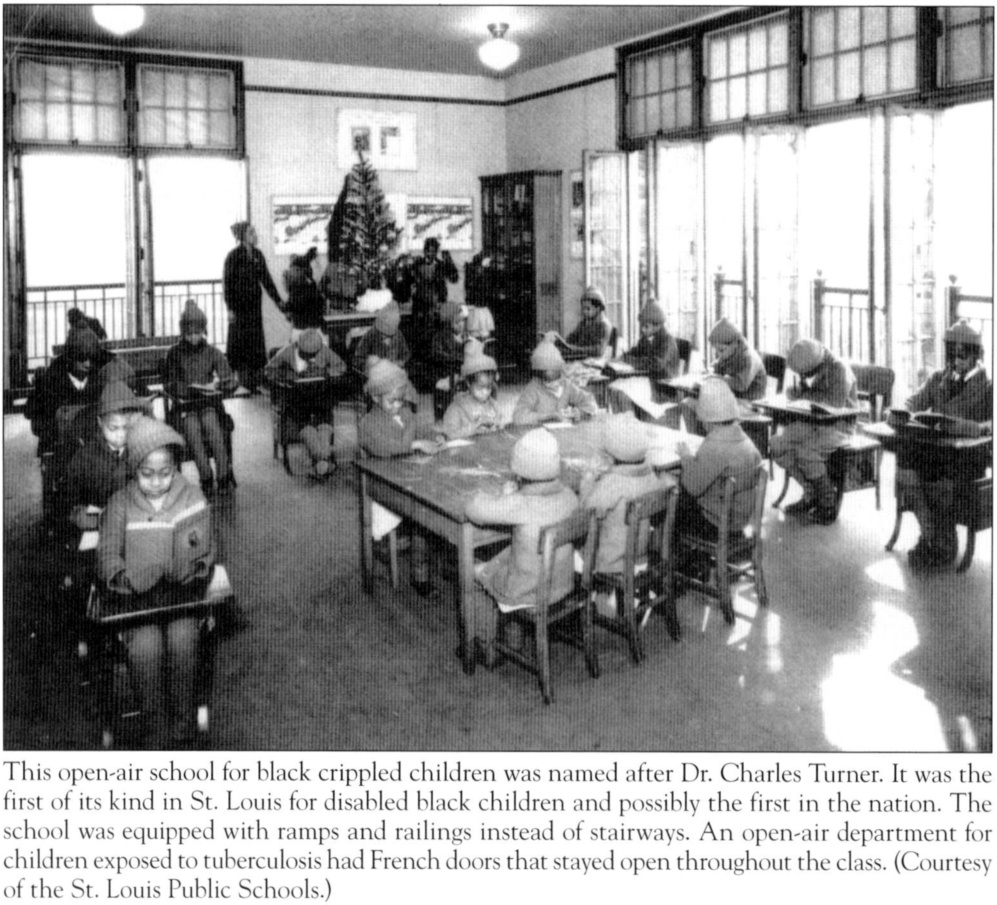

This open-air school for black crippled children was named after Dr. Charles Turner. It was the first of its kind in St. Louis for disabled black children and possibly the first in the nation. The school was equipped with ramps and railings instead of stairways. An open-air department for children exposed to tuberculosis had French doors that stayed open throughout the class. (Courtesy of the St. Louis Public Schools.)

The first YMCA was organized in 1887 under the leadership of John Boyer Vashon. It was called YMCA for Colored Men and became a branch of the Metropolitan St. Louis YMCA in 1912. Although it was a branch of the Metropolitan YMCA, it remained segregated. This building was dedicated on March 25, 1919. During the last days of World War I, it was used for housing and feeding troops. (Courtesy of John A. Wright Sr.)

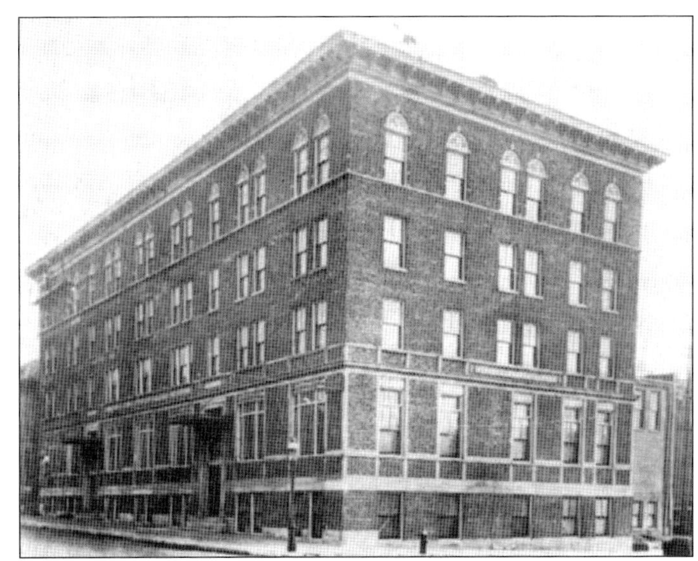

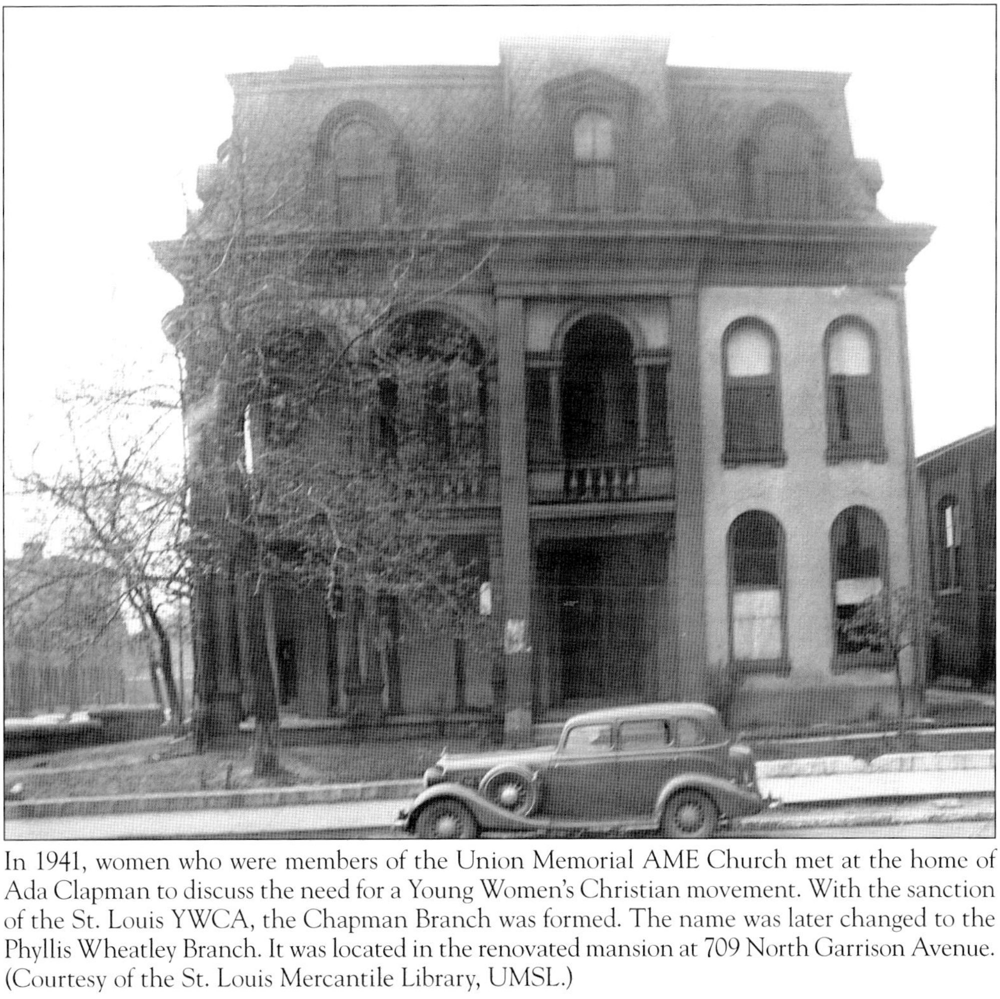

In 1941, women who were members of the Union Memorial AME Church met at the home of Ada Clapman to discuss the need for a Young Women's Christian movement. With the sanction of the St. Louis YWCA, the Chapman Branch was formed. The name was later changed to the Phyllis Wheatley Branch. It was located in the renovated mansion at 709 North Garrison Avenue. (Courtesy of the St. Louis Mercantile Library, UMSL.)

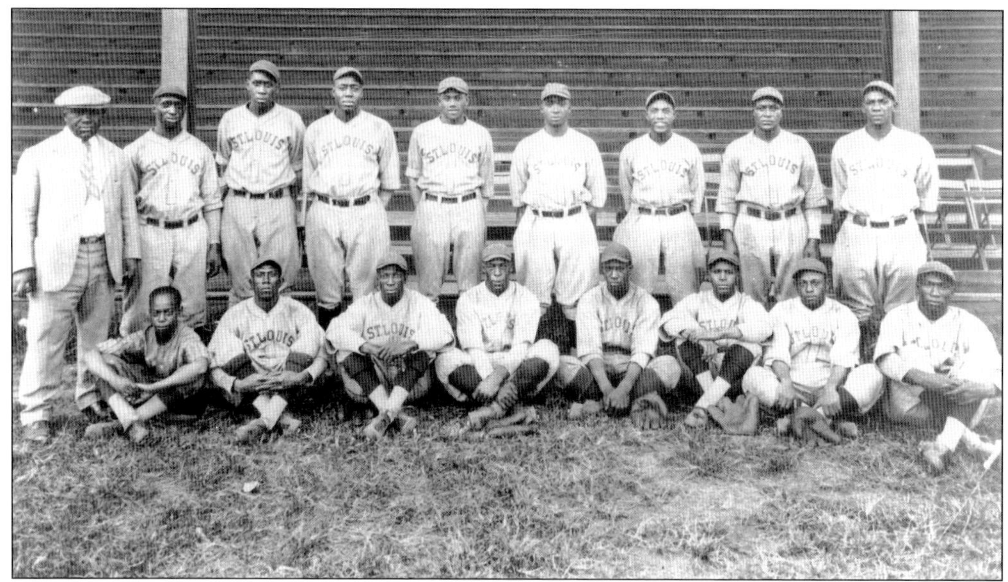

Since blacks were not permitted to play baseball in white leagues, they formed their own league. The first professional black team was the St. Louis Giants, founded in 1909. The team first played at Finley Park before moving to Stars Park in 1931, where the first permanent lights for night games were installed in St. Louis. (Courtesy of National Baseball Hall of Fame Library.)

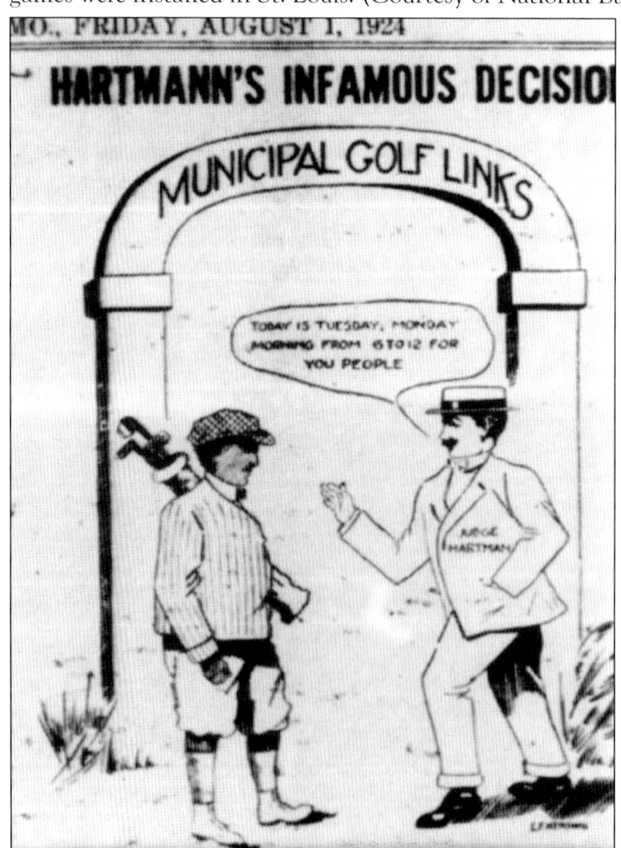

The recreational facilities in Finley Park were segregated. In 1922. Albert Howard asked the St. Louis Circuit Court to compel the park commissioner to issue golf permits. A decision was made to issue permits for blacks to play on Mondays from 6:00 a.m. to noon. A whistle blew at the end of the period, and black golfers were expected to leave the course. (Courtesy of the Missouri Historical Society.)

Searching for a better life, several thousand blacks in St. Louis joined the Pacific Movement of the Eastern World, a pro-Japan organization because of their desire for full equality, whether achieved within or outside the borders of the United States. The organization embraced the back-to-Africa movement and endorsed colonization projects in Brazil and Japan. The organization faded after Japan lost the war. (Courtesy of the Washington University Archives.)

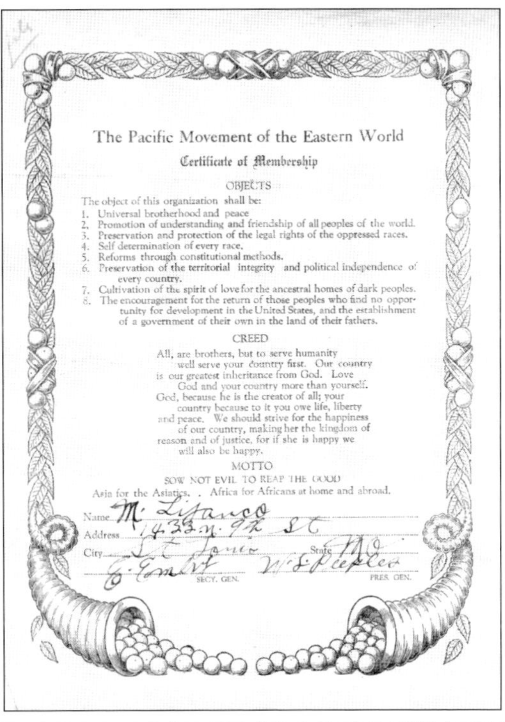

The Pacific Movement of the Eastern World

Certificate of Membership

OBJECTS

The object of this organization shall be:

1. Universal brotherhood and peace
2. Promotion of understanding and friendship of all peoples of the world.
3. Preservation and protection of the legal rights of the oppressed races.
4. Self determination of every race.
5. Reforms through constitutional methods.
6. Preservation of the territorial integrity and political independence of every country.
7. Cultivation of the spirit of love for the ancestral homes of dark peoples.
8. The encouragement for the return of those peoples who find no opportunity for development in the United States, and the establishment of a government of their own in the land of their fathers.

CREED

All, are brothers, but to serve humanity well serve your country first. Our country is our greatest inheritance from God. Love God and your country more than yourself. God, because he is the creator of all; your country because to it you owe life, liberty and peace. We should strive for the happiness of our country, making her the kingdom of reason and of justice, for if she is happy we will also be happy.

MOTTO

SOW NOT EVIL TO REAP THE GOOD

Asia for the Asiatics. . Africa for Africans at home and abroad.

Name

Address

City State

SECY. GEN. PRES. GEN.

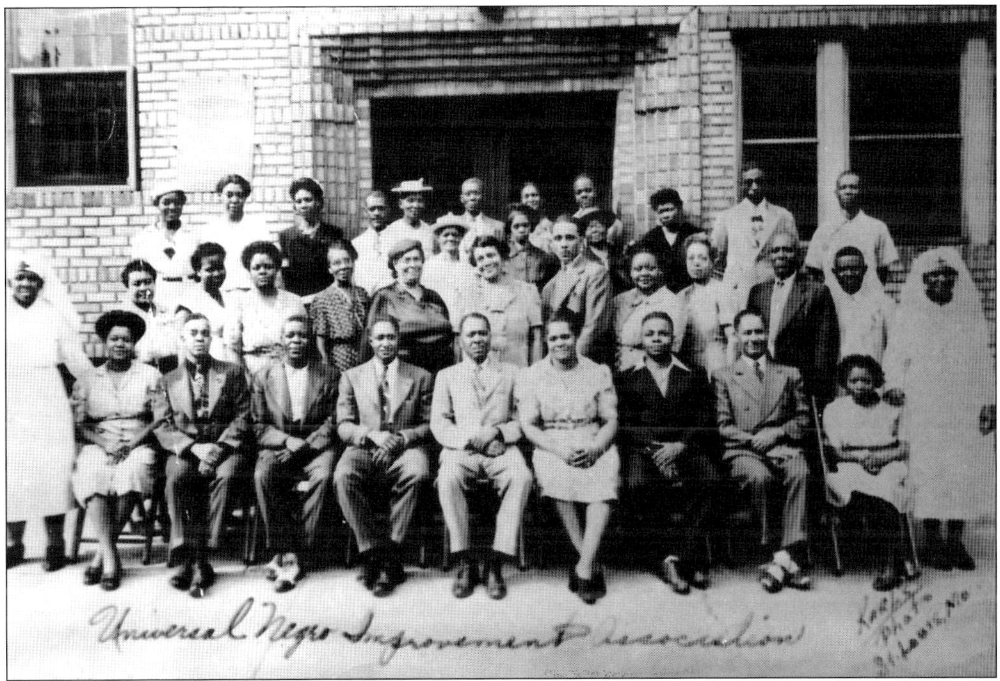

These are members of the Universal Negro Improvement Association founded by Marcus Garvey in front of Jackson Funeral Home at 2649 Delmar Boulevard. The organization came to America in 1916, and its national membership soon grew to about two million. It established a chain of cooperative grocery stores, restaurants, steam laundries, tailoring and dressmaking stores, and a publishing house to meet the needs of the black community. (Courtesy of Samella Woodson.)

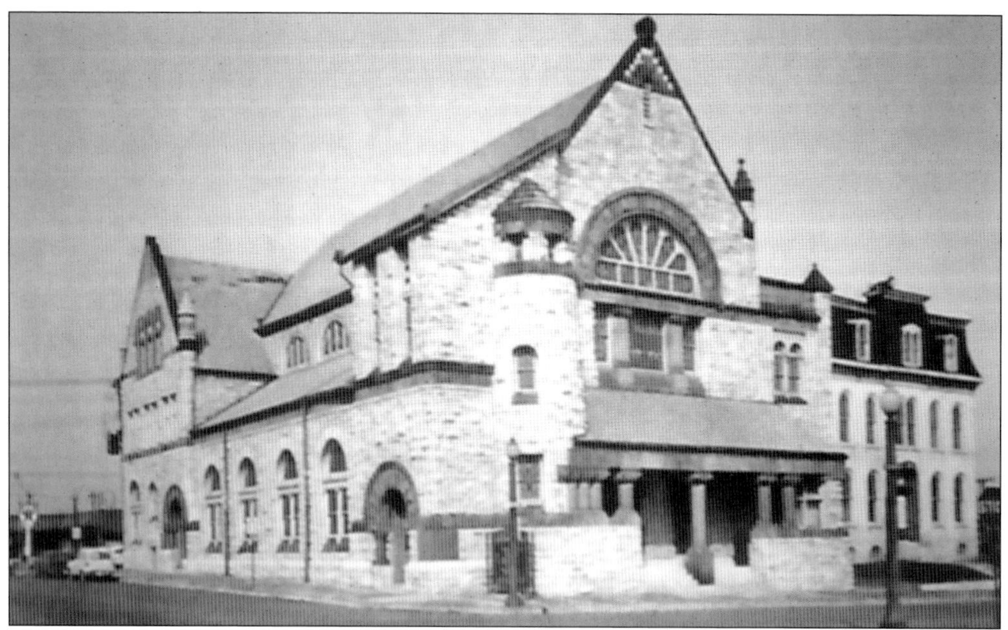

After Union Memorial AME experienced a growth in its congregation, it purchased a large Presbyterian church at the northeast corner of Lucas and Garrison Avenues. When the white Union Methodist Episcopal Church discovered the purchase, it offered to pay the difference if the church would move. Since it was near their church and they did not confuse the name, the church then purchased the former Temple Israel. (Courtesy of the St. Louis Landmark Association.)

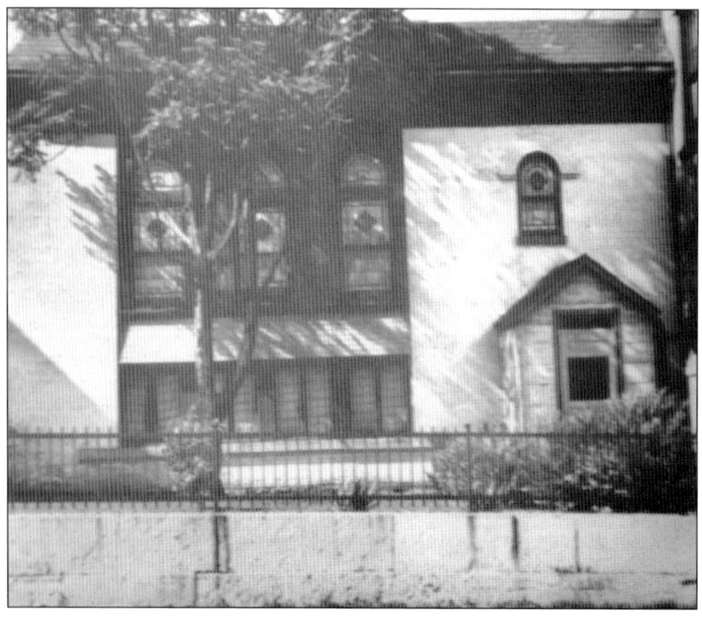

Although Roman Catholic parishes in St. Louis were never officially segregated, African Americans were often excluded from white congregations. In 1875, the refurbished Vinegar Hill Hall at Fourteenth and Gay Streets was dedicated as St. Elizabeth Church for the use of African Americans. The church was moved to this facility at 2721 Pine Street in 1912. (Courtesy of the St. Louis Archdiocese.)

Four

Separate and Unequal

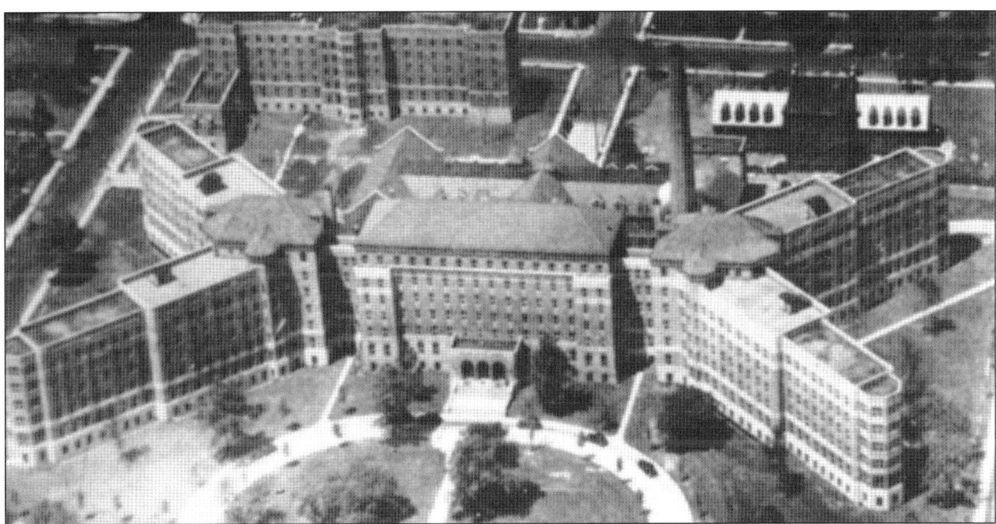

Homer G. Phillips Hospital was dedicated on February 22, 1937. The city argued that an earlier bond issue did not include the building of a hospital for blacks. However, once it was decided a hospital would be built, blacks were not allowed to work on its construction because of union objections. The city officials rejected applications from blacks, even those with union cards. (Courtesy of the Western Manuscript Collection, UMSL.)

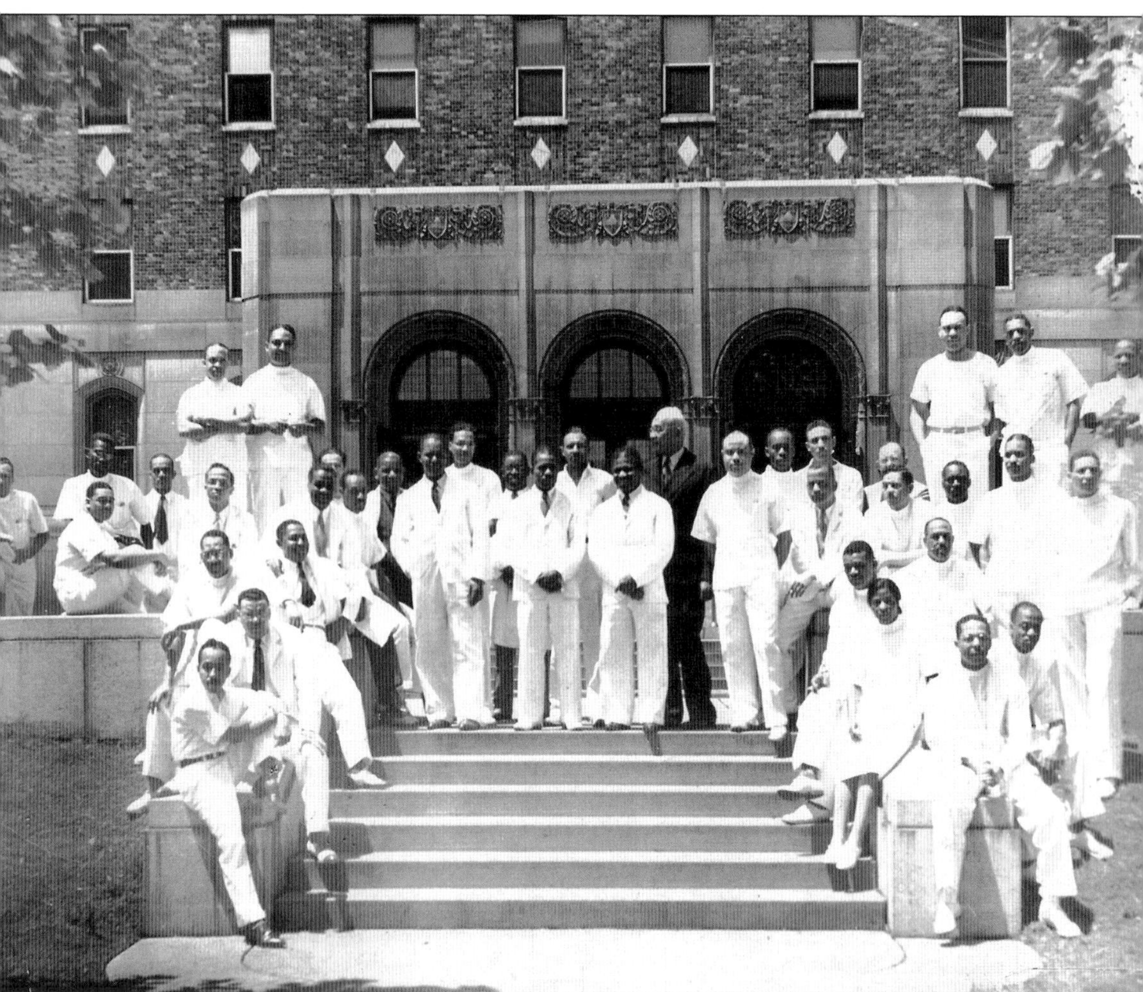

Homer G. Phillips Hospital was a Class A hospital approved for junior internships and assistant residencies by the American Council on Medical Education and the American College of Surgeons. There were small numbers of black graduates from predominantly white medical schools, who were not considered for hospital training in those institutions after earning their medical degrees. Over half the black medical doctors at the time received their training at this hospital. (Courtesy of Vivian Dreer.)

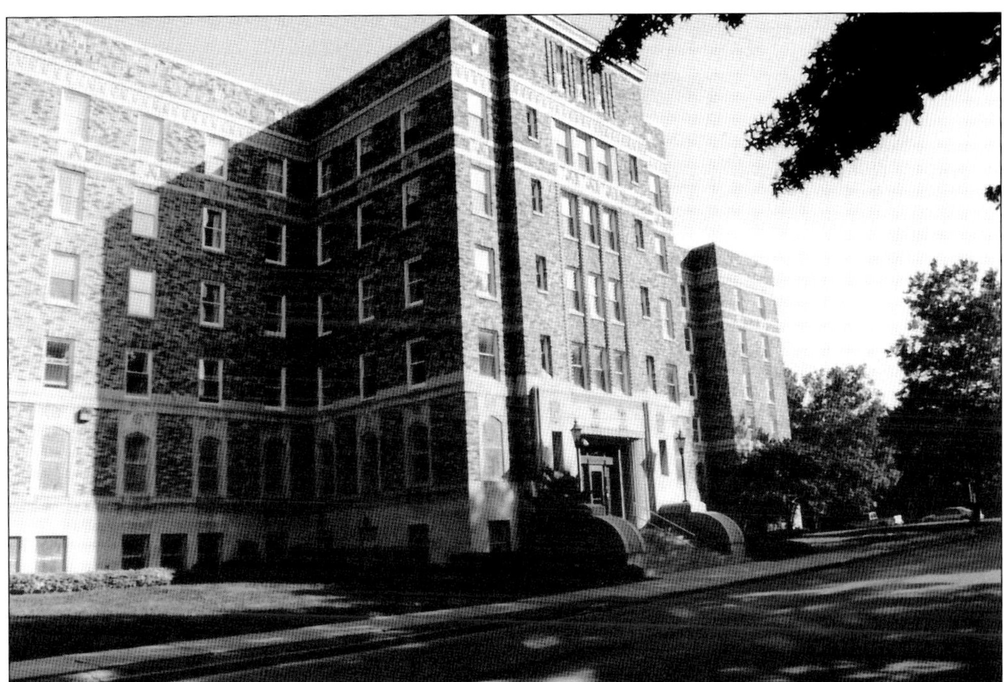

A nursing school and residence was part of the hospital complex, with a connecting tunnel to the hospital. The facility provided living quarters for 147 students and 14 faculty members. (Photograph by John A. Wright Sr.)

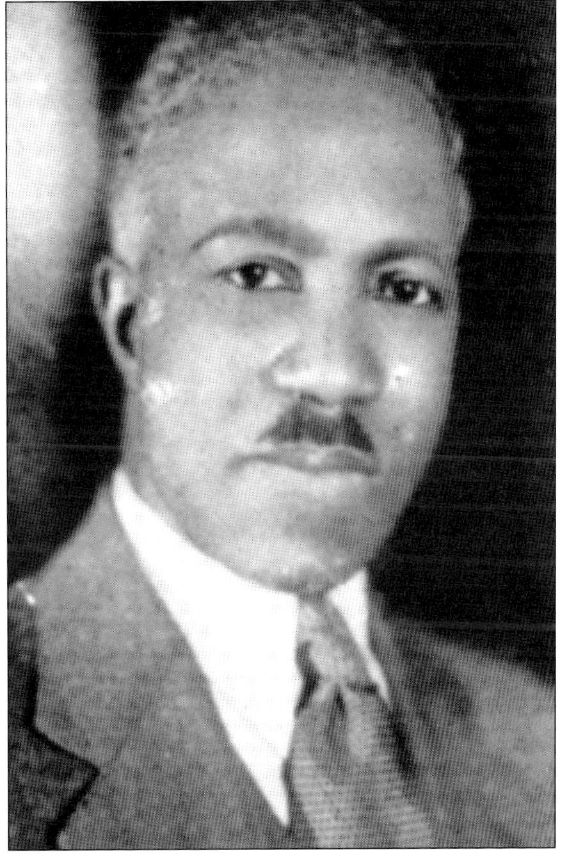

After the city refused to allow black tradesmen to work on the construction of Homer G. Phillips Hospital, John Clark, head of the St. Louis Urban League, assisted skilled black workers to form a union: the International Laborers and Builders Corporation. A letter from Washington ordered the Local Civil Work Administration to cooperate with local administration, which meant they could exclude blacks from working. (Courtesy of John A. Wright Sr.)

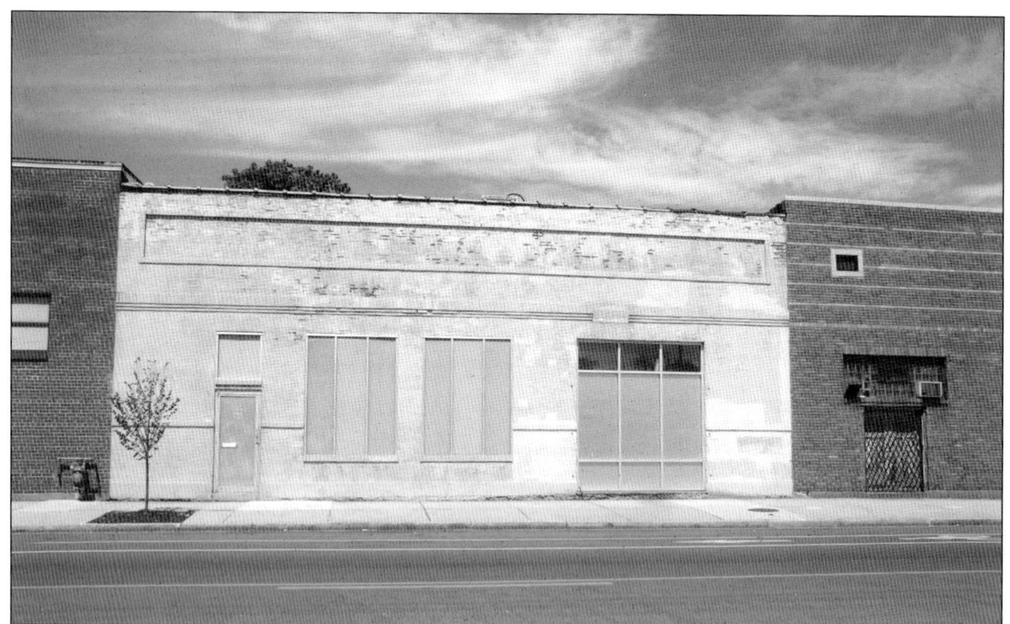

In 1933, about 1,000 black women walked off the job for higher wages. R.E. Funsten Company was paying white women 4¢ to 6¢ per pound to sort through pecans, and African American women 3¢ or 4¢ per pound to shell them. The women won all their demands, doubling their salaries and setting an important precedent for the labor movement. This is an R.E. Funsten Company site at 4241 Easton Avenue (Photograph by John A. Wright Sr.)

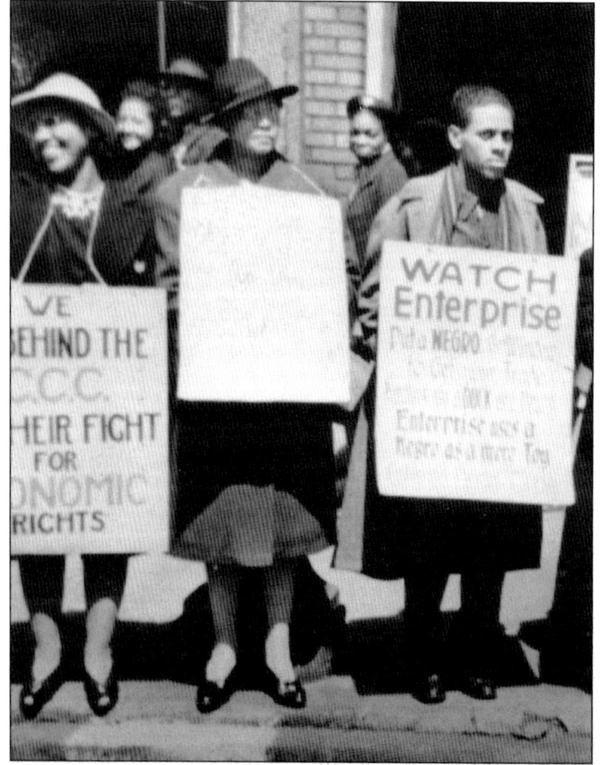

The Colored Clerks Circle, pictured here, were waging a fight for equal employment. With the assistance of the Urban League, they pressured Woolworth on Sarah Street and Easton Avenue to employ more African American clerks. (Courtesy of the Western Manuscript Collection, UMSL.)

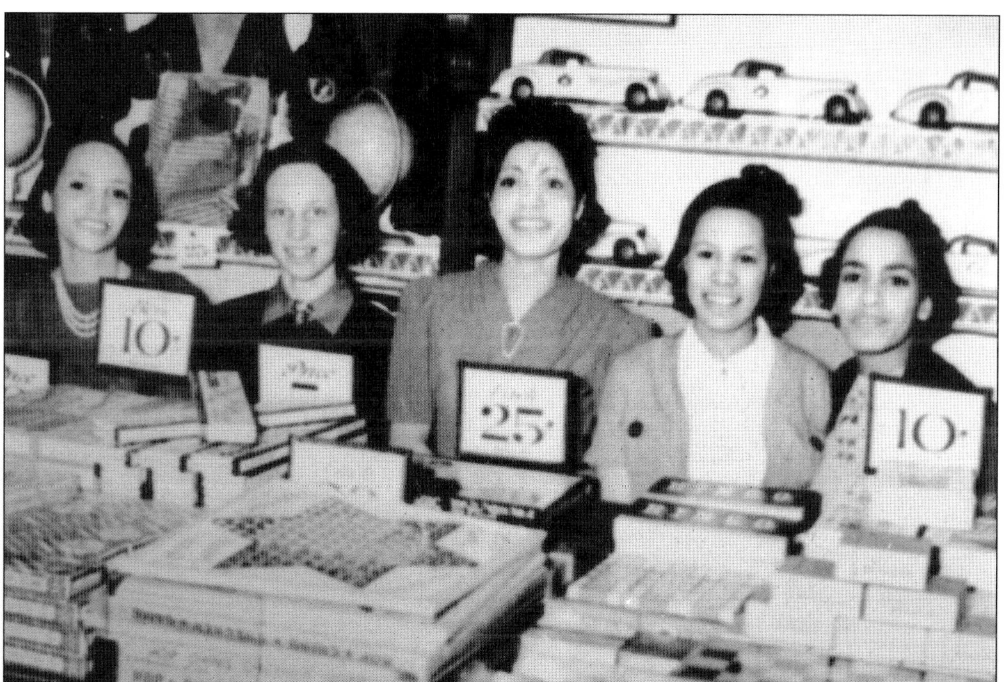

Pictured here are the first clerks hired at the Woolworth department store on Franklin Avenue in the heart of the black community. They are, from left to right, Ruby Cockrell, Helen Hollway, Evelyn Woods, Paris Jones, and Dorothy Bolar. These women had light complexions. The closer they came to looking white, the better their chances of getting hired. (Courtesy of the Urban League of Metropolitan St. Louis.)

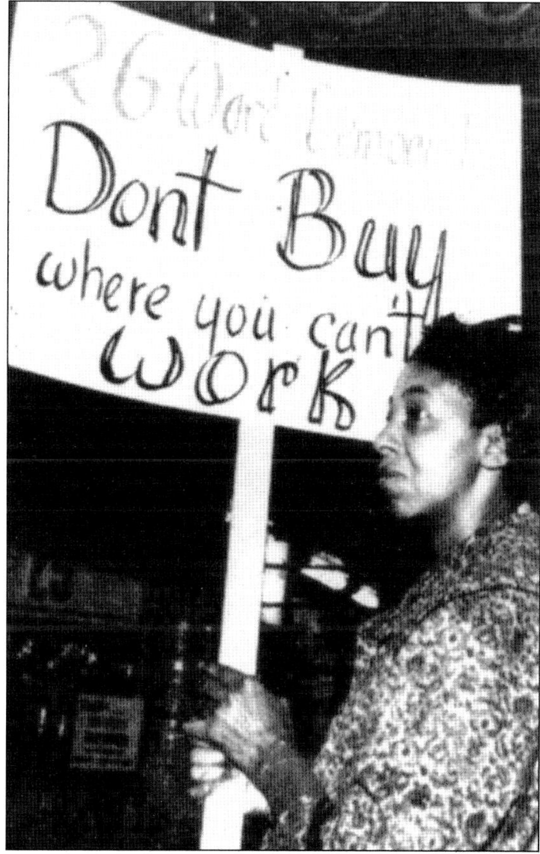

During the Depression, many economic gains made by African Americans were lost. They were the last hired and the first fired. In 1931, the St. Louis Urban League led a boycott against a white-owned store chain that employed only whites although its trade was largely with blacks. Picketers carried signs in front of businesses that read, "Don't Buy Where You Can't Work." (Courtesy of the Western Manuscript Collection, UMSL.)

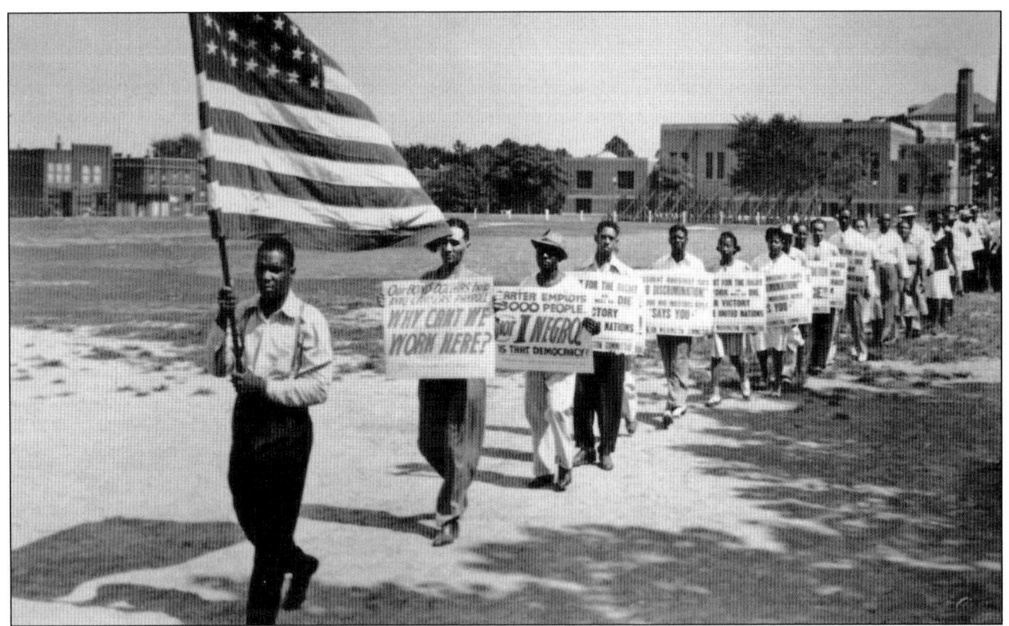

In August 1942, several hundred men and women marched from Tandy Park in the Ville to the Carter Carburetor plant at 2840 North Spring Avenue to protest the company's reluctance to hire African Americans. Not one black employee was among the company's workforce of 3,000. The plant had a government contract to manufacture shell fuses for the US War Department. (Courtesy of the St. Louis Mercantile Library, UMSL.)

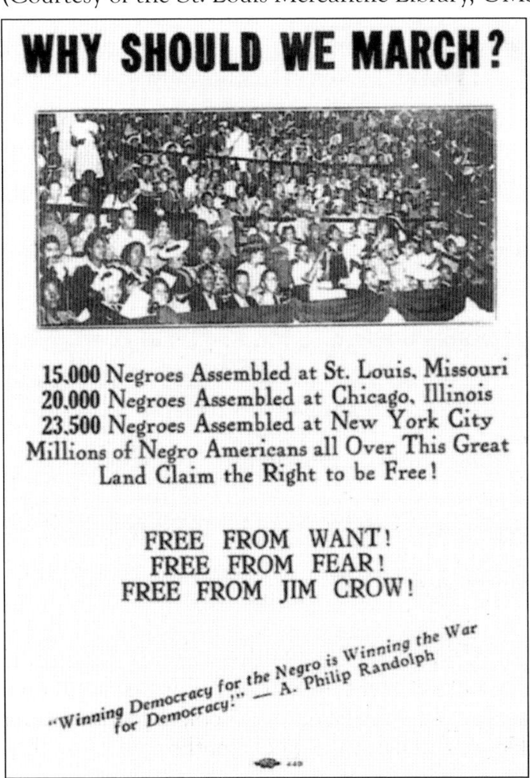

In 1942, St. Louis was part of the national March on Washington Movement, whose aim was to demand an increase in wages for black porters, admittance to training schools for defense plant jobs, and employment of black women. Defense plants gradually hired blacks in St. Louis. Fifty black women a week were hired as matrons after the Carter Carburetor march. (Courtesy of the National Archives.)

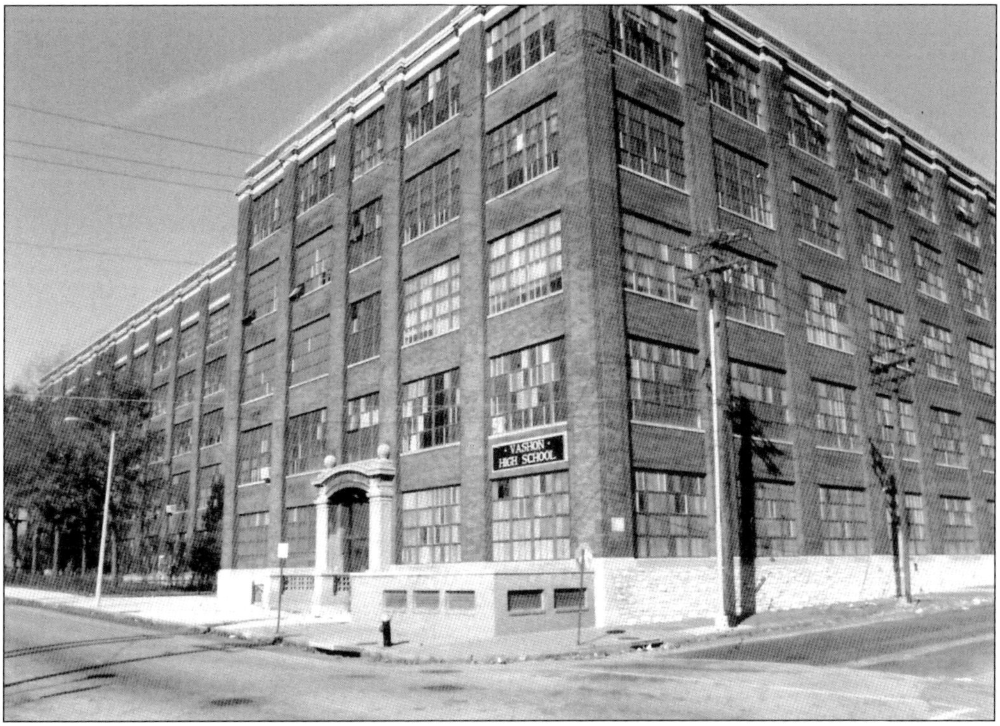

In 1947, the NAACP brought a suit against the St. Louis Board of Education to require Hadley Technical High School to allow access for black students to an aeromechanics program that was only offered to white students. The court ruled that the students had to be admitted, or provided with a similar program. Rather than make the program available to all, it was closed down. (Courtesy of John Wright Sr.)

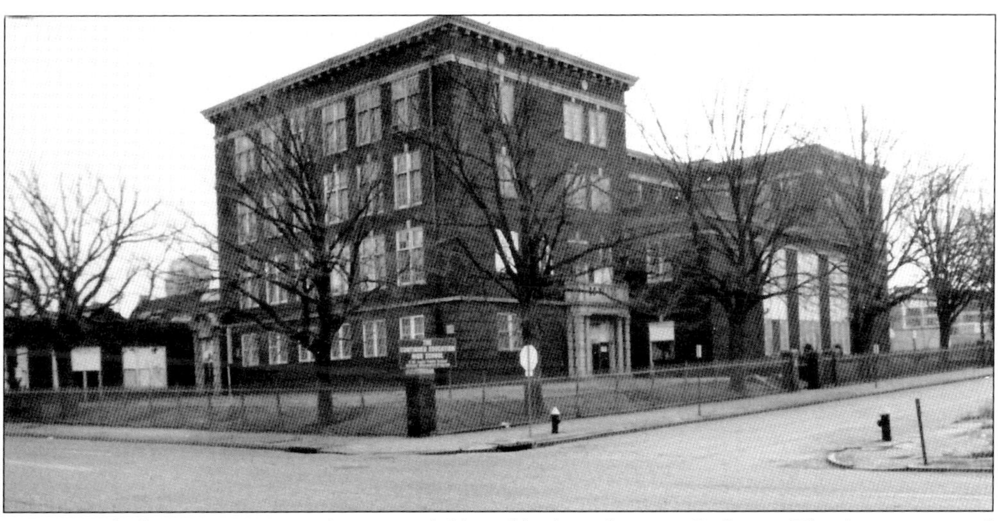

Vocational education was not always available to black students in St. Louis. The first vocational high school was opened in September 1929 at Carr Lane Elementary School, formerly used for whites. In 1937, the school was relocated to Henry Elementary School, another school used by whites. (Courtesy of John A. Wright Sr.)

THE FRANKLIN DISTRICT NEIGHBORHOOD ASSOCIATION

An organization of taxpayers, business and professional men and women, parents, and interested citizens who believe in the future of this entire district.

The immediate reopening of Franklin School to elementary and intermediate white children is not only good business, but a square deal for the property owners and parents of this district.

> We believe in fair play; and in the policy of LIVE AND LET LIVE. We are not antagonistic to any group of citizens. We wish to help them. We do not ask to take anything from them. But we do ask—most emphatically—to KEEP WHAT WE HAVE.

This neighborhood is coming back to its former substantial quality. The critical situation facing us has brought together all sorts of organizations which will work for the **immediate restoration** of Franklin School as an elementary and intermediate school **for white children.**

Due to the widening of Franklin Avenue and other major improvements, we, the taxpayers and business men of the entire Franklin district have suffered keenly during the past two years. We have borne these difficulties and heavy expenses in the hope of **future prosperity**. Now, when we are at a point to realize on our investment, IT IS UNFAIR TO CLOSE FRANKLIN SCHOOL TO ELEMENTARY AND INTERMEDIATE WHITE CHILDREN.

> **Many white families who were driven from this neighborhood, wish to return. We want them; we need them!!!**

This district is convenient to good schools, good stores, good doctors, good churches and missions; Day Nursery; and unusual recreational facilities for boys and girls. Also there is a branch of the Community Music Schools Foundation (violin, piano and other instruments); and a modern Social Settlement with gymnasium, showers, meeting rooms, library, craft rooms, workshop, outdoor porches and outside playground. This is for the use of boys and girls, men and women.

> We are in the heart of St. Louis! Fifteen minutes from everywhere! The rents are reasonable.
>
> The reopening of Franklin School as an elementary and intermediate school for white children will help us rebuild this entire district.

"WE DO NOT WANT TO TAKE. WE WANT TO KEEP"

The Franklin District Neighborhood Association
and Associated Organizations

The Franklin District Neighborhood Association objected to the black vocational high school replacing its white elementary school. The St. Louis Community Council, a municipal group, and the Urban League took up the issue and decided to approve the St. Louis School Board's plan to relocate the school from Carr Lane Elementary to Henry Elementary. (Courtesy of Washington University Archives.)

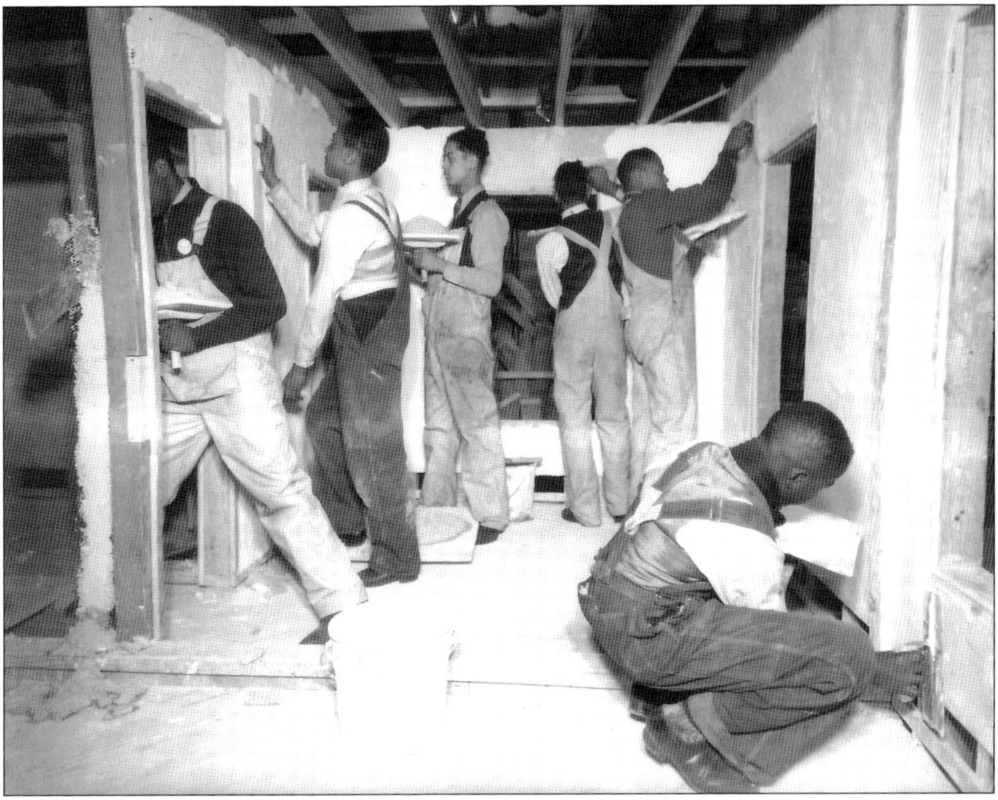

The Urban League and black civic leaders requested that students be provided technical skills similar to those in the white schools. F.J. Jeffrey, assistant superintendent in charge of vocational schools, stated, "I am offering courses that I think your people can get jobs, and I am not going to offer courses that will not enable them to get jobs." (Courtesy of St. Louis Public Schools.)

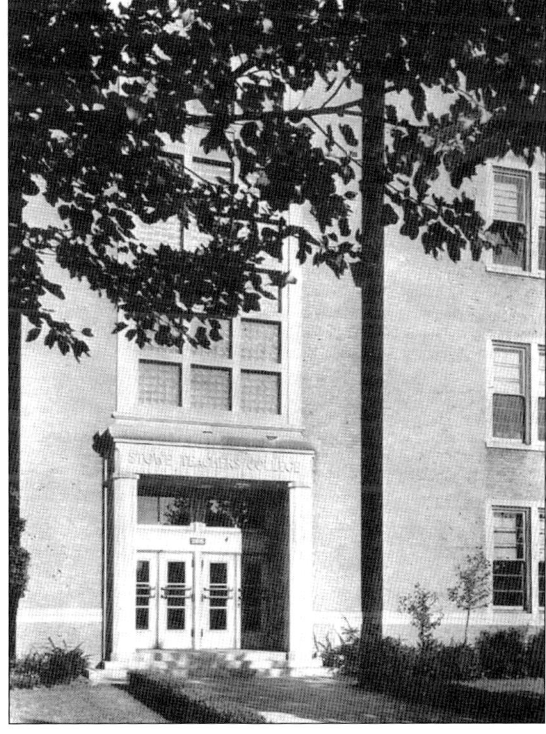

In 1950, a black student attending Stowe Teachers College, a teacher training institution maintained by the City of St. Louis for black students, applied for admission in Harris Teachers College, Stowe's white counterpart. The application was denied. The student then sought to compel the college to admit him through a writ of mandamus. The applicant contended there was a vast difference between the two facilities. This request was denied. (Courtesy of Gerdine Johnson.)

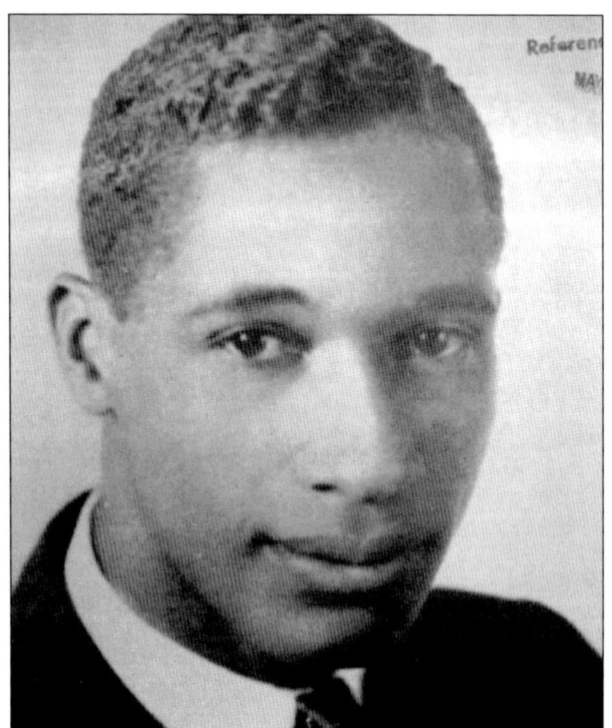

Lloyd Gaines graduated first in his class from Vashon High School in 1951. He then enrolled in Stowe Teachers College, where he earned 26 credits and transferred to Lincoln University in Jefferson City on a scholarship. After graduation, he applied for admission to the University of Missouri. He was advised by the university to apply for an out-of-state scholarship. (Courtesy of Lincoln University Archives.)

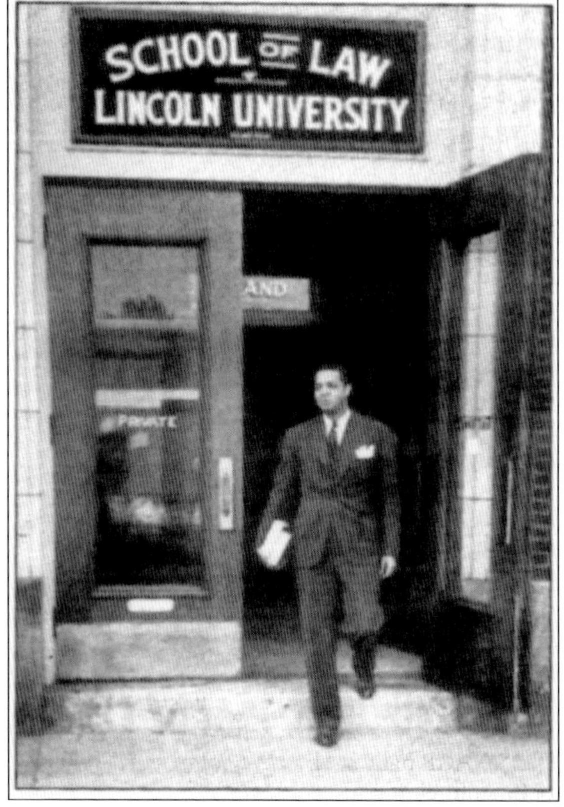

With the assistance of the National Association for the Advancement of Colored People, a legal team was assembled to enroll Gaines in the University of Missouri's Law School The team won in the US Supreme Court. But instead of admitting Gaines, the state passed a bill providing $275,000 for the establishment of Lincoln Law School. Lincoln University established its school in St. Louis. (Courtesy of Lincoln University Archives.)

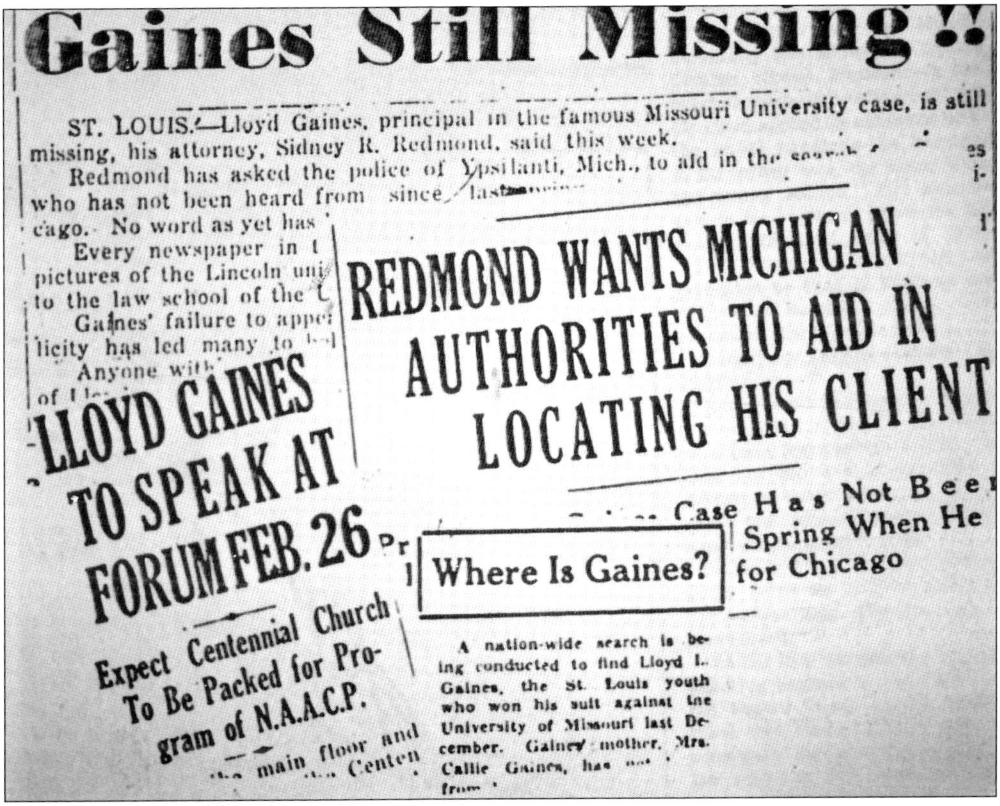

Gaines Still Missing!!

ST. LOUIS.—Lloyd Gaines, principal in the famous Missouri University case, is still missing, his attorney, Sidney R. Redmond, said this week.

Redmond has asked the police of Ypsilanti, Mich., to aid in the search ... who has not been heard from since last ... cago. No word as yet has ...

Every newspaper in t... pictures of the Lincoln uni... to the law school of the U...

Gaines' failure to appe... licity has led many to b...

Anyone with ... of ...

REDMOND WANTS MICHIGAN AUTHORITIES TO AID IN LOCATING HIS CLIENT

LLOYD GAINES TO SPEAK AT FORUM FEB. 26

Expect Centennial Church To Be Packed for Program of N.A.A.C.P.

... main floor and ... Centen...

... Case Has Not Been ... Spring When He ... for Chicago

Where Is Gaines?

A nation-wide search is being conducted to find Lloyd L. Gaines, the St. Louis youth who won his suit against the University of Missouri last December. Gaines' mother, Mrs. Callie Gaines, has not ... from ...

News articles like those pictured here were reported a few months after Gaines's Supreme Court victory. He left a Chicago fraternity house, telling the housekeeper he was going to purchase some stamps. Taking only the clothes he wore, he disappeared into the night and has never been seen or heard from since. The reason for his disappearance has remained a mystery. (Courtesy of Lincoln University Archives.)

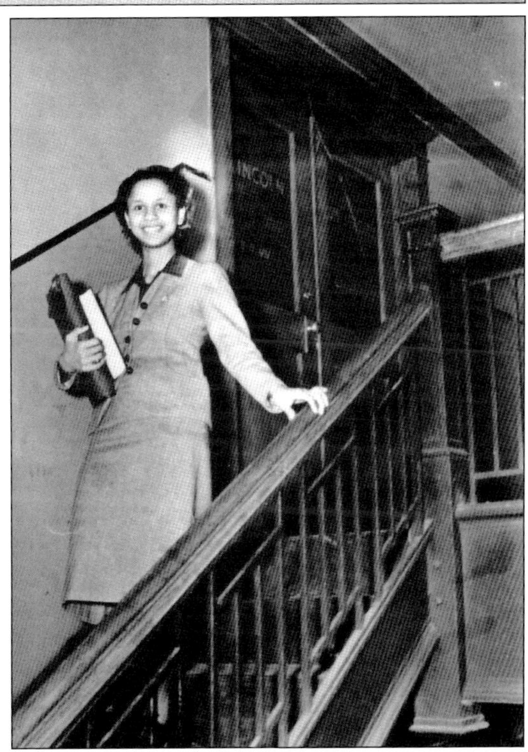

Margaret Bush Wilson is pictured on the stairs in the Lincoln Law School after graduation. She helped her father, realtor James Busch, with legal documents for the *Shelly* v. *Kramer* suit. She became the assistant attorney general for Missouri and acting deputy director for the St. Louis Model City Agency, among other accomplishments. In 1975, she became the first black woman to chair the NAACP national board. (Courtesy of Lincoln University Archives.)

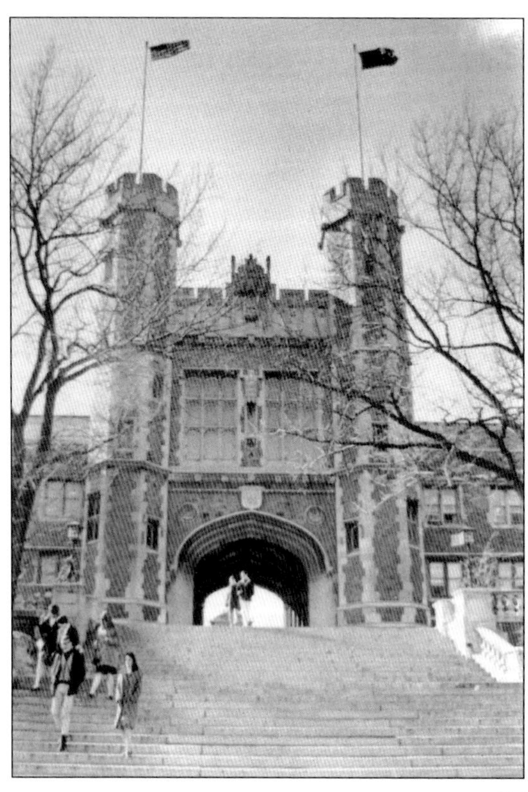

Washington University was founded in 1853 by William Elliot. The University had no formal policy regarding the admission or exclusion of black students. Walter Farmer, a black man, graduated in 1889. By the 1900s, there were no blacks enrolled. The city was beginning to experience a decline in revenue and wanted the university to pay taxes on its city property. The city lost in court. (Courtesy of Washington University Archives.)

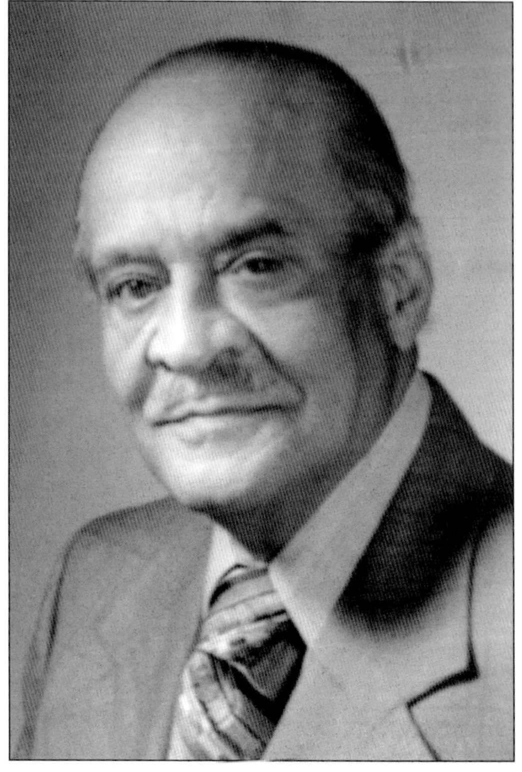

When the city tried again to collect taxes on the university's property, attorney David Grant, president of the local branch of the NAACP, requested permission to enter the case as a friend of the court. He argued that hundreds of nonresidents were getting an education at the expense of blacks who paid taxes for them. The university ended racial discrimination admission in 1951. (Courtesy of the City of St. Louis.)

During the Great Depression, Dr. Herman Dreer reopened Douglass University to assist black scholars. Dreer was refused admission by St. Louis University and Washington University to work on his doctorate because of his race. This was despite the fact he had graduated from Bowdoin College in Brunswick, Maine, in three years, graduated magna cum laude, and was a member of Phi Beta Kappa Society. (Courtesy of John A. Wright Sr.)

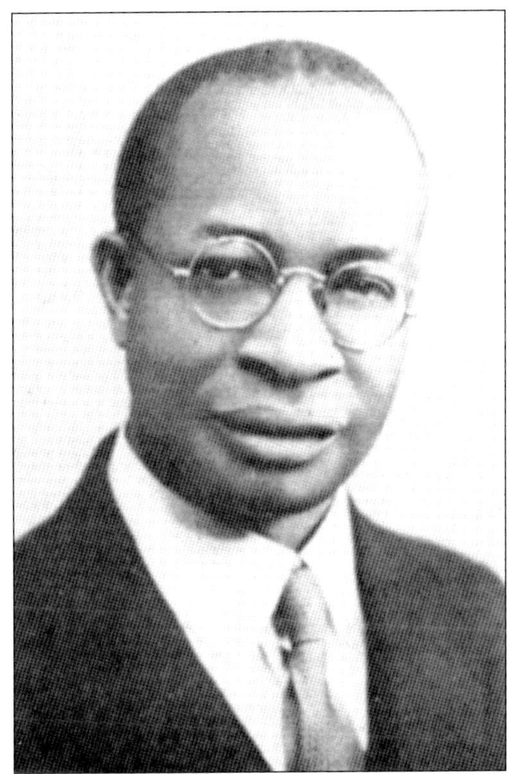

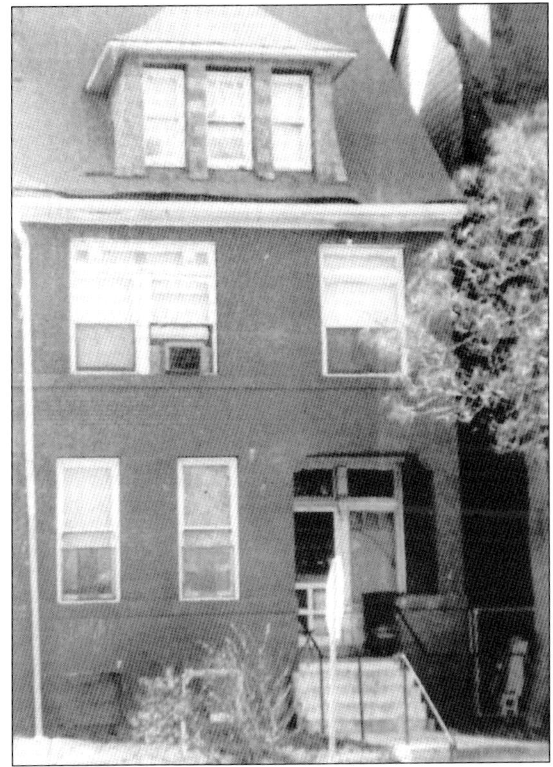

Despite many drawbacks, the university operated successfully. Many teachers volunteered their time, and Dreer used his own money to keep the doors open. The school closed in 1941 after Stowe Teachers College relocated to its new building. (Photograph by John A. Wright Sr.)

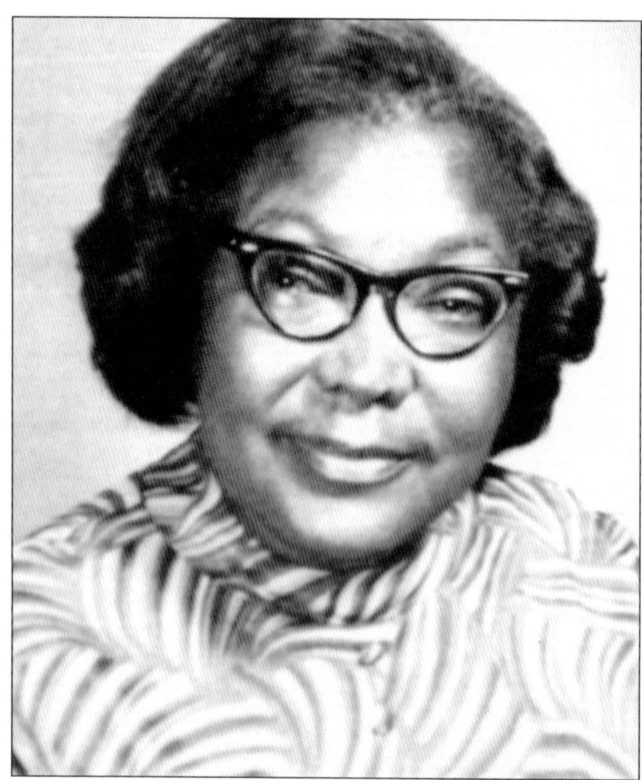

Sumner High School teacher Olivia Perkins is credited with bringing about a change in St. Louis school board policy that denied married women employment. Perkins secretly married a co-worker who died during World War II, after which Perkins started using her married name. The marriage was discovered by the board, Perkins was issued a letter of reprimand, and the policy gradually faded from use. (Courtesy of John A. Wright Sr.)

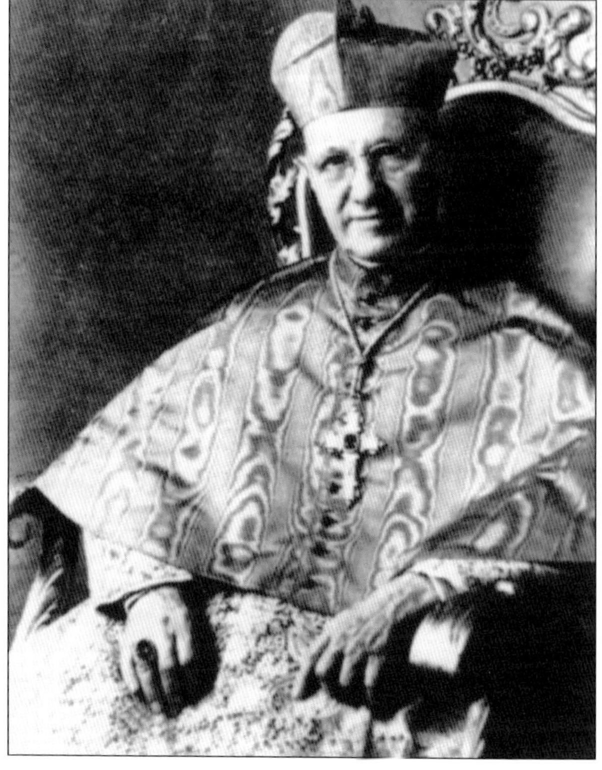

St. Louis University and all the Catholic educational institutions were integrated in 1947 by Cardinal Joseph Ritter. He wrote letters to all pastors saying that he expected them not only to admit negros, but to go and find them and bring them in. His orders were not well received by many, but he remained firm in his commitment to the integration of all educational institutions under his authority. (Courtesy of the St. Louis Mercantile Library, UMSL.)

Cardinal John Glennon, who preceded Cardinal Ritters, followed the city customs regarding segregation and made no effort to move in a different direction. He made his feelings known as a strong supporter of segregation. (Courtesy of the Archdiocese of St. Louis.)

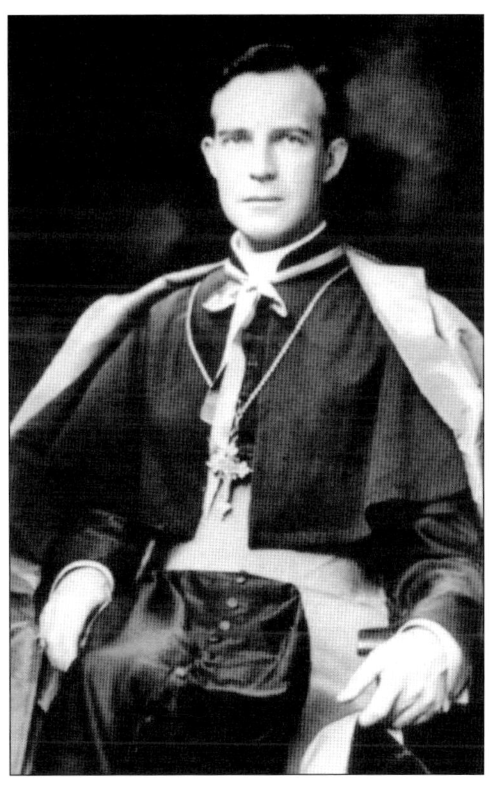

Municipal Athletic Association

Organized in 1912

CENTRAL COUNCIL
330 MUNICIPAL COURTS BUILDING
MAIN 5560, STA. 662 OR STA. 676

DWIGHT F. DAVIS,
ONORARY PRESIDENT

HON. CHARLES W. STEINER,
HONORARY SECRETARY

ST. LOUIS, MO. April 25, 1946

Father P. J. Molloy
4575 Evans
St. Louis
Missouri

Dear Sir:

Re: Visitation Baseball Team.

We regret to inform you that the application of the Visitation Baseball Team for entry into the Municipal Baseball Association has been rejected.

We are returning herewith your entry fee of $4.00.

Please acknowledge receipt as soon as possible.

Very truly yours

John A. Turner

JOHN A. TURNER
Chairman Executive Committee
Municipal Baseball Association

CC to Father Klario

JAT/W

Through the efforts of Fr. Patrick Malloy, who coached the boys in sports, St. Joseph High School played a dramatic part in opening integrated activities between schools. This is a copy of a letter Father Malloy received from the Missouri High School Association implying that they were unaware they were approving integrated athletics. (Courtesy of Msgr. Patrick J. Malloy.)

90 Per Cent of 375 Members Ask Exclusive Sections for Blacks.

Practically 90 per cent of the 375 "realtor" members of the Real Estate Exchange have approved of the establishment of negro sections in certain outlined districts of the city through a referendum of the organization, W. W. Kay, executive secretary of the exchange, announced yesterday.

Official action by the exchange would have to be taken by the Board of Directors which has not as yet considered the question other than to provide for the vote by mail. Adoption of the plan to establish the negro sections would mean the exchange would recommend that none of its members sell or rent property outside of the designated districts to negroes.

Associate and other members of the organization who are not in the real estate business were not called upon

In 1923, members of the Real Estate Exchange voted to establish exclusive sections of the city for blacks. This meant that their members would not sell or rent to blacks outside of these sections. This article from the *Globe-Democrat* newspaper describes the boundaries of each section (Courtesy of the St. Louis Mercantile Library, UMSL.)

After the US Supreme Court ruled the ordinance calling for the legal segregation of negros unconstitutional, white relators resorted to the establishment of black sections in the city through the use of race restrictive covenants. Pictured here is a map of the locations of the race restrictive housing covenants in St. Louis in 1945. (Courtesy of John A. Wright Sr.)

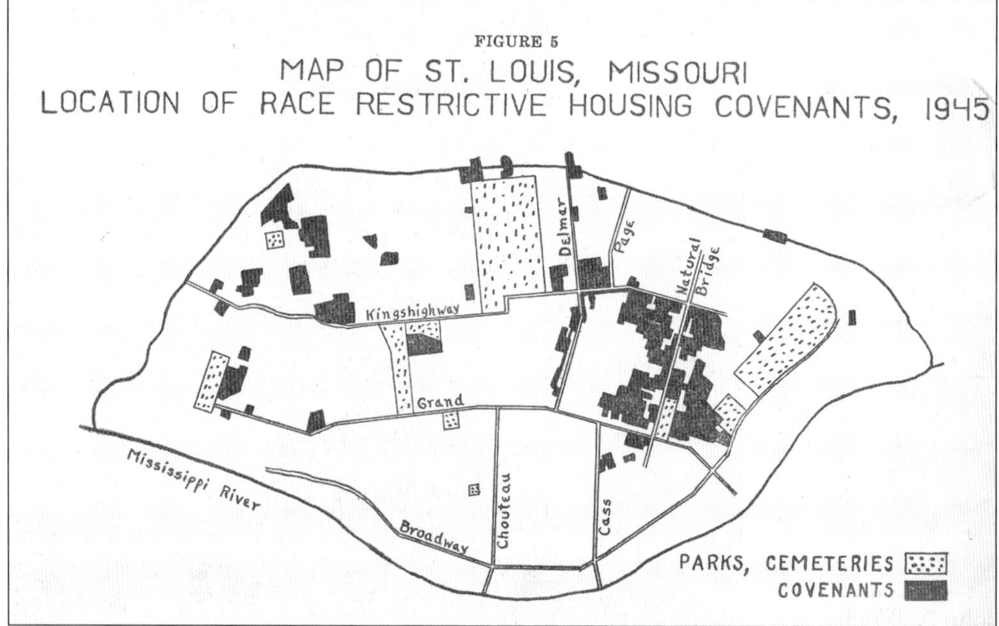

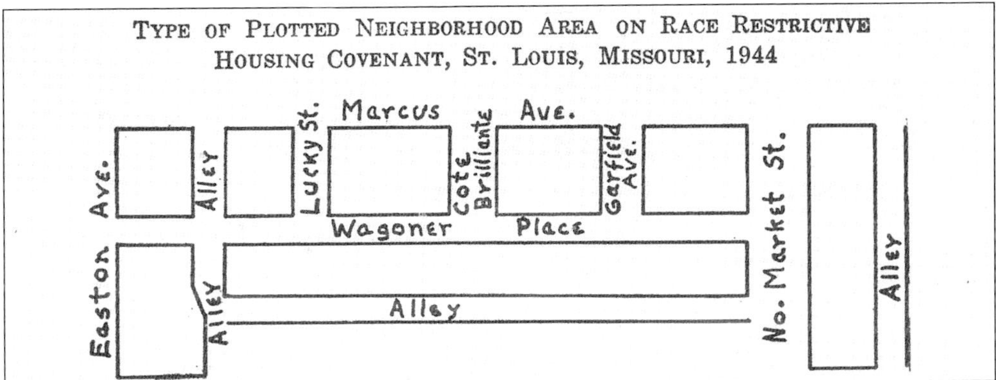

The St. Louis neighborhood covenants carried no provisions for their extension after 20 years had elapsed. There was an implicit understanding among the parties involved at the time of the agreement that it would be renewed at the end of the period. The agreement carried a map, as seen here, enacted by the Marcus Avenue Improvement Association. (Courtesy of John A. Wright Sr.)

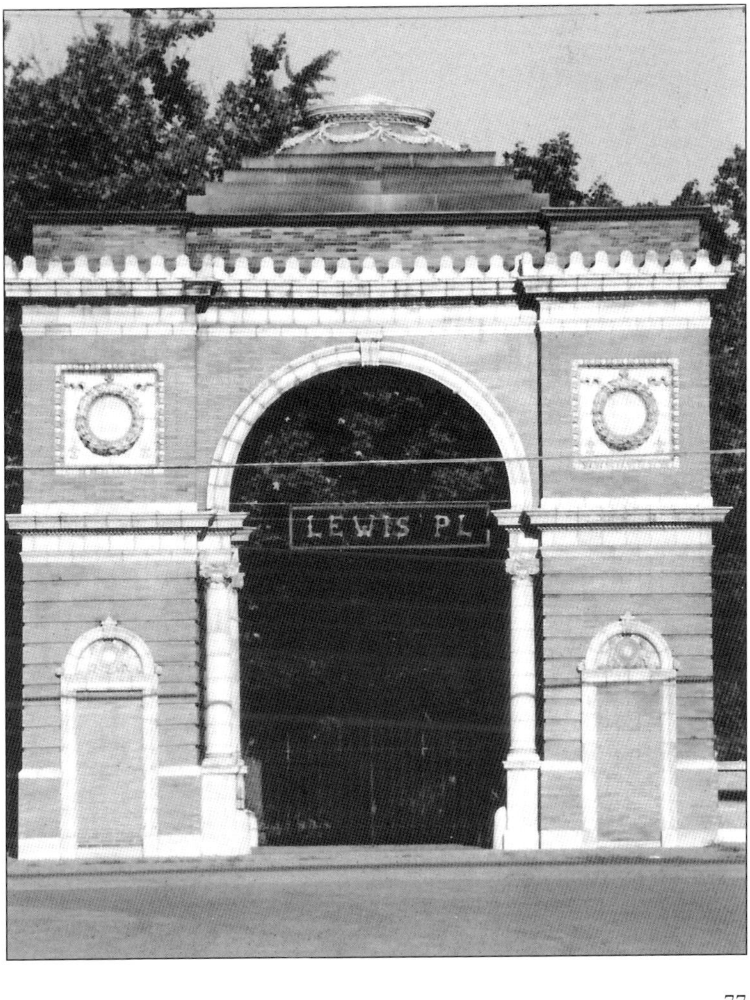

In the 1940s, a group of black St. Louisans led by Robert Witherspoon decided to fight the Lewis Place covenant. They persuaded fair-skinned blacks to "pass for white" to purchase several homes. They then transferred the deeds to the actual owners of the properties who voted down the restrictive covenants on the street. (Courtesy of John A. Wright Sr.)

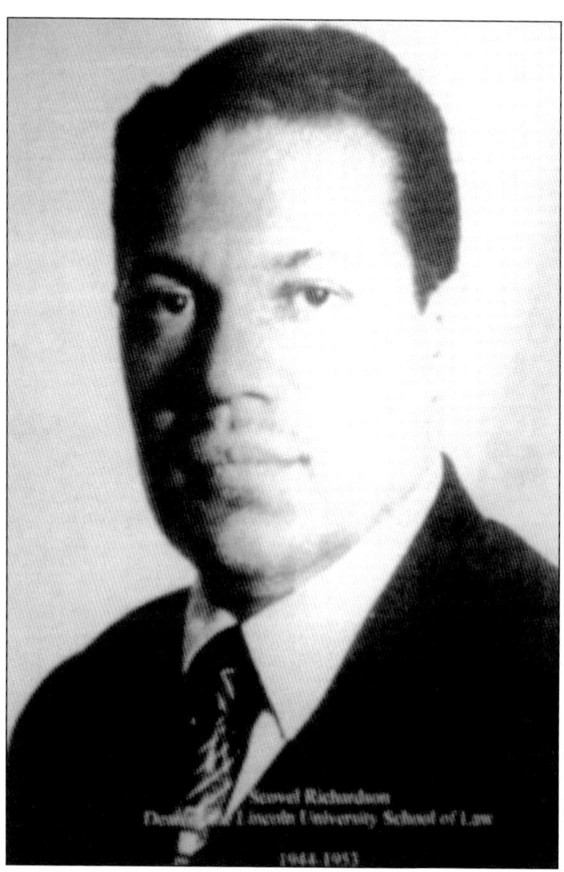

In October 1941, Scovel Richardson bought a home at 4635 North Market Street that was covered by a restrictive covenant that did not expire until December 1942. Richardson and his wife were able to delay the case in court until the covenant had expired. When the case *Dolan* v. *Richardson* came to trial it was thrown out because the plaintiffs had no grounds to sue. (Courtesy of Dr. Arnold Parks.)

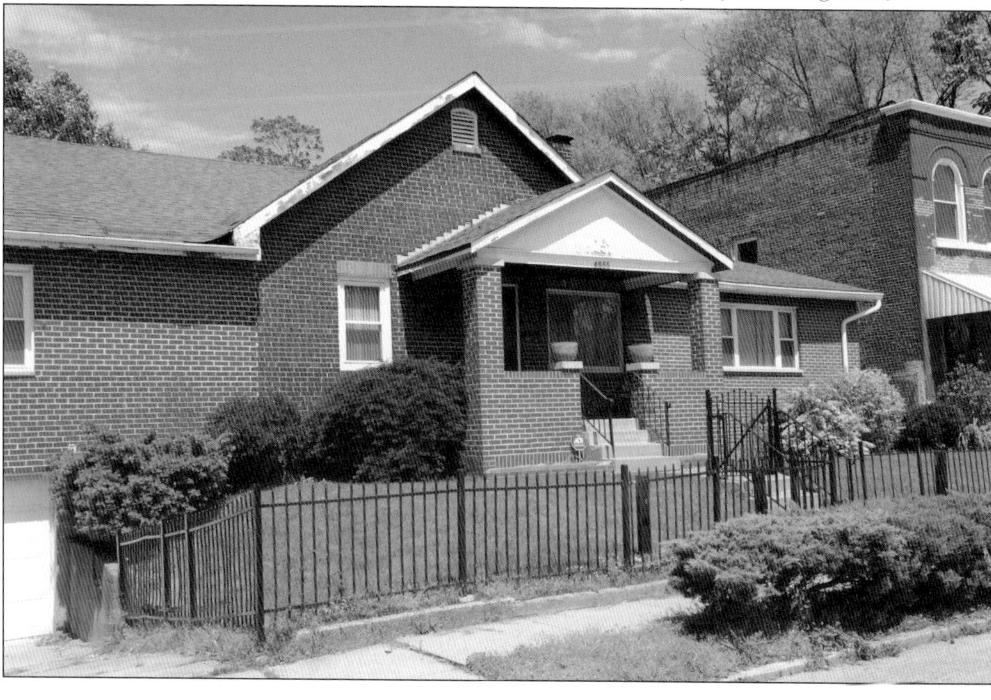

Dr. and Mrs. Vaughn Payne moved to 4655 North Market Street in September 1941 after negotiating the sale directly with the former owner. Unlike much of the property on the block, there was no restrictive covenant on it. The Paynes were subjected to prolonged campaigns of terror and annoyance. They received no assistance from the police until they threatened to arm and protect themselves. (Courtesy of John Wright Sr.)

In 1939, J.D. Shelley and his wife purchased a home at 4600 Labadie Avenue that had a 50-year covenant barring its sale to non-whites. The case was taken to court with the assistance of James T. Bush Sr. In 1948, the Supreme Court ruled in *Shelley* v. *Kraemer* that the use of restrictive covenants was a violation of the 14th Amendment. (Photograph by John A. Wright Sr.)

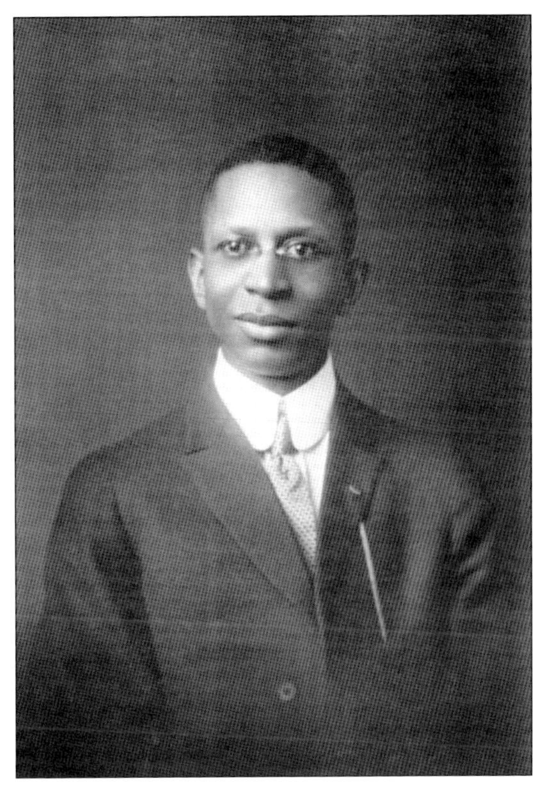

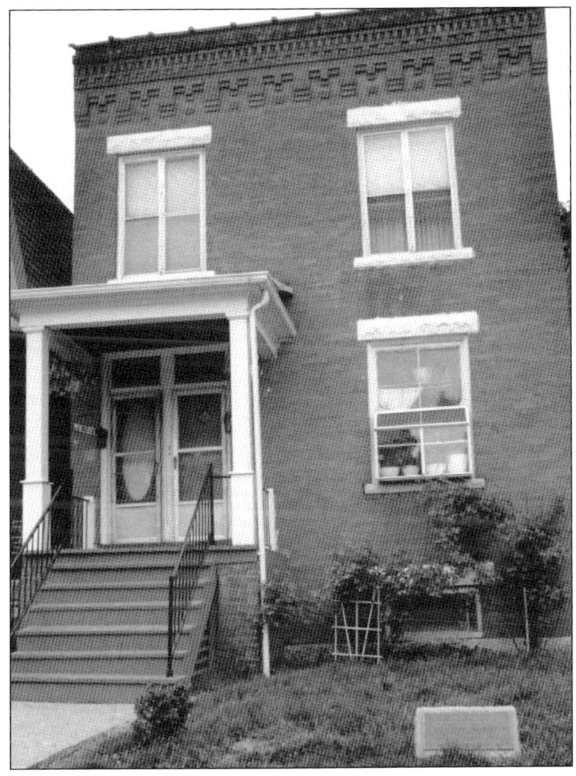

Despite the Shelly decision, a decade later, the 95,000 blacks who moved to St. Louis would find only 100 new homes available. (Photograph by John A. Wright Sr.)

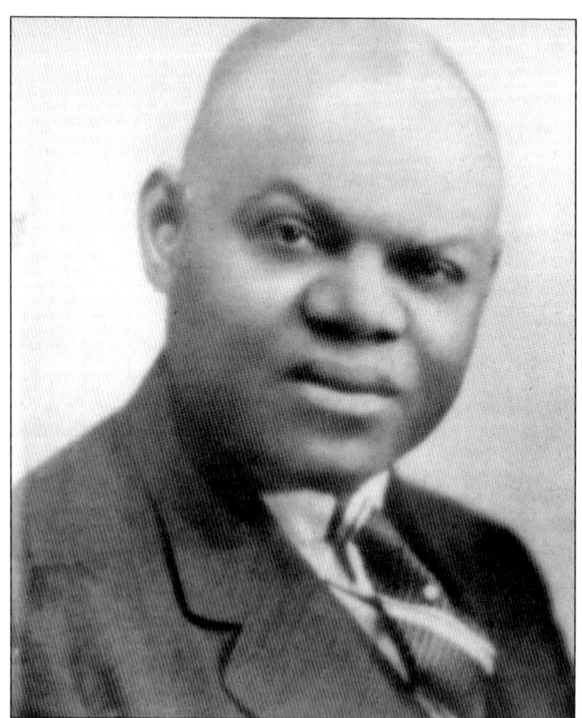

Attorney George Vaughn successfully litigated the *Shelly* v. *Kramer* case before the Supreme Court that put an end to racially restrictive covenants as a legal consideration in the sale of housing. Vaughn was the first president of the Mound City Bar Association and editor of the *St. Louis Argus* newspaper. He served for many years on the executive board of the NAACP. (Courtesy of Murphy Park.)

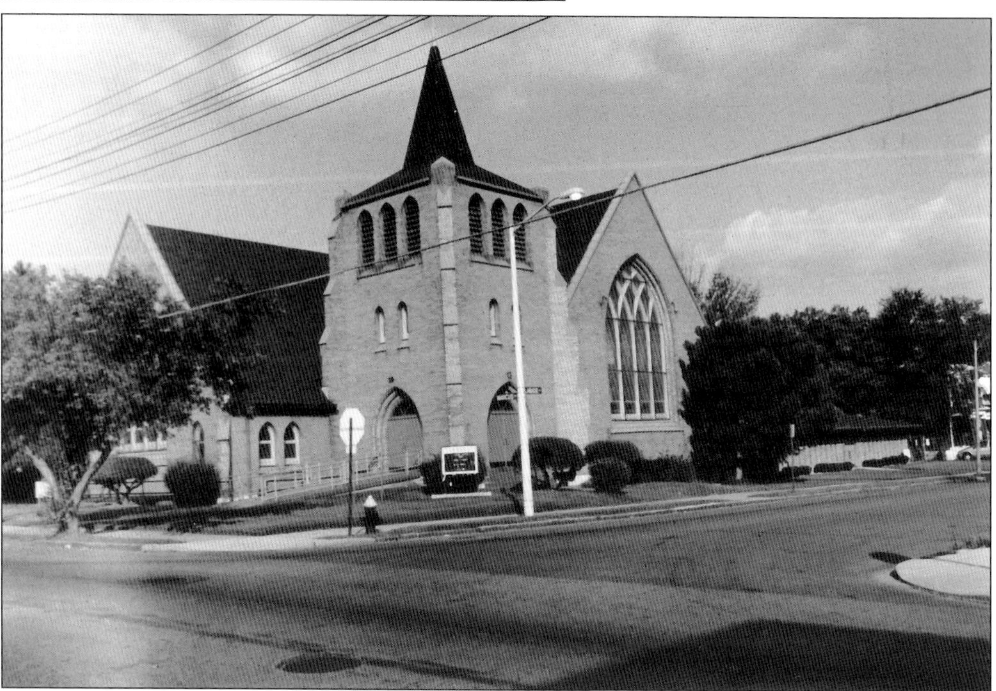

The Marcus Avenue Improvement Association was founded in 1910 to prevent the purchase of homes to African Americans from Natural Bridge to Easton Avenue, and from Newstead Avenue to Kingshighway Boulevard. The association used Cote Brilliante Presbyterian Church as its headquarters. When the neighborhood became integrated, the congregation moved. (Photograph by John A. Wright Sr.)

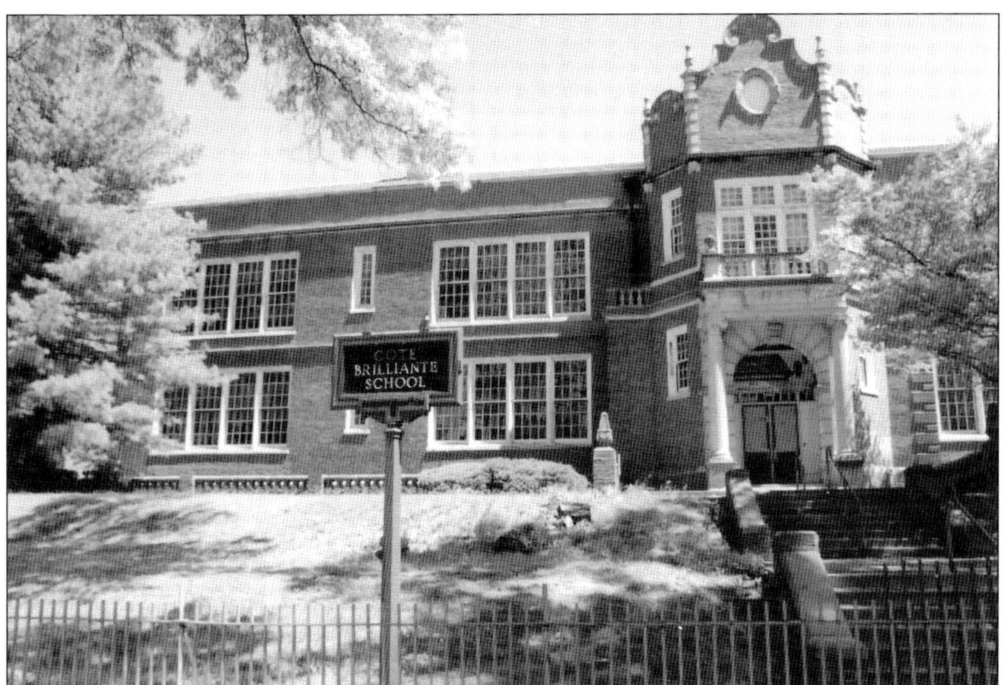

The Marcus Avenue Improvement Association marshaled its forces to keep the Cote Brilliante Elementary School white. Because of their petition, the school was closed from September 12, 1944, to September 1, 1945. It only opened because of community pressure to relieve the overcrowded schools in the Ville community. (Photograph by John A. Wright Sr.)

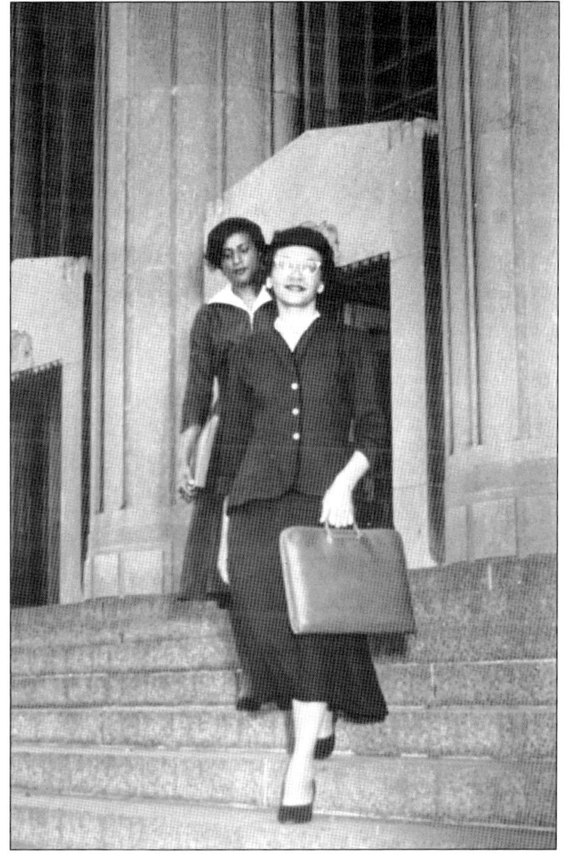

On June 20, 1952, attorney Frankie Freeman filed a class action suit, *Davis et al* v. *the St. Louis Housing Authority*, in the US District Court for the Eastern District of Missouri. It challenged the city's practice of discrimination in public housing. On December 27, 1955, the St. Louis Housing Authority was "forever enjoined" from refusing to lease or rent to qualified negro applicants. (Courtesy of Frankie Freeman.)

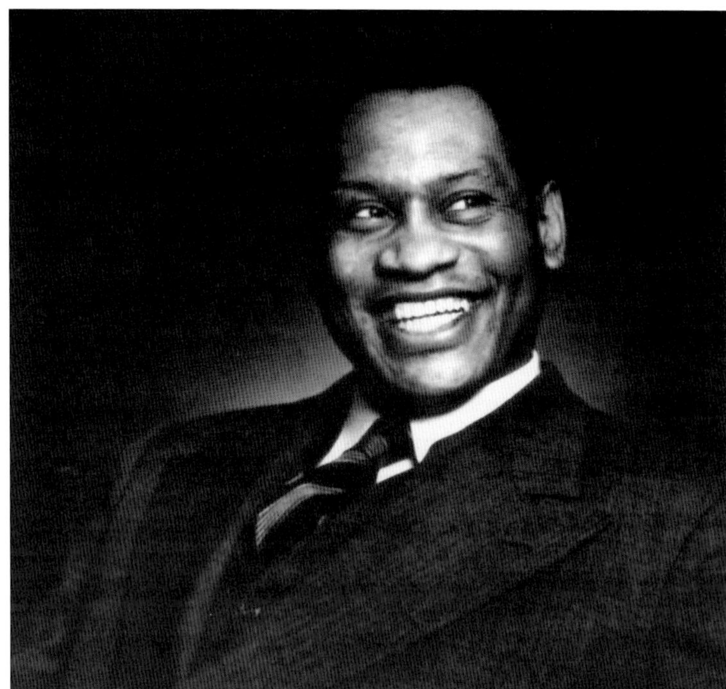

On January 25, 1947, Paul Robeson, a famous actor and singer, led the picket line outside the American Theatre to protest segregated seating. Black patrons were forced to sit in the upper balcony. According to the newspaper, their inspiration was the showing of the musical *Carmen Jones*, about black characters. In October 1952, without announcement, the American Theater opened all seats to blacks. (Courtesy of the National Archives.)

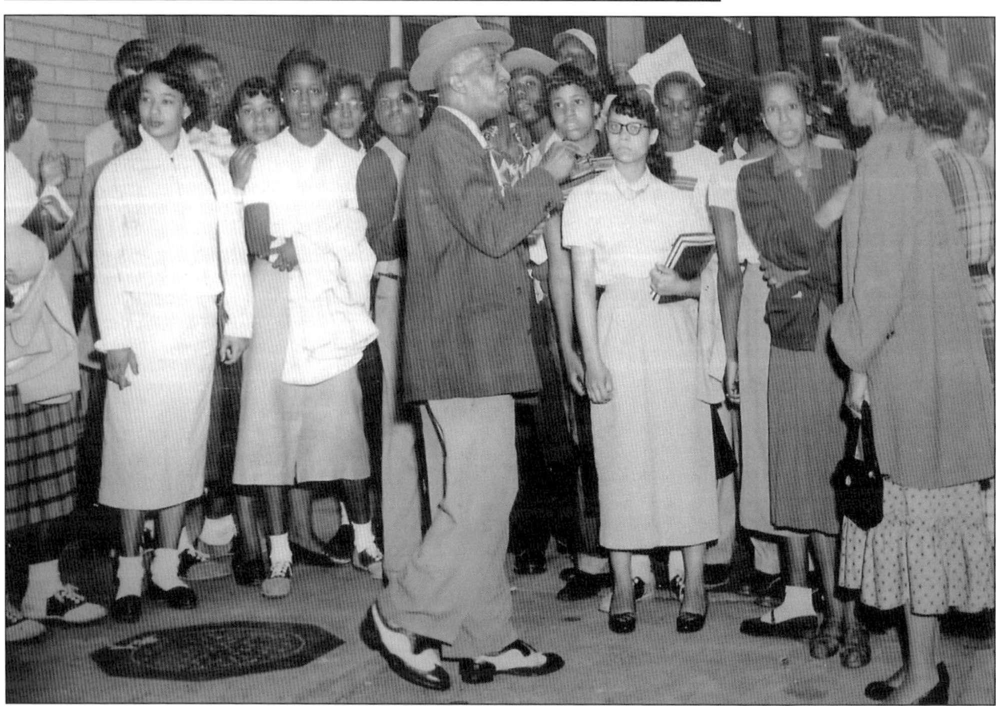

Henry Wheeler, besides being a leader in the picket line outside the American Theater, was also an organizer in the post office. When the American Federation of Postal Employees refused membership to African Americans, he worked for the establishment of the all-black National Alliance of Postal Employees. He became its spokesman and led demonstrations against postal policies. (Courtesy of the St. Louis Mercantile Library, UMSL.)

On May 14, 1944, three black women and one white woman sat down at the Stix Baer and Fuller lunch counter to get the store to open its lunch counter to blacks, without success. For the next two months, African Americans demonstrated twice a week at the department store. When 40 black and 50 white demonstrators sat at the counters of two stores in July, the stores closed the restaurants. (Courtesy of the St. Louis Mercantile Library, UMSL.)

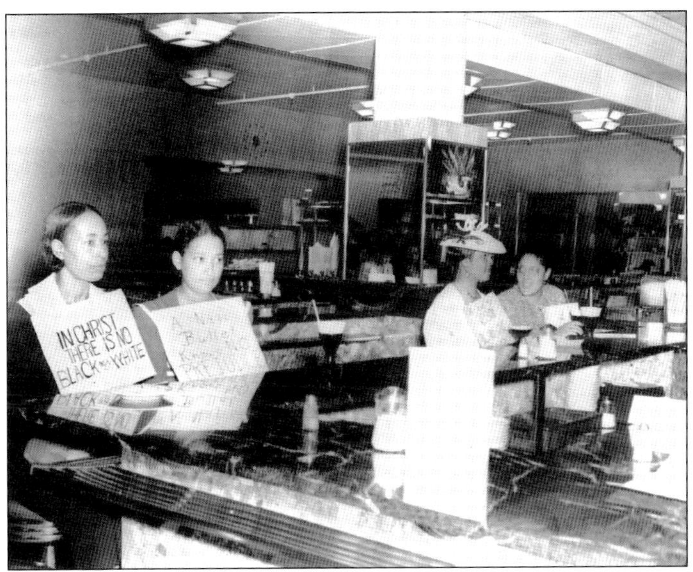

FOUR STUDENTS IN RESTAURANT INCIDENT FINED

Four Washington University students were found guilty last night of trespassing in a University City restaurant where they had been denied service. They were fined $20 each by Police Judge Victor A. Wallace of University City, who also found three of them guilty of unlawful assembly. He assessed additional fines of $10 each on the unlawful assembly charges.

Appeals were filed and the St. Louis county chapter of the National Association for the Advancement of Colored People supplied bonds of $200 each. Three of the students are Negroes.

They are Robert B. Curtis, 23 years old, 4421 McPherson avenue; Miss Elner Jane McCraty, 20, 1475A Shawmut place, and Miss Elanore Ann True, 25, 5949 Bartmer avenue. The fourth defendant is Miss Susan L. Friedman, 20, 6841 DeGiverville avenue, president of the university N.A.A.C.P. chapter.

Approximately 400 persons crowded into the courtroom to listen to the testimony. Robert Santoro, operator of Santoro's Restaurant, 37[illegible] North Big Bend boulevard, described events Feb. 14 leading to the arrests of the students.

Santoro said Curtis entered the restaurant Feb. 14 and was refused service. Police were called when he refused to leave, the proprietor said. The women students arrived later, he said. They were told the table at which they seated themselves was reserved for a private party. They refused to leave and police were called, Santoro said.

Negro students, including the accused, had unsuccessfully sought service in the establishment on 50 to 60 earlier occasions, he said. Santoro said he reserved the right to refuse service to anyone. Defense Counsel Charles R. Oldham's question as to what standards were used in deciding to refuse service was blocked by the prosecution's objection.

The court found all four students guilty of trespassing, and the three women students guilty of unlawful assembly. Curtis was acquitted of a charge of peace disturbance.

The University City ordinance relating to unlawful assembly makes it illegal for three or more persons to do an unlawful act with force or violence against the property or peace of another.

When four Washington University students were arrested in 1959 for participating in a sit-in at Santoro's, it marked the beginning of the civil rights movement in University City. As a result of the students' arrest, a group of citizens who represented the major religions formed an ad hoc committee to study racial issues and to make recommendations. One recommendation was to pass a public accommodations law. (Courtesy of the St. Louis Mercantile Library, UMSL.)

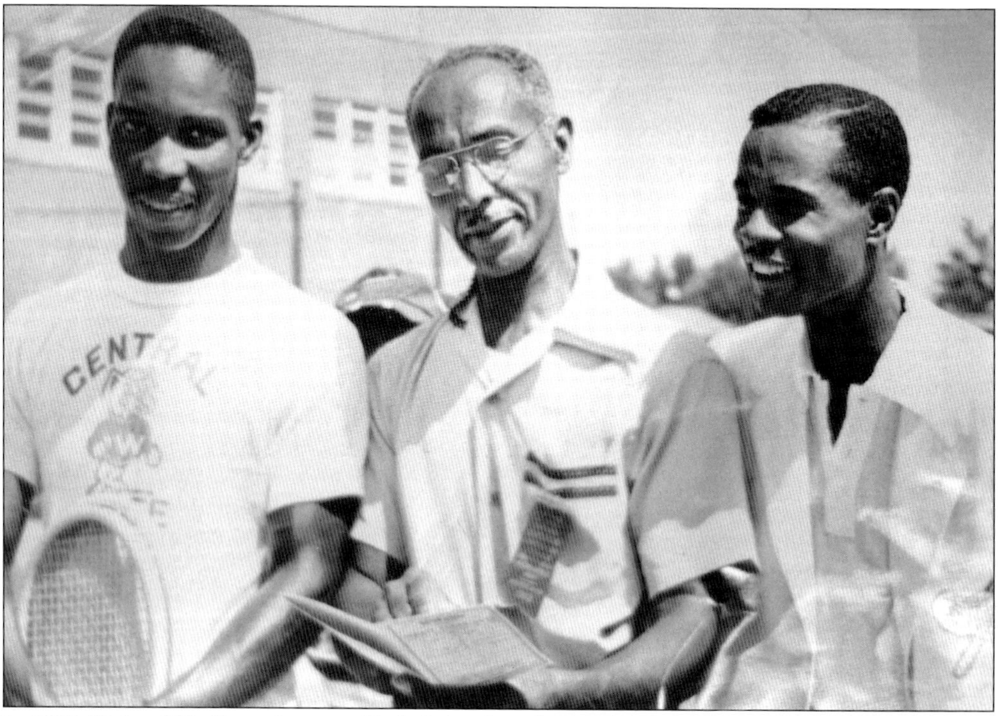

In 1941, Richard Hudlin, a Sumner High School teacher and tennis coach, brought a lawsuit in an attempt to compete in the city's tennis championship in Forest Park. To participate, a player had to belong to a tennis club affiliated with the Municipal Tennis Association. Hudlin, being black, was not permitted to join such a club. The court ruled the association was a private organization and could not intervene. (Courtesy of the St. Louis Mercantile Library, UMSL.)

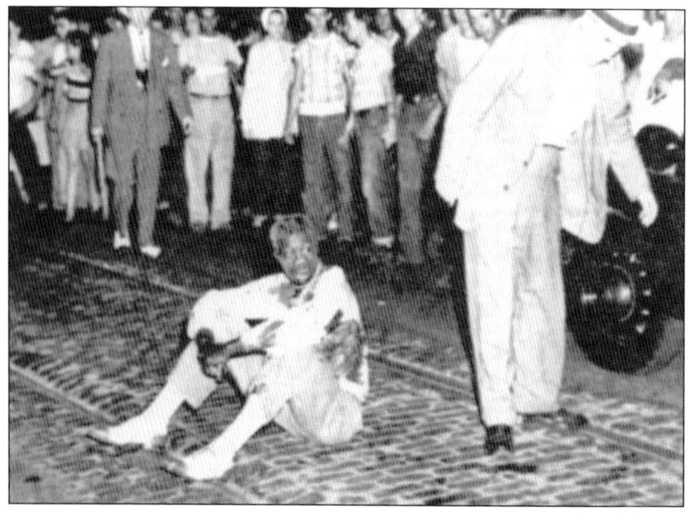

In 1949, Fairground Park was the scene of a racial incident that took place when Mayor Joseph Darst ordered the opening of city swimming pools to blacks. When 50 black youth attempted to enter the pool, they were violently attacked by some 200 teenage white boys. The mayor rescinded the order. The US District Court ordered the city to open all swimming pools to blacks. (Courtesy of Billy Crumpton.)

Five

CHALLENGING SEGREGATION

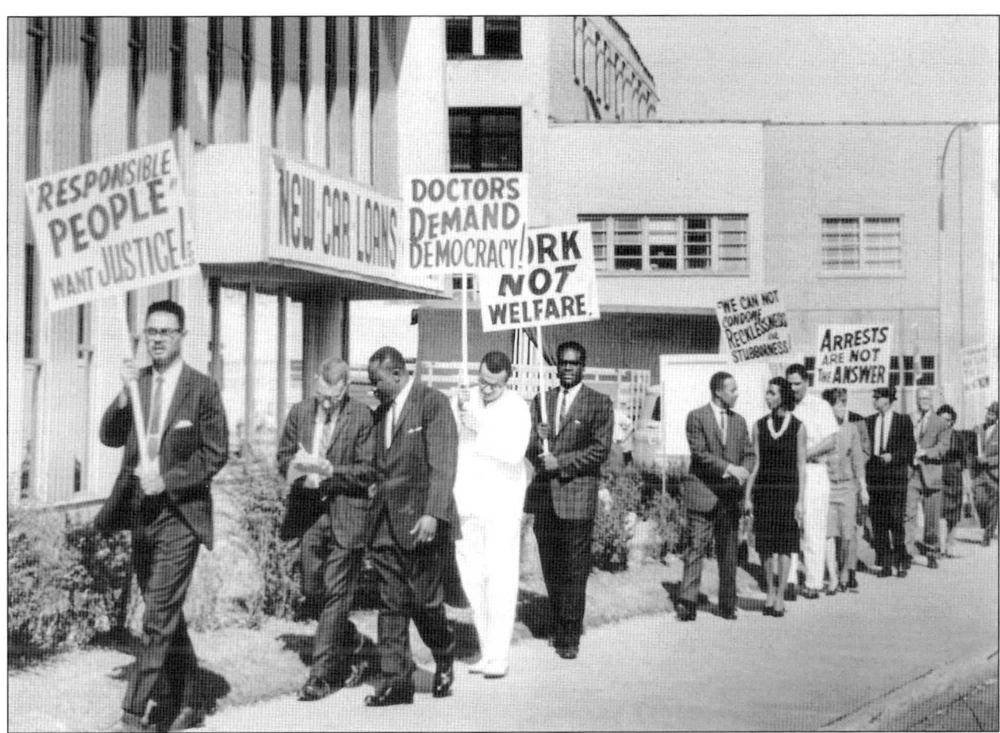

Jefferson Bank and Trust was the scene of a seven-month-long demonstration in 1963 organized by the St. Louis chapter of Congress of Racial Equality (CORE) aimed at forcing the bank to hire four black workers. Although the bank was in a black community and served mainly black clients, it had no black clerks. The protest ended in 1964 when five black clerks were hired. (Courtesy of the St. Louis Mercantile Library, UMSL.)

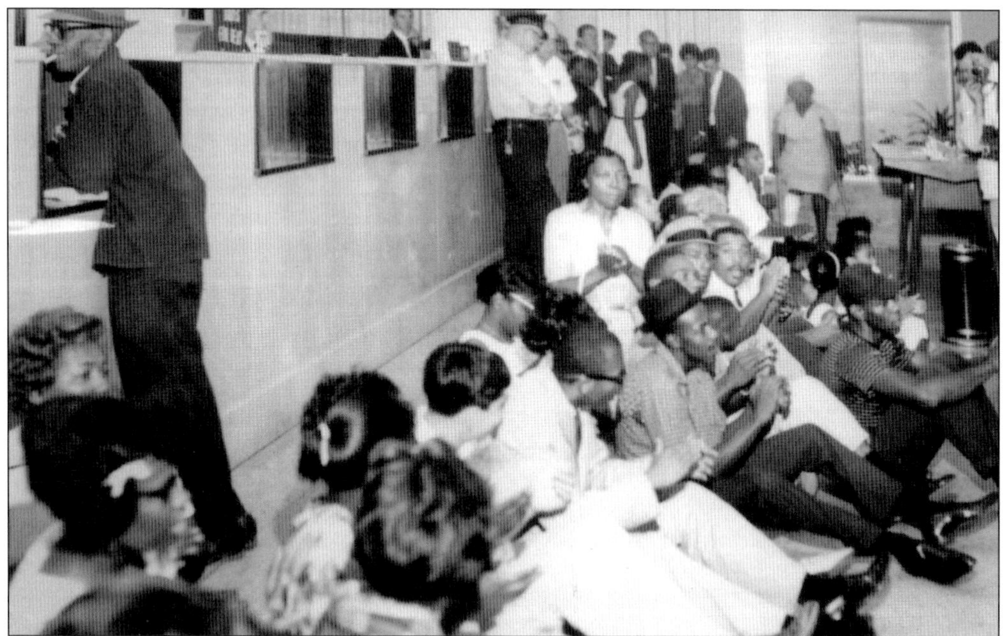

Organizers first wrote a letter to the bank urging them to employ four black clerks. At the time there were more than 5,000 workers in local banks, but only 277 were black and 99 percent of them were doing menial jobs. According to one report, the bank responded, "There were not four blacks in the city fit to do clerical work." This did not deter the protesters. (Courtesy of the St. Louis Mercantile Library, UMSL.)

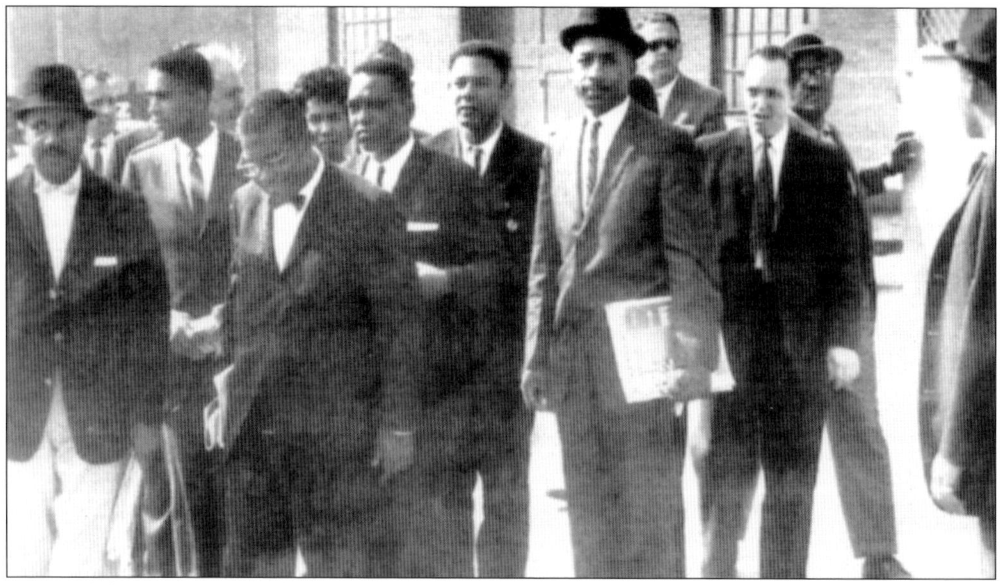

Many of the Jefferson Bank protesers were arrested. The protest proceeded despite injunctions by the bank to halt them. Among those taking part were 26th Ward alderman William Clay, elected to the US House of Representatives in 1968; Louis Ford, a state senator and community leader; Robert Curtis, president of CORE; Norman Seay; Herman Thompson; Lucian Richards; and Charles and Marian Oldham. (Courtesy of the St. Louis Mercantile Library, UMSL.)

Unemployment was a major issue in St. Louis. In 1959, St. Louis black workers' income was 60 percent of white workers. A 1960 study by the Human Rights Commission found that "in St. Louis, more than 10 percent of all non-white males in the labor force were unemployed compared with 2.8 percent of white males." Employment sit-ins were held in the city treasurer's office (Courtesy of the St. Louis Mercantile Library, UMSL.)

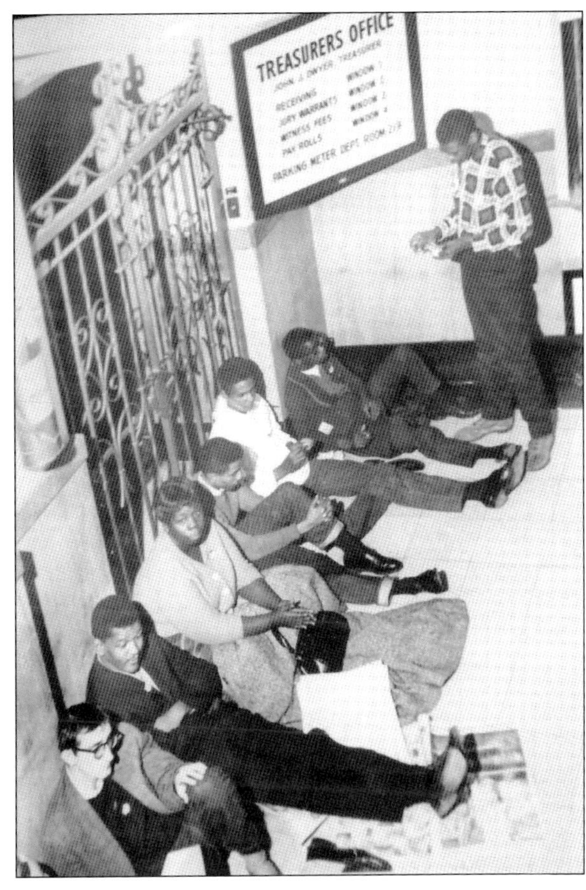

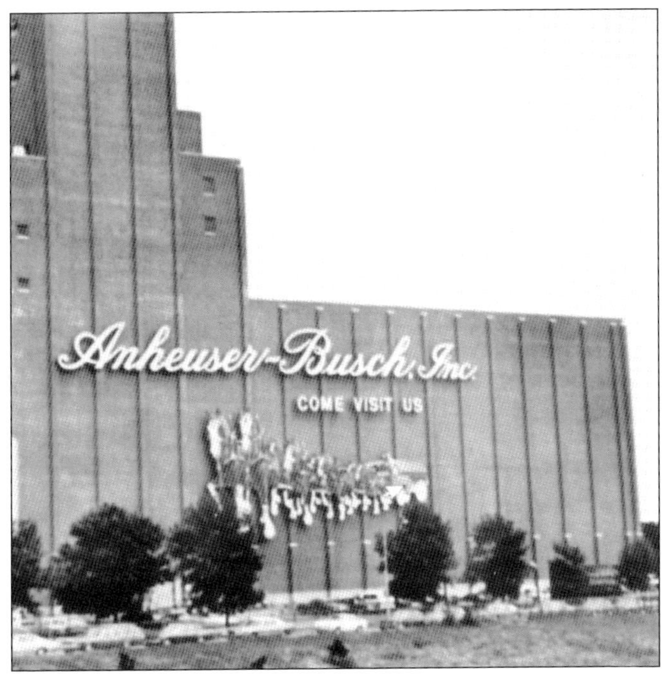

In 1970, a boycott was conducted against Anheuser-Busch and its products. Flyers were passed out urging citizens to "drink something else. . . . Because only 2 percent of the Busch workforce in St. Louis is black in a city whose black citizens make up 50 percent of the population." (Courtesy of the St. Louis Mercantile Library, UMSL.)

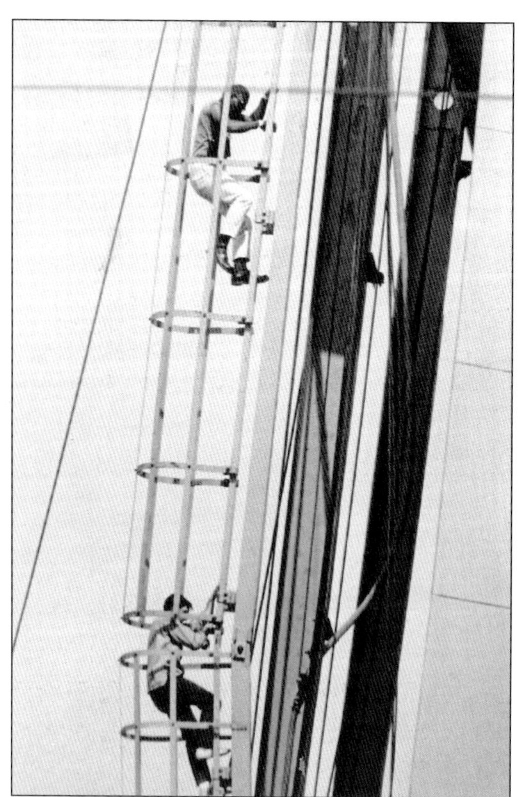

In 1964, ACTION president Percy Green and fellow activist Richard Daly focused attention on the lack of African American employment on the Gateway Arch project through a series of direct action. The most dramatic occurred on July 14, when they climbed the work ladder on the outside of the arch. (Courtesy of the St. Louis Mercantile Library, UMSL.)

The actions of Green and Daly forced the US Department of Justice to file its first "pattern or practice" suit against the St. Louis branches of the American Federation of Labor and Congress of Industrial Organizations (AFL-CIO) Building and Construction Trades Council and four of its member unions for violation of Title VII of the Civil Rights Act of 1964. (Courtesy of the St. Louis Mercantile Library, UMSL.)

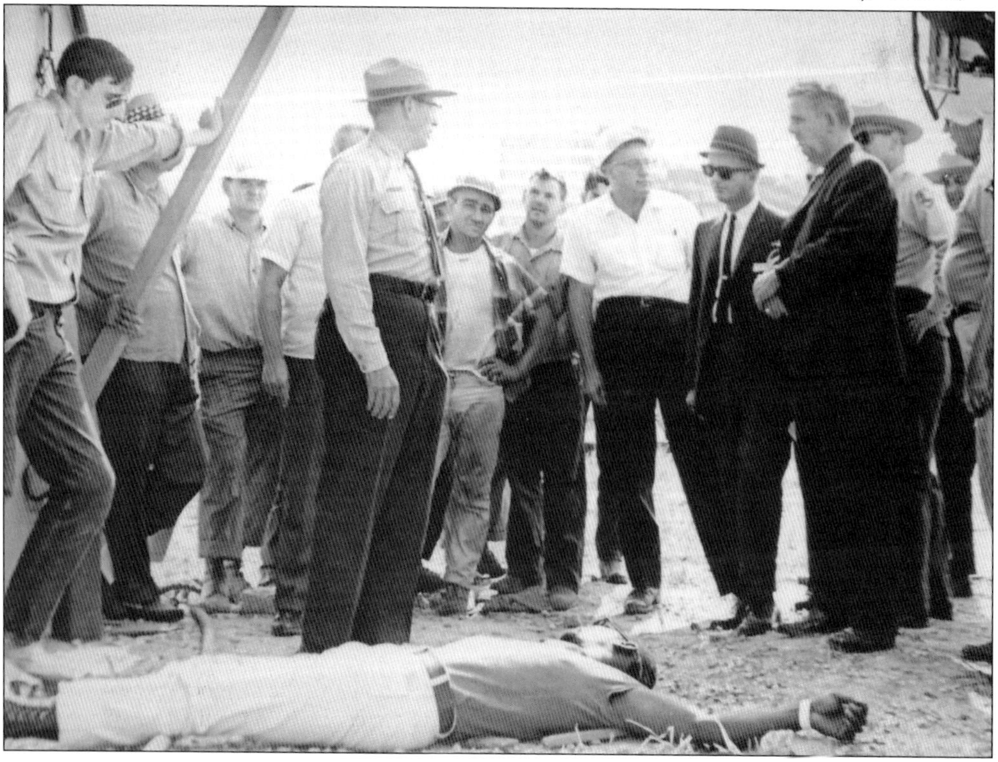

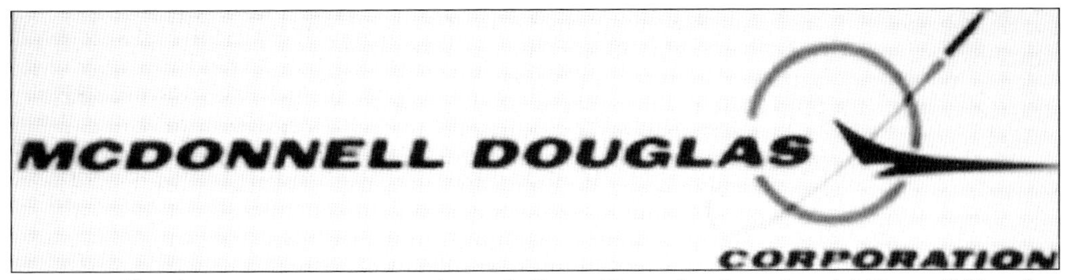

Because of his direct action protest at the arch, Percy Green lost his job at McDonnell Douglas. When the company refused to rehire him after layoffs, he sued, alleging racial discrimination. The suit went to the Supreme Court, which ruled unanimously in his favor. *McDonnell* v. *Green* provided a framework for dealing with discrimination in the workplace. (Courtesy of John A. Wright Sr.)

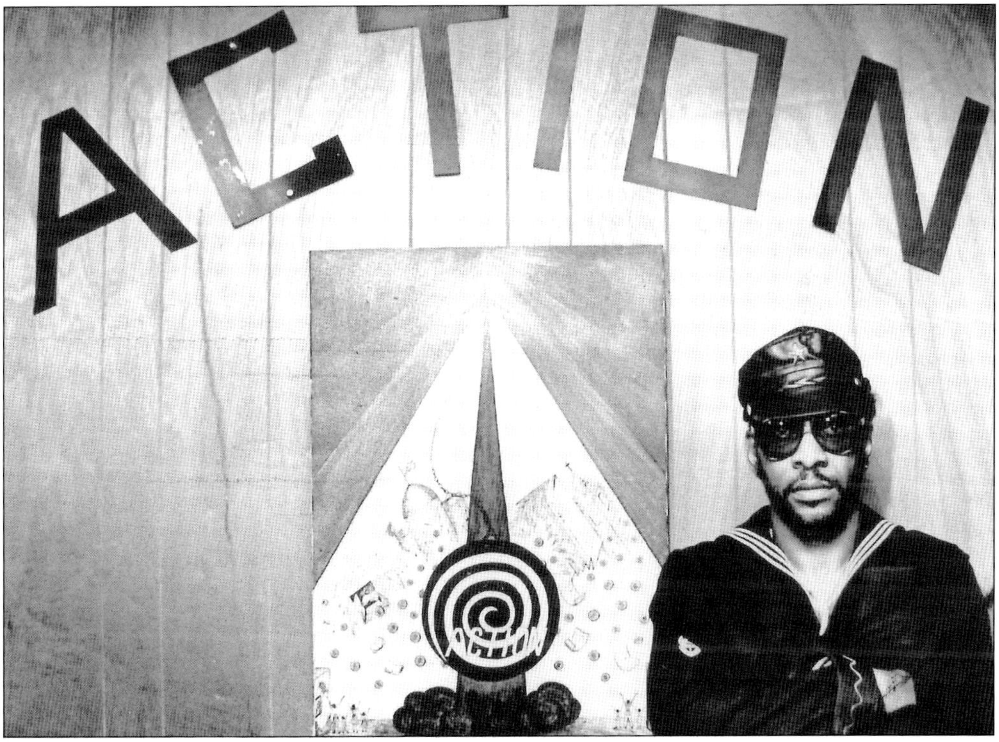

ACTION, an interracial, human rights, and protest organization, was founded in the early 1960s after a philosophical disagreement developed among members of the St. Louis chapter of the Congress of Racal Equality. After the Jefferson Bank protest, not all the members were up to more arrests. Some members wanted to continue non-violent protest by being deliberately annoying. (Courtesy of the St. Louis Mercantile Library, UMSL.)

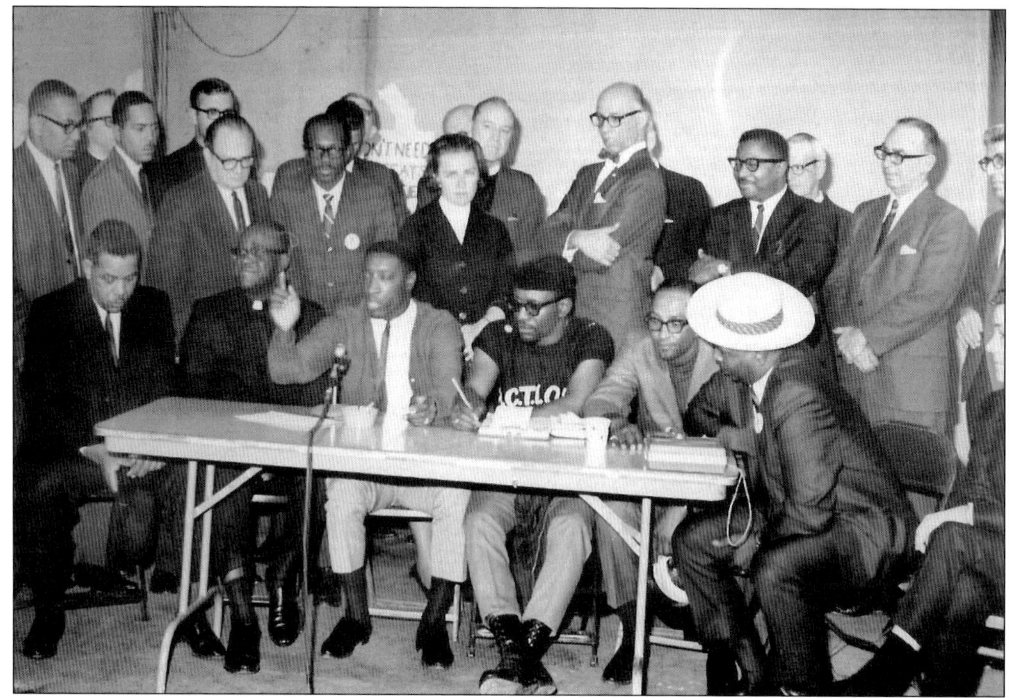

Members of ACTION are shown here presenting issues to community leaders. Although ACTION's methods were non-violent, they were confrontational. Their protests included deliberately tying up traffic on St. Louis highways and passing out leaflets telling drivers about unfair practices, and demonstrations in churches pointing out the responsibility of the church to eradicate racism in employment. (Courtesy of the St. Louis Mercantile Library, UMSL.)

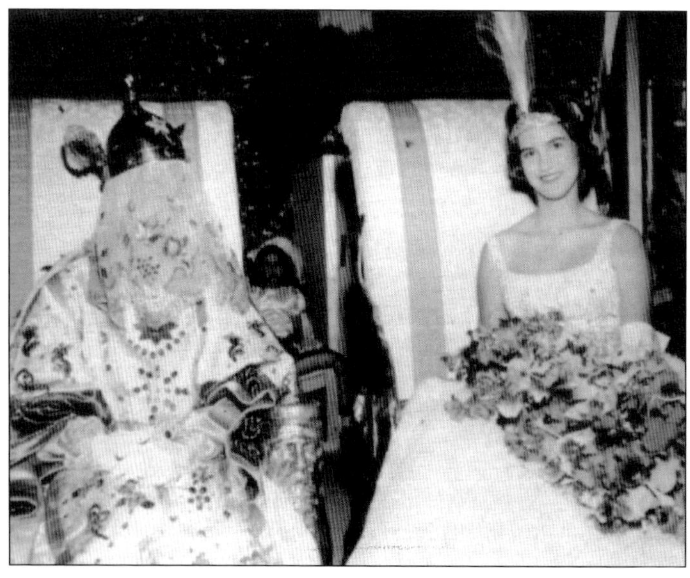

In 1972, ACTION was involved in one of St Louis's most famous civil rights protests against the Veiled Prophet Ball, founded in 1878 by former Confederate general Charles Slayback. During the event, one of ACTION's members unveiled the Veiled Prophet. ACTION considered the organization elitist and racist. Blacks and Jews were not admitted. (Courtesy of the St. Louis Mercantile Library, UMSL.)

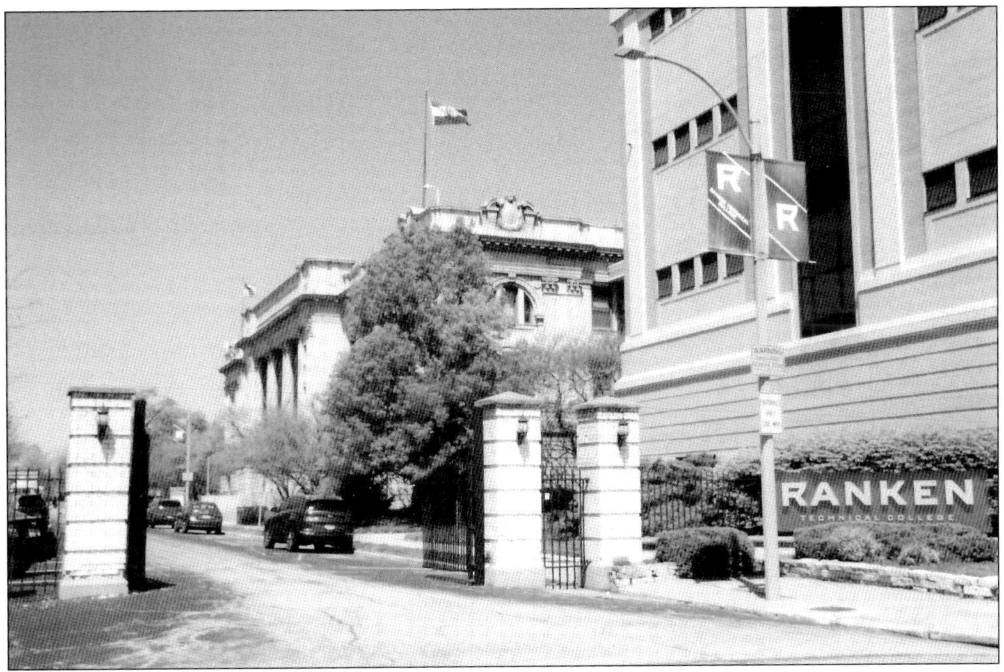

The David Ranken Jr. School of Mechanical Trade was founded in 1907 as a private, nonprofit educational institution to train students for employment in a variety of technical and mechanical occupations. It was established with a foundation deed of more than $1 million. Although the school was in a black community, it was not open to African Americans. (Photograph by John A. Wright Sr.)

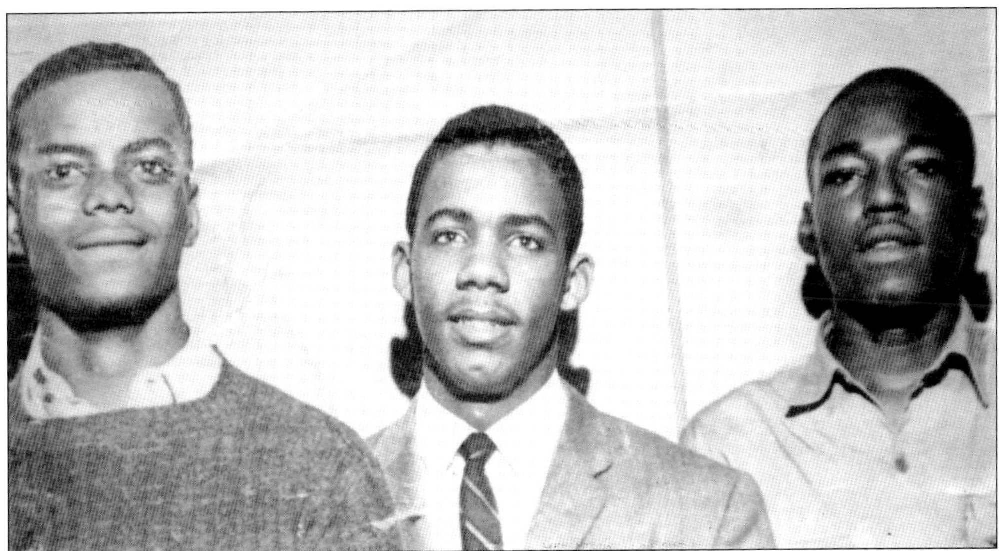
In 1963, after many years of protest, the David Ranken Jr. School of Mechanical Trade opened its doors to African Americans with the admission of Henry Talifarrio, Arthur Kennedy, and Mitchell Washington. If the school had failed to admit African Americans, its graduates would have been denied the ability to work on construction projects supported by federal funds. (Courtesy of John A. Wright Sr.)

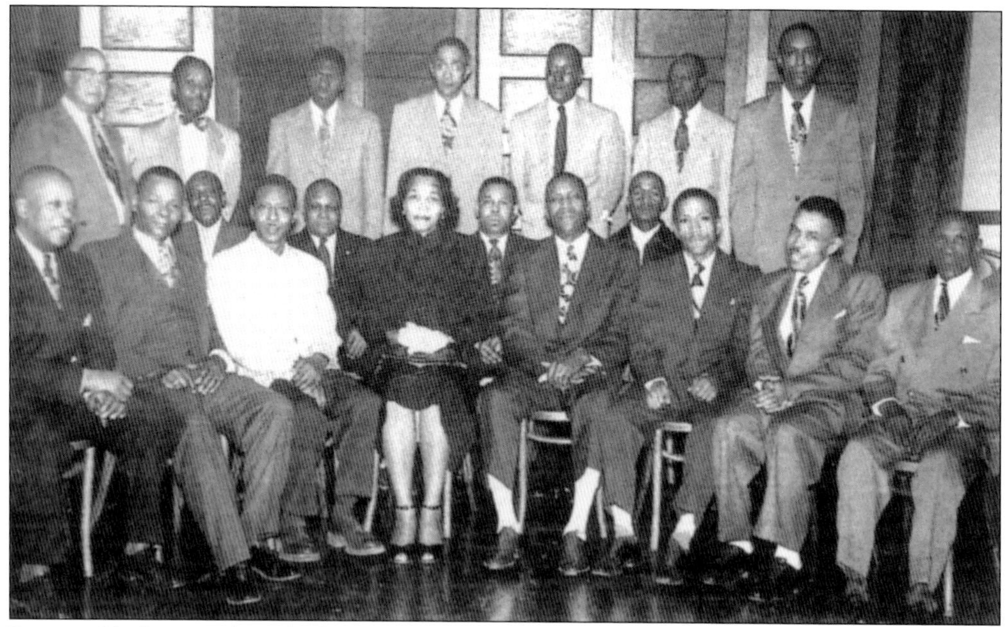

Because blacks were denied admission into the white union, they established one of their own. Pictured here are officers of Local 6063, comprising 16 local lodges representing 14 railroads in the St. Louis and East St. Louis areas in 1954 during an installation. (Courtesy of John A. Wright Sr.)

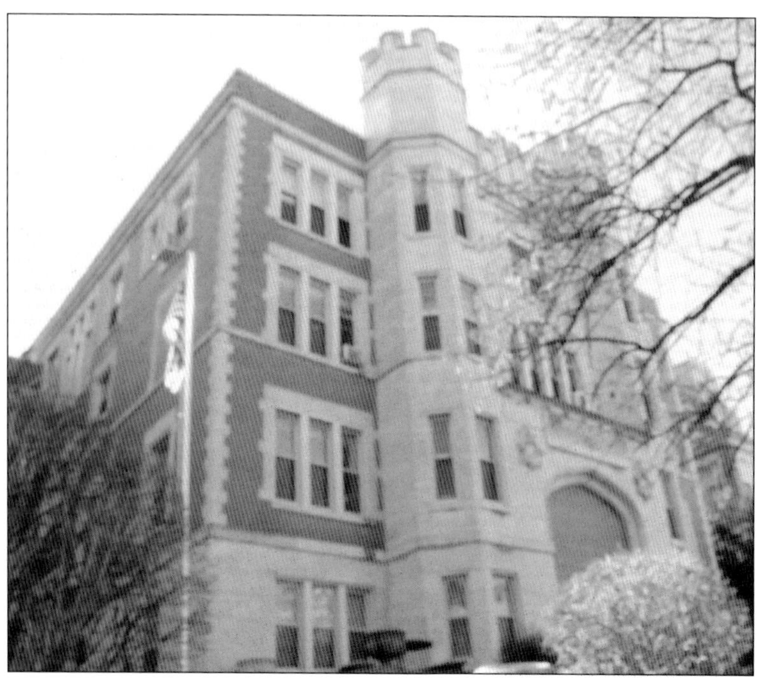

In 1956, one of the early issues facing the union was the integration of Frisco Hospital at 4960 Laclede Avenue. Although the company provided funds to the hospital for all its employees, black employees were not admitted. The union wrote a letter to the hospital trustees threatening action if their requests were not met. (Courtesy of John A. Wright Sr.)

As the city began to reduce its budget for healthcare facilities, it also began discussions to close or merge Homer G. Phillips with the Mac C. Starkloff Memorial Hospital. These proposals led to pickets and sit-ins from citizens. At that time, the hospital employed 800–900 people and was the major source of employment in the Ville. (Courtesy of the St. Louis Mercantile Library, UMSL.)

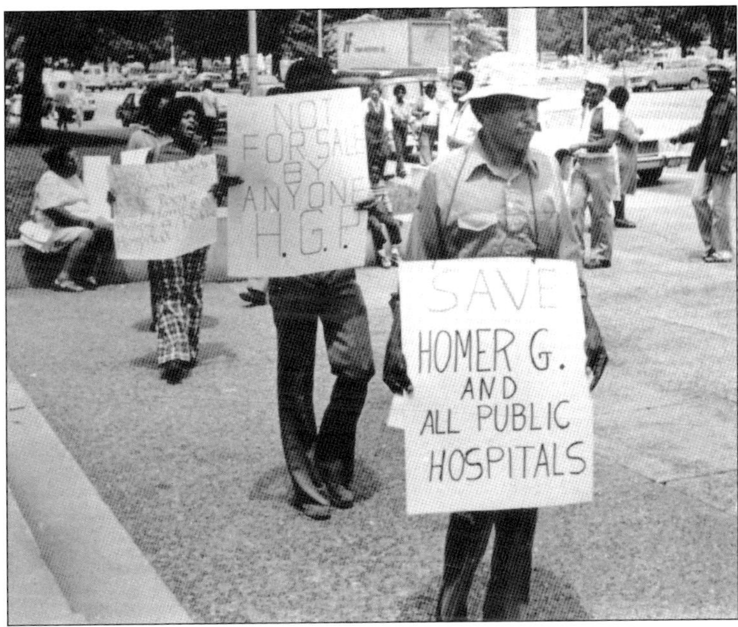

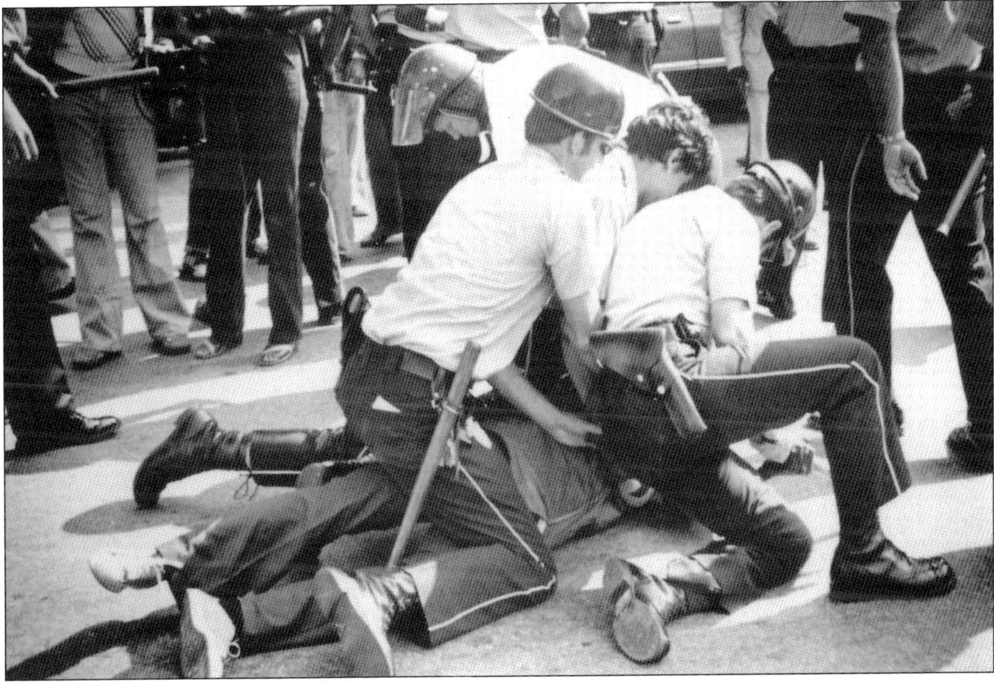

In 1973, St. Louis commissioned two separate audits of the city hospitals. Both recommended the closing of City No. 1 and retaining Homer G. Phillips hospital. However, in 1979, Homer G. Phillips closed its doors. The decision did not go down well in the community. Several hundred police officers were needed to keep the peace as the last patients were removed. (Courtesy of the St. Louis Mercantile Library, UMSL.)

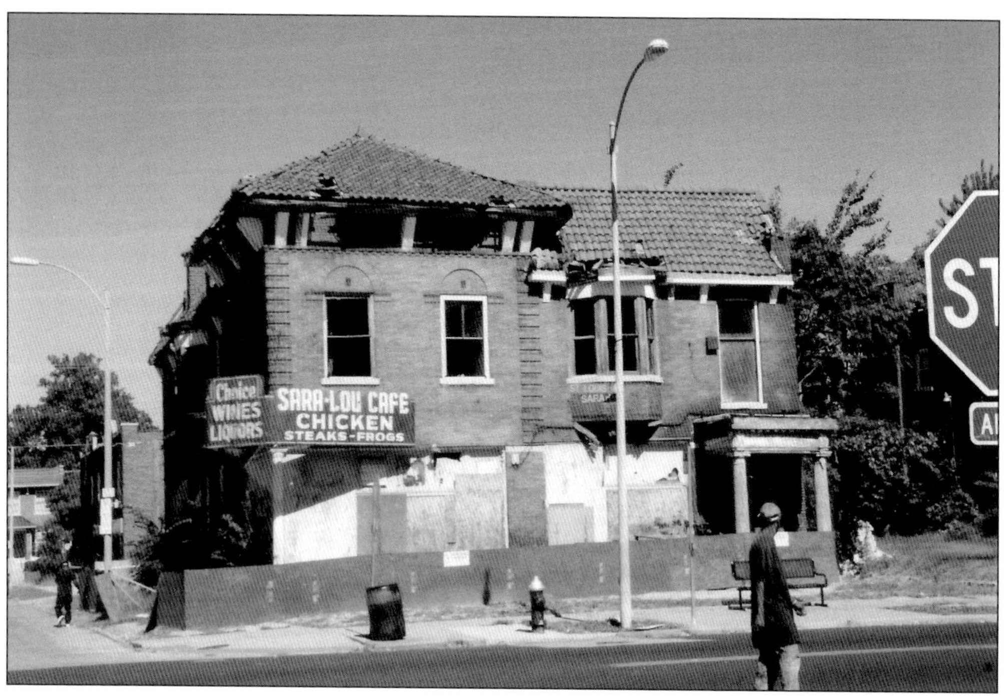

The closing of the hospital had a devastating effect on the community. Many who worked in the hospital lived in the community and shopped in the community. Once the hospital closed, residents began to move and businesses closed. Money no longer circulated several times before it left the community. (Both photographs by John A. Wright Sr.)

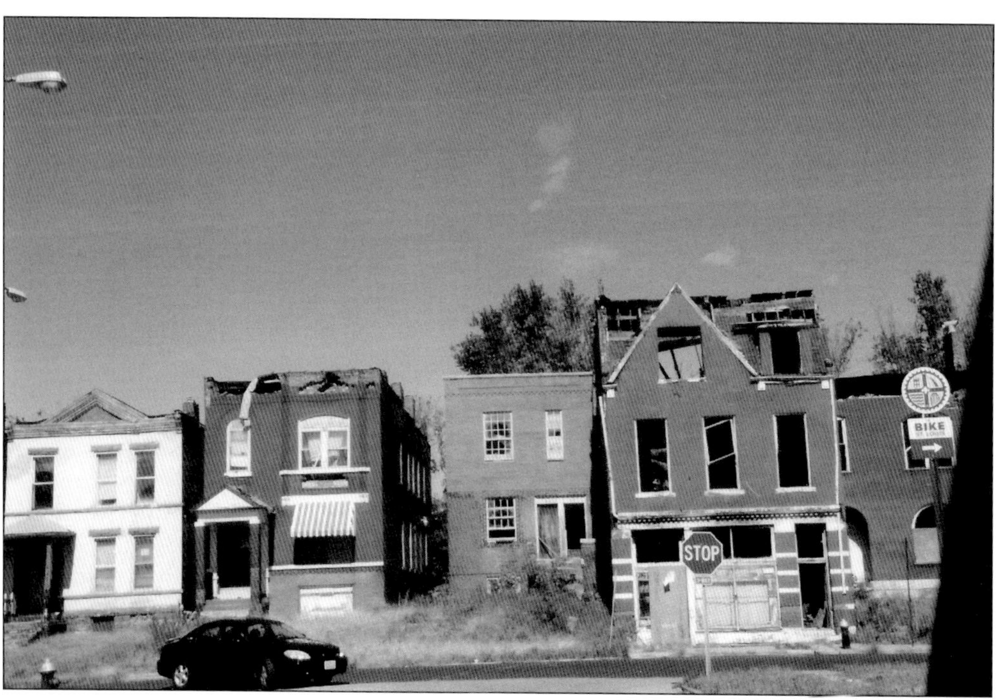

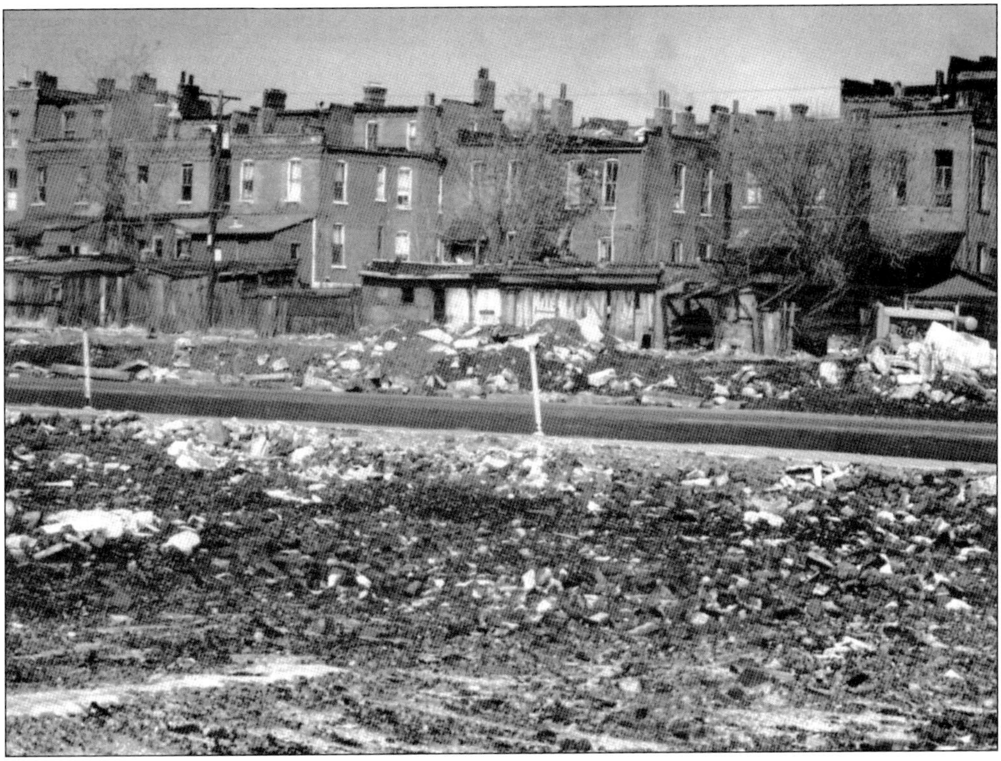

By 1950, time had taken its toll on the African American community in downtown St. Louis, as can be seen here. Many of the homes and businesses that once served the community were removed for good. Some were replaced by housing projects. (Above, courtesy of the Missouri Historical Society; below, courtesy of the St. Louis Mercantile Library, UMSL.)

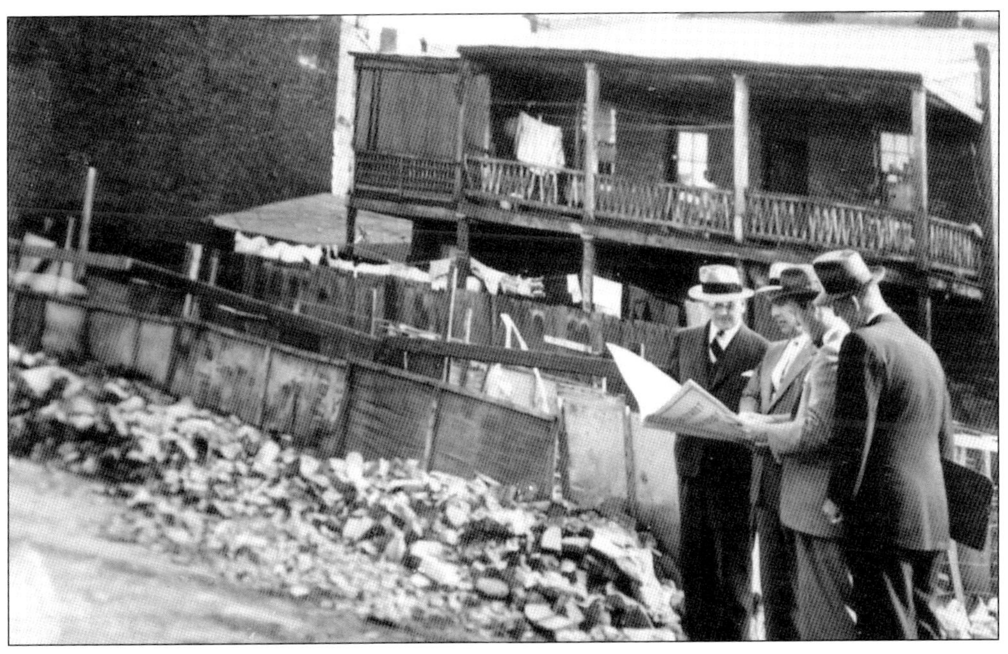

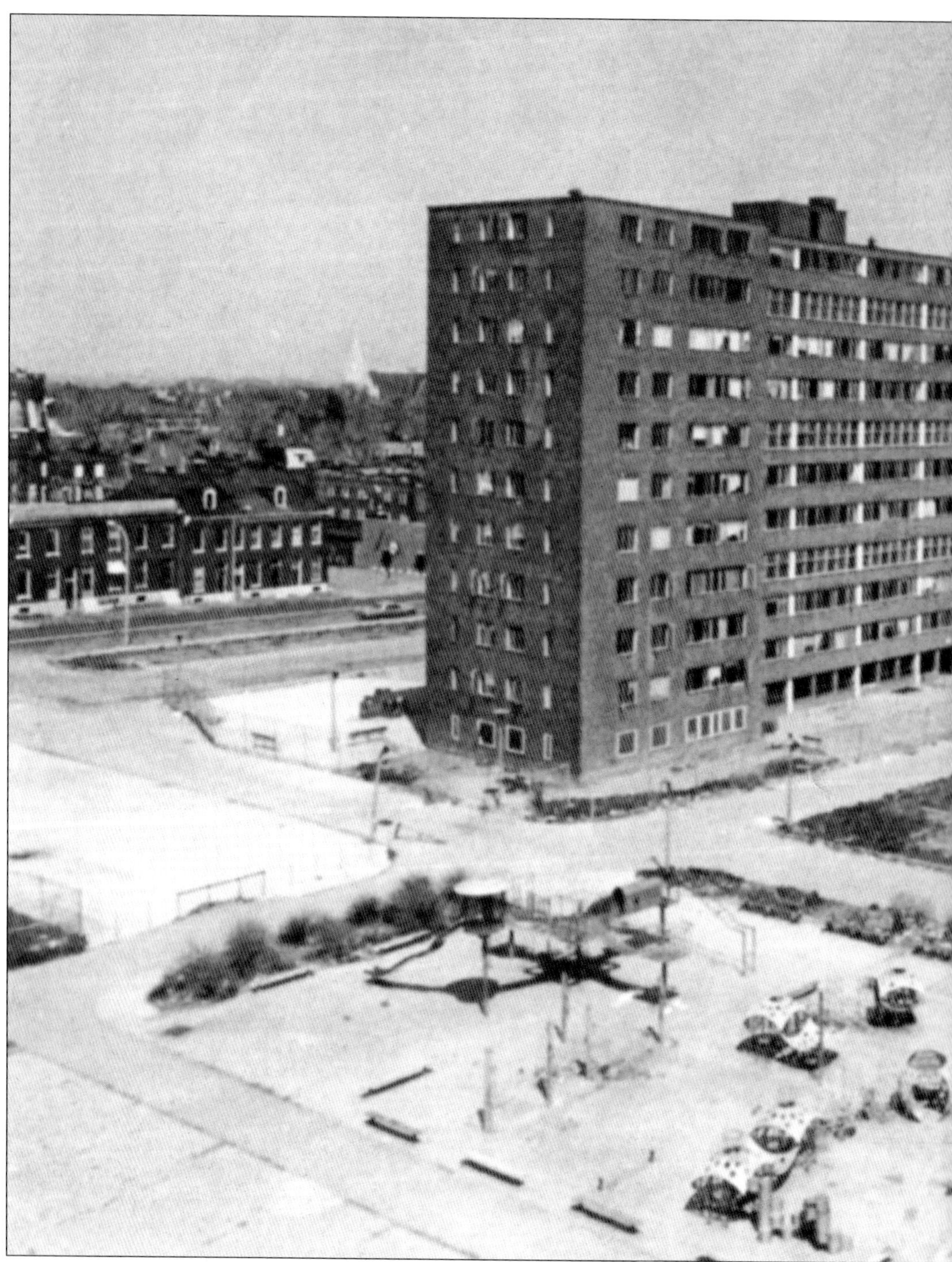

With the passage of federal legislation in 1937 and state legislation in 1939, St. Louis embarked upon a program of building low-rent housing. The most ambitious of the programs was the Pruitt-Igoe Housing Project. It was touted as one of the best-designed public housing projects of the post–World War II era. The city planned two projects: Pruitt for blacks, and Igoe for whites. Because of the ruling in the US District Court in *Davis et al* v. *the St. Louis Housing Authority* in

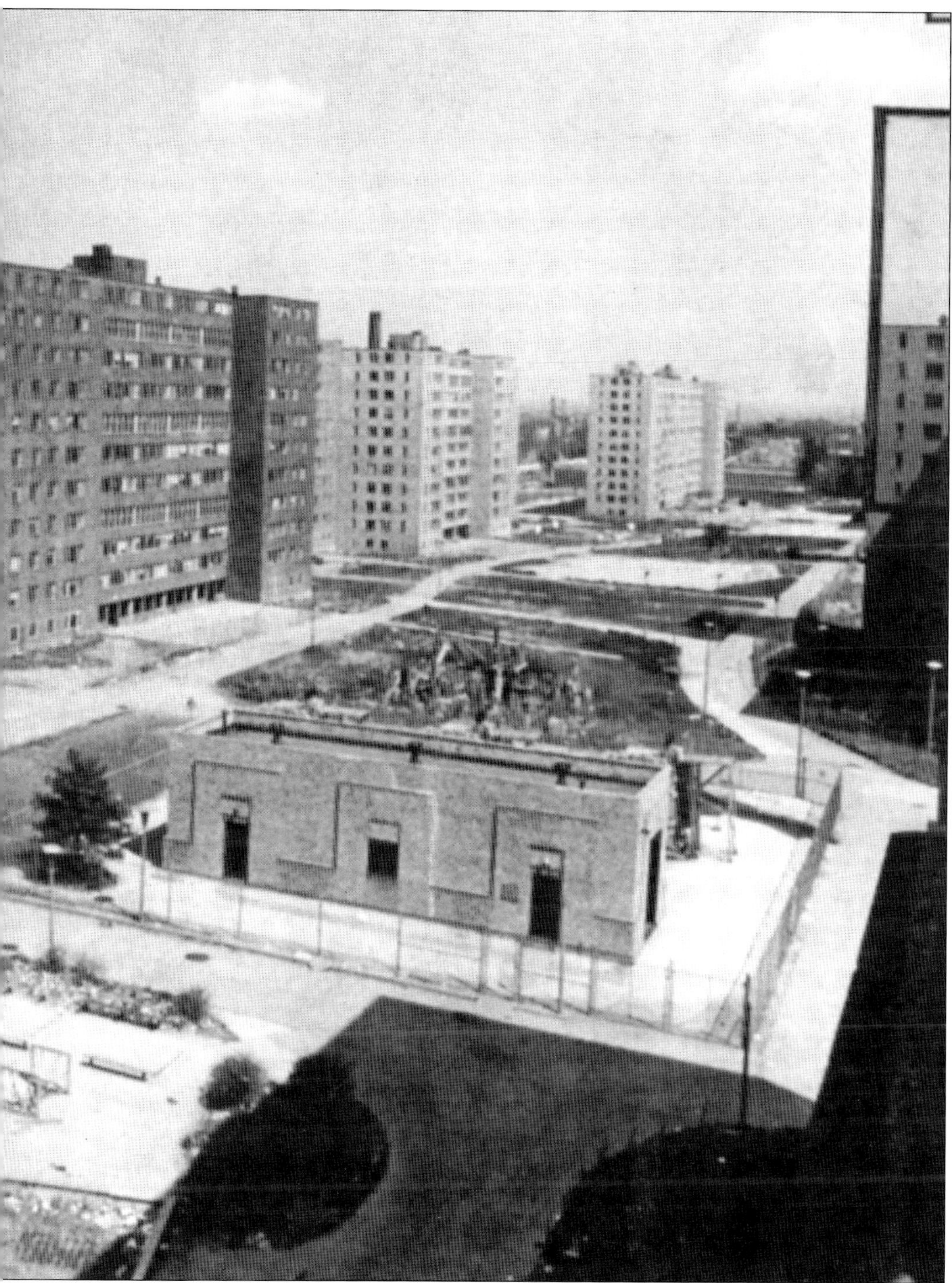

1952, all the buildings had to be open to everyone. The St. Louis Housing Authority said it "had a duty and responsibility under the law to preserve peace and order in the community for the protection and welfare of both races and, in the interest of public safety, to prevent racial conflict and violence." (Courtesy of the St. Louis Mercantile Library, UMSL.)

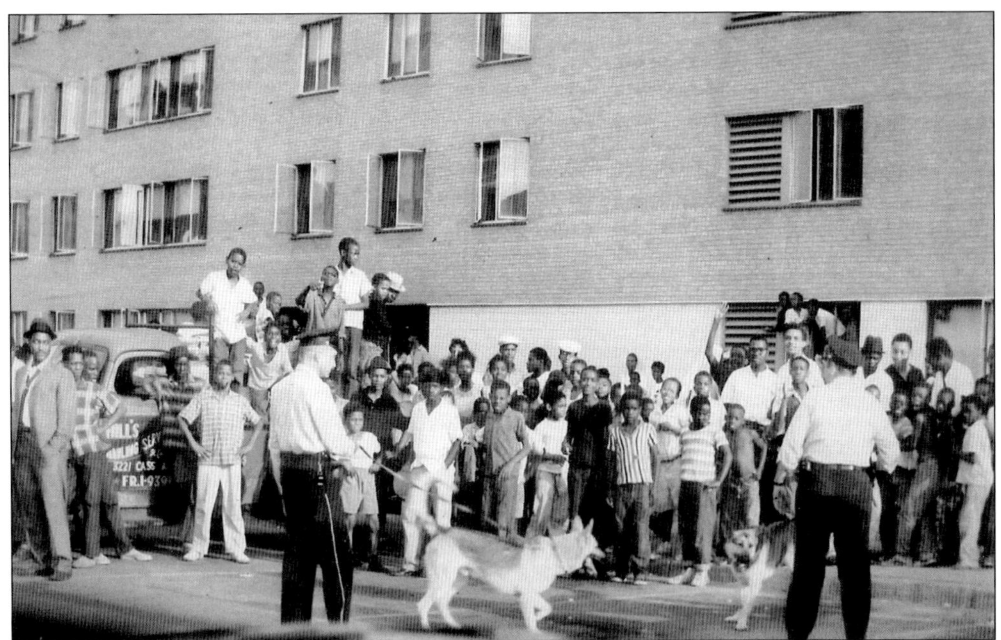

During the hot summer, the Pruitt-Igo housing projects were often the scene of unrest. Once completed, the projects soon became a national scandal, viewed by many as a concentration camp without basic services. (Courtesy of the St. Louis Mercantile Library, UMSL.)

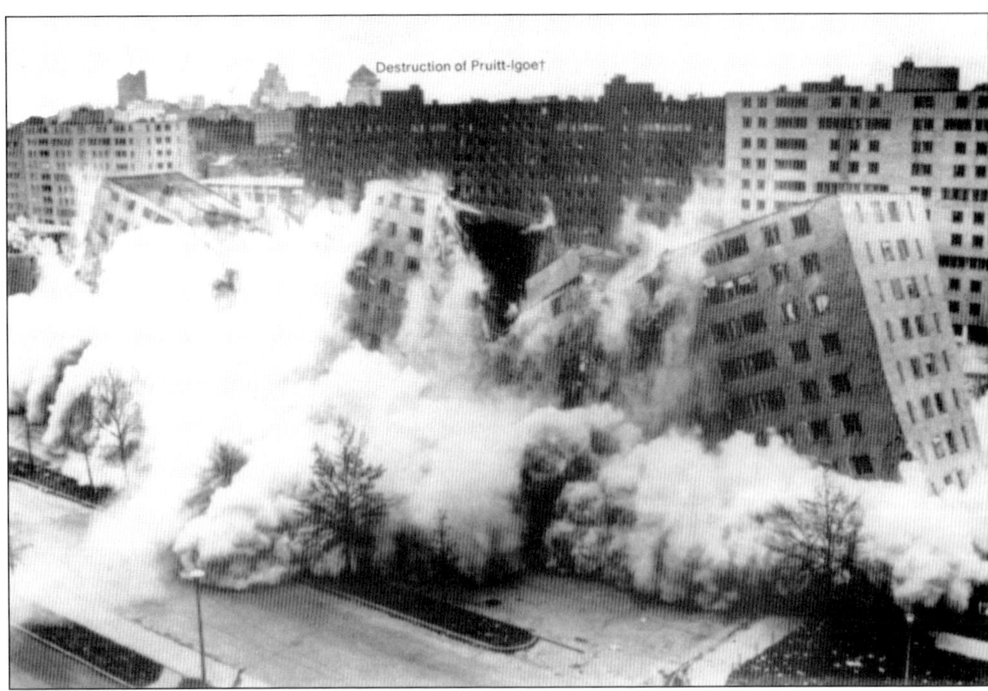

The buildings were demolished in the mid-1970s. They were poorly planned and badly managed. Elevators stopped on every other floor, there were no restrooms on the ground floor, it had no shopping or health services or adequate transportation, and children who lived there had no planned recreation space. Some viewed the housing projects as concentration camps. (Courtesy of Michael Willis.)

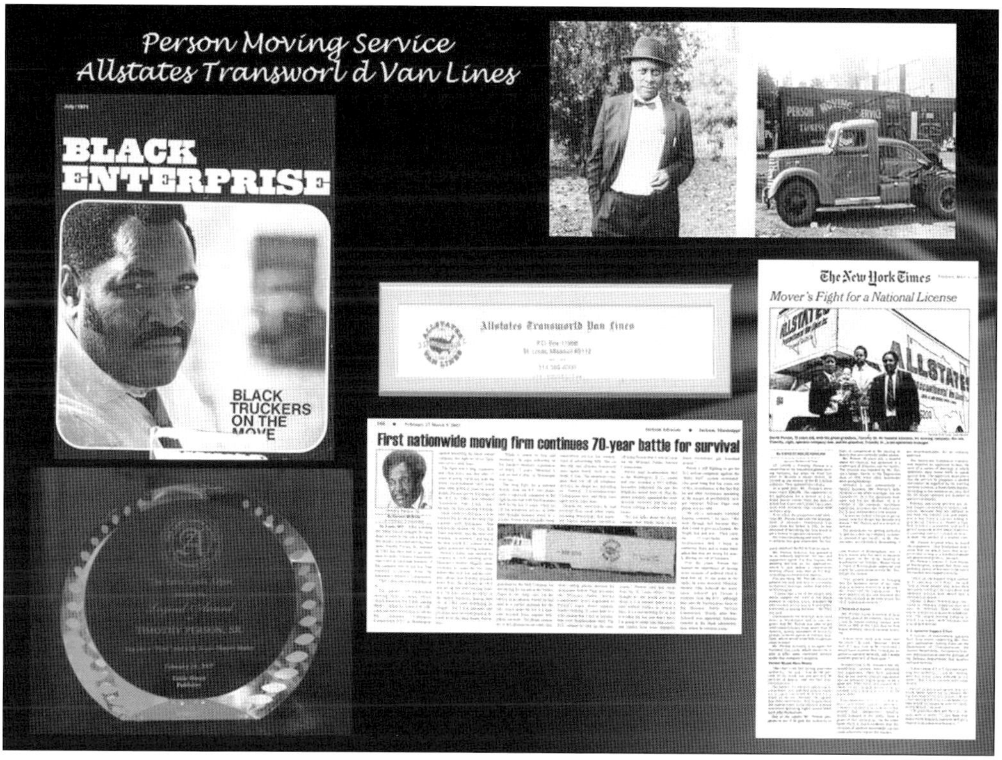

Person Moving Service
Allstates Transworl d Van Lines

BLACK ENTERPRISE

BLACK TRUCKERS ON THE MOVE

First nationwide moving firm continues 70-year battle for survival

The New York Times

Mover's Fight for a National License

Allstate Transworld Van Lines had its beginning in 1929 when David Person began the family moving business. It was taken over by his son Timothy, who began a battle to obtain an interstate moving license in 1964. The battle lasted until 1981, when Allstate became the first black company to obtain a license, one of 20 such companies in America. (Courtesy of Timothy Person.)

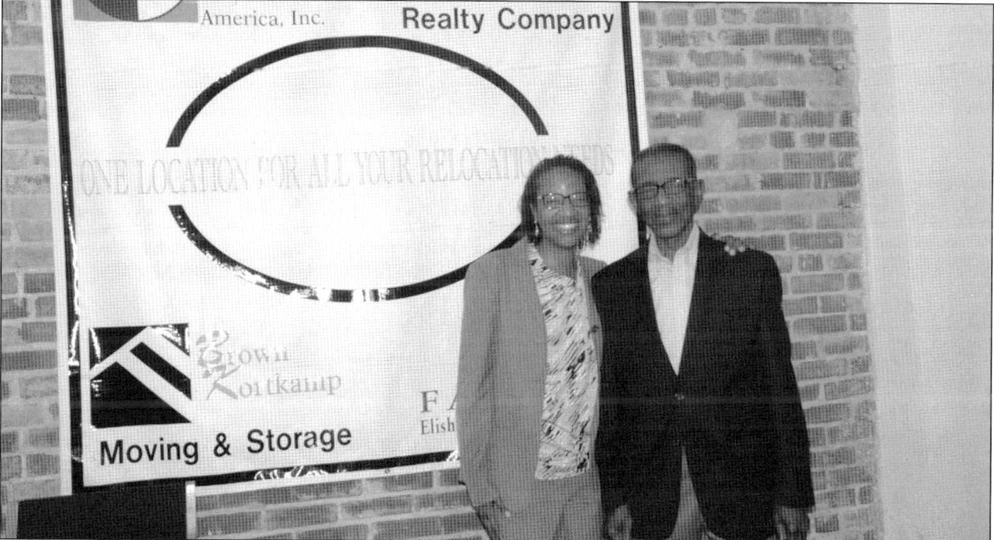

Elisha Brown was the founder of Brown-Kortkamp Moving and Storage Company. He formed the company in 1960 to provide a full spectrum of services. He was unable to obtain a license to provide moving services. To get around this obstacle he purchased a white moving company, Kortkamp. (Courtesy of John A. Wright Sr.)

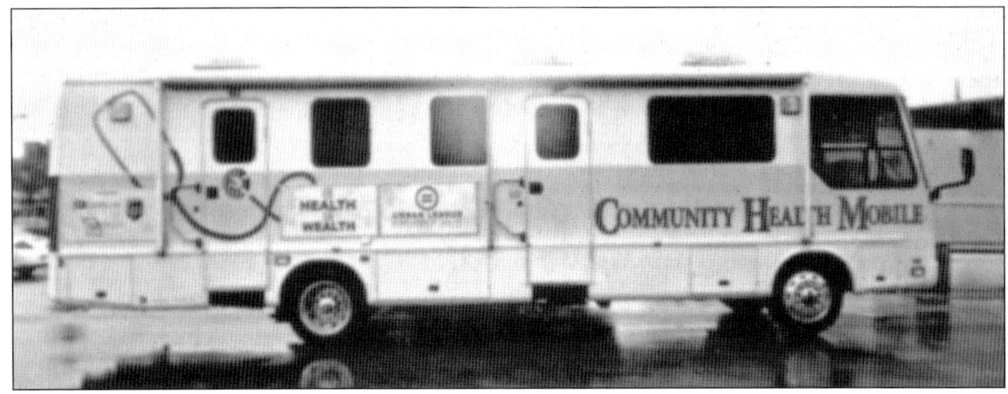

In 2017, a study by the Urban League showed that there was a lack of primary care and prevention services in predominantly African American communities. In north St. Louis, there are 25 physicians for every 10,000 residents, a number that is 70 percent less than the rest of the city. The report pointed out the fact that a child born in the Jeff-Vander-Lou neighborhood, where 95 percent of the residents are African American, can expect to live 18 fewer years than a child born in Clayton, where 80 percent of the residents are white. The Urban League acquired this vehicle from Anheuser-Busch to serve the community. (Courtesy of the Urban League of Metropolitan St. Louis)

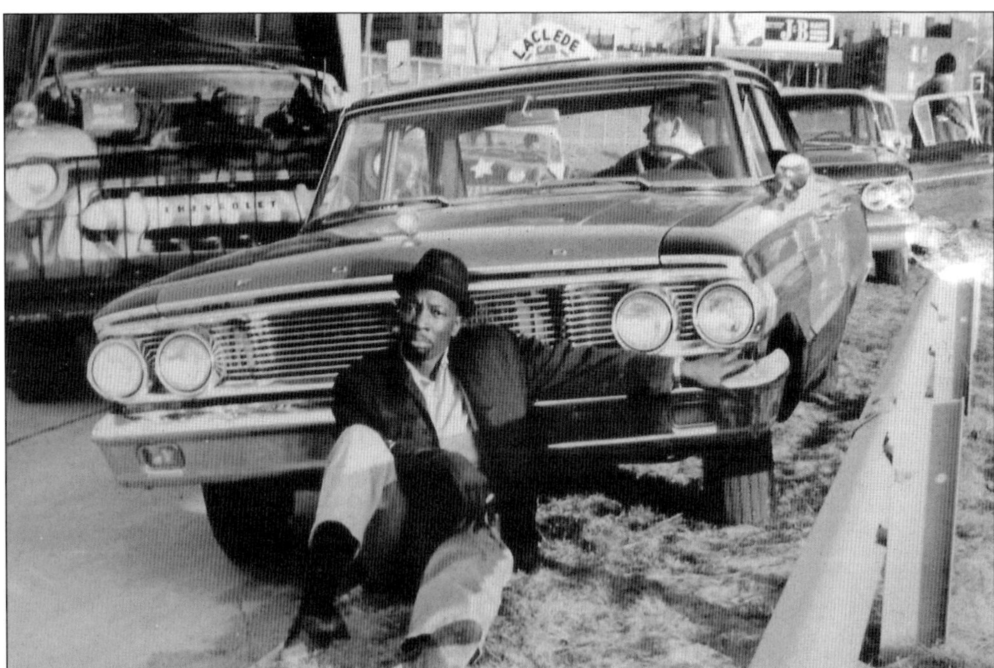

In March 1965, civil rights activists Ivory Perry and Ernest Gilkey created a massive traffic tie-up at rush hour on a busy highway exit ramp in St. Louis. The demonstration was designed to awaken the public to the violence taking place against peaceful civil rights demonstrators in Alabama. First, the two men disabled their truck at the ramp. Then Perry laid down and blocked the path of oncoming cars. (Courtesy of the St. Louis Mercantile Library, UMSL.)

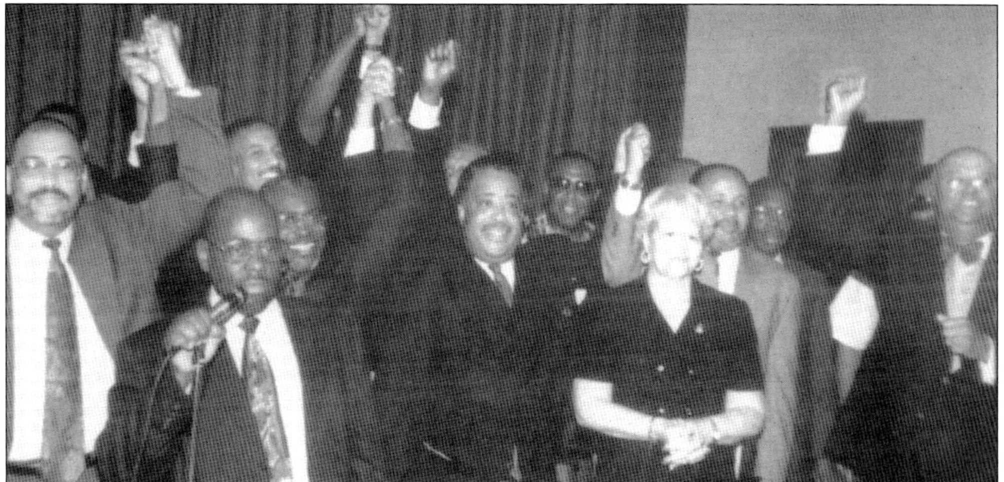

In 1999, protesters were arrested for blocking Interstate 70. They protested the lack of minorities hired to do road repair. A 1995 study commissioned by the State of Missouri and conducted by an out-of-state consulting firm found that in the previous five years, 3.9 percent of the available black construction firms received only 0.48 percent of the construction dollars. (Courtesy of the Urban League of Metropolitan St. Louis.)

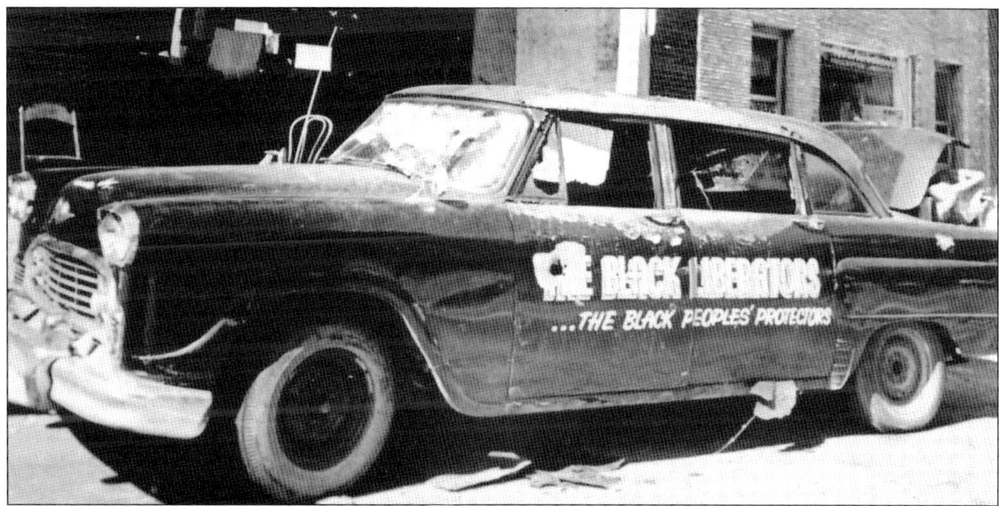

In the spring of 1968, a short-lived militant civil-rights group was formed known as the Black Liberators. It adopted a five-point program for better human development. In 1969, a police precinct was shot into by an unknown assailant, along with a firebombing of an African American member of the police board. This was followed by the Liberators' headquarters being substantially damaged. (Courtesy of the St. Louis Mercantile Library, UMSL.)

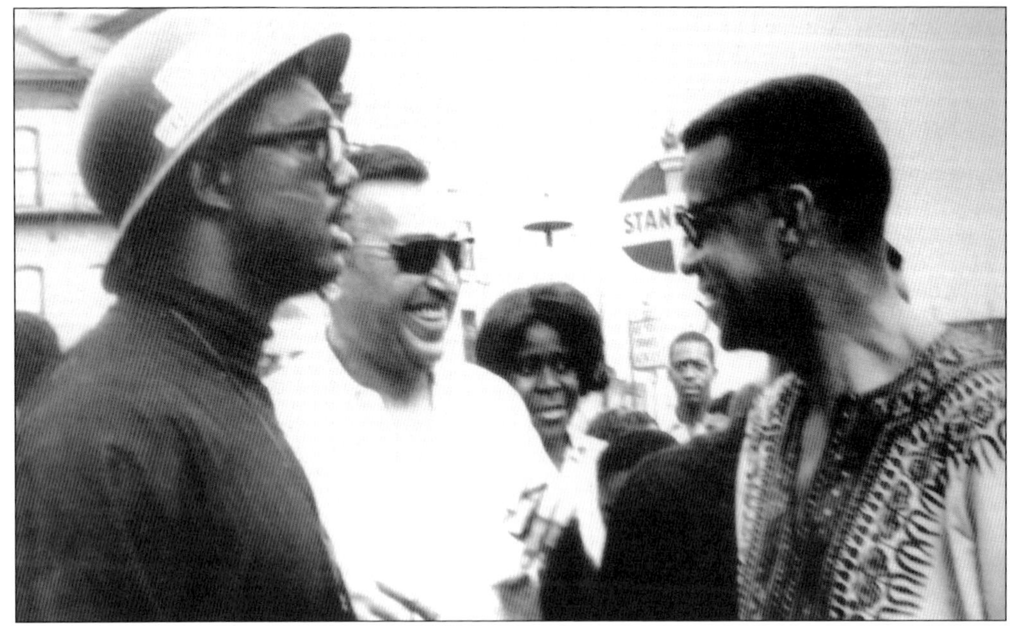

Members of the Black Liberators are pictured here outside of their headquarters at 2810 Easton Avenue (now Dr. Martin Luther King Drive) during a visit by Congressman Adam Clayton Powell. The group was viewed as a threat, like many groups during the civil rights movement. They were constantly undermined by law enforcement agencies. The membership gradually declined and the group eventually disbanded. (Courtesy of the St. Louis Mercantile Library, UMSL.)

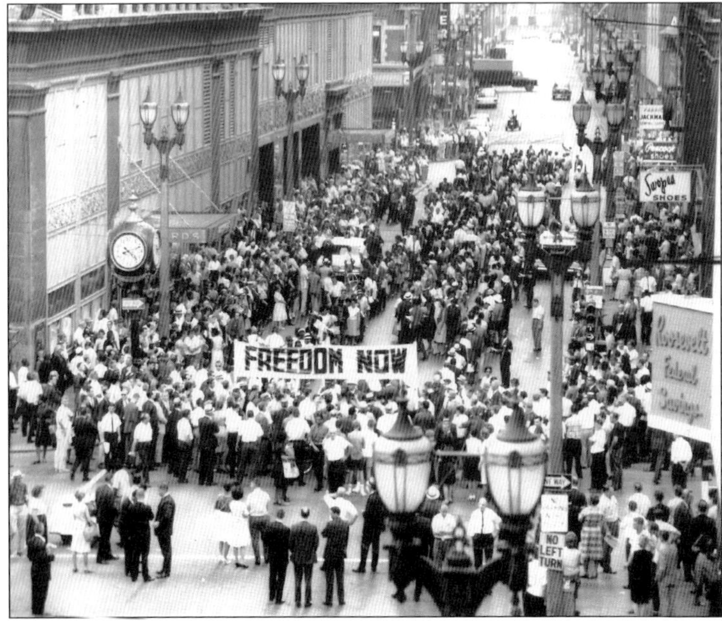

In June 1963, the NAACP organized a demonstration in front of the St. Louis Board of Education, calling for the integration of the total school system. The school system was in a practice of busing 6,000 students from overcrowded black schools to white schools. Once at school, they were kept in separate sections of the building and given separate lunch and playground periods. (Courtesy of the St. Louis Mercantile Library, UMSL.)

In 1972, parent Minnie Liddell filed a successful class-action lawsuit against the St. Louis Board of Education in the City of St. Louis for violation of the 14th Amendment's equal protection clause. Her action served as a landmark event in the desegregation of the city's public schools and sparked the largest school-choice program in the United States at the time. (Courtesy of John Wright Sr.)

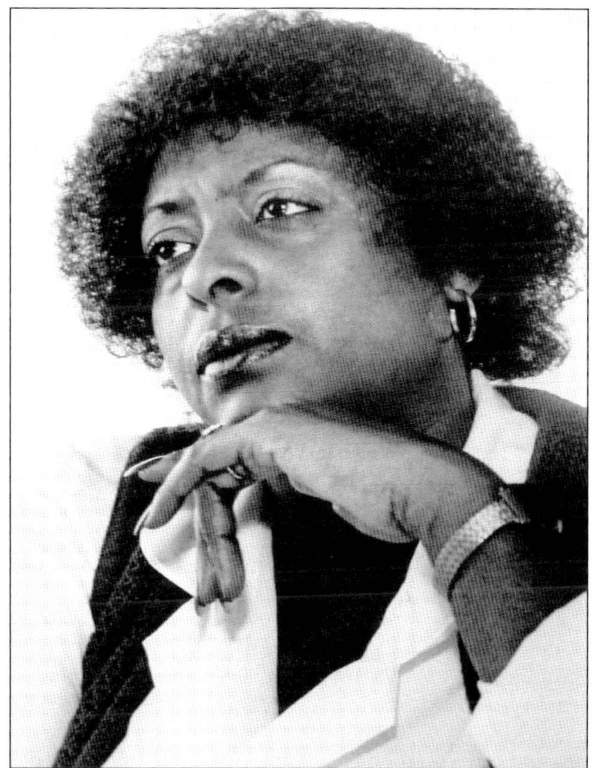

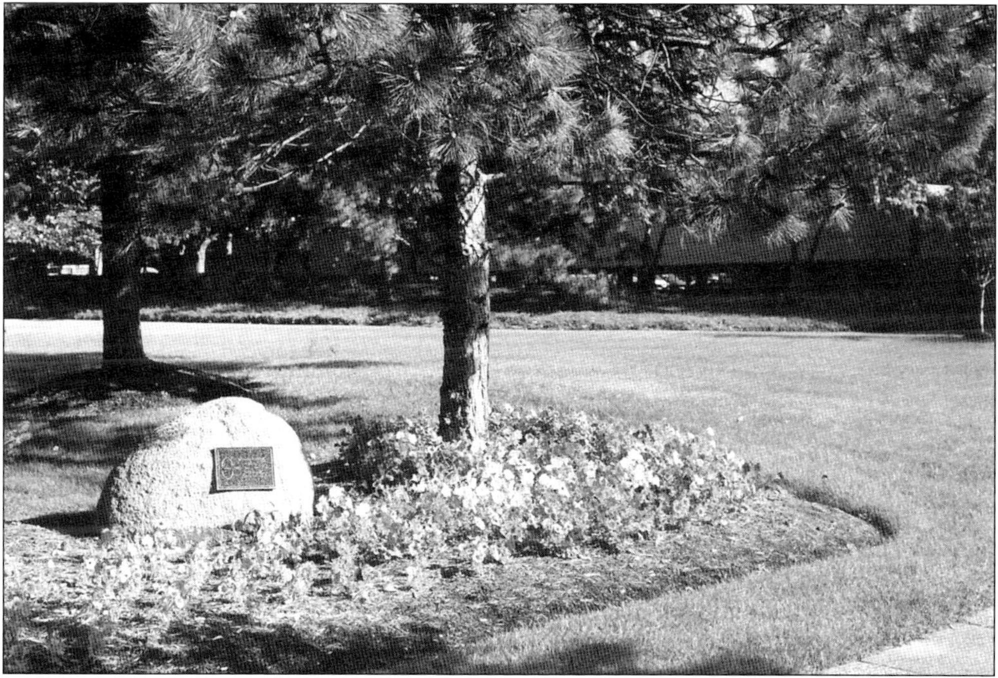

On March 11, 2001, the St. Louis Board of Education dedicated Lindell Park next to its central Office. Minnie Lindell is known as the mother of school desegregation. (Photograph by John A. Wright Sr.)

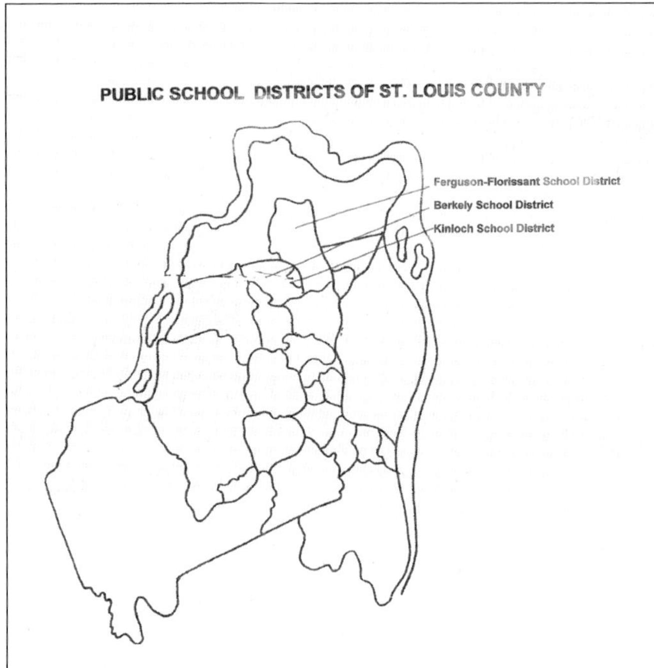

In 1975, the federal court ordered the merger of the all-black Kinloch, semi-integrated Berkeley, and mostly white Ferguson-Florissant School Districts to merge for desegregation purposes. In 1938, the whites in Kinloch pulled away from Kinloch to form the City of Berkeley to establish a white school district, taking away the resources. The Ferguson-Florissant School District had reorganized in 1948. (Courtesy of John A. Wright Sr.)

IN THE

SUPREME COURT OF THE UNITED STATES

OCTOBER TERM, 1975

No. ....

KINLOCH SCHOOL DISTRICT and JOHN A. WRIGHT, Superintendent, Petitioners,

vs.

UNITED STATES OF AMERICA; STATE OF MISSOURI; MISSOURI STATE BOARD OF EDUCATION; ARTHUR L. MALLORY, Commissioner of Education; F. BURTON SAWYER, President, SIDNEY R. REDMOND, W. C. BANTA, JOHN M. MORRIS, DALE M. THOMPSON, JACK WEBSTER, ELEANOR B. GRIFFITH, HARVEY B. YOUNG, JR., Members of the Missouri State Board of Education; ST. LOUIS COUNTY BOARD OF EDUCATION, GEORGE W. VOSSBRINK, Superintendent, ROBERT S. WEINSTOCK, President, QUINTON C. KELLER, PAUL A. LEUPOLD, FRED R. SMALL, GLENN A. SWEET, CLARENCE J. WOHLWEND, Members of the St. Louis County Board of Education, Respondents.

PETITION FOR WRIT OF CERTIORARI

To the United States Court of Appeals for the Eighth Circuit

MARVIN S. WOOD
230 South Bemiston—Suite 900
St. Louis, Missouri 63105
Attorney for Petitioners, Kinloch School District and John A. Wright, Superintendent

The Kinloch School District appealed to the US Supreme Court over the court-ordered merger, without success. The district wanted to merge with only Berkeley so that it could maintain its schools, lower its tax rate, and avoid a great deal of travel for its students. In the end, all its schools were closed and its students were bussed to the northern part of the Ferguson-Florissant School District. (Courtesy of John A. Wright Sr.)

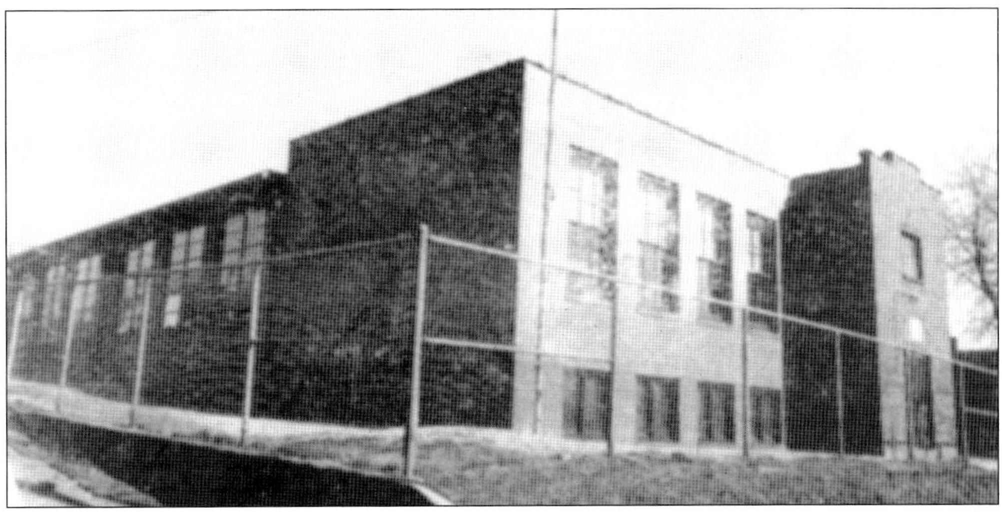

Not all school districts responded to the 1954 Brown decision. Vernon Elementary School in the Ferguson-Florissant School District remained segregated until it closed in 1967. The decision to close was caused by pressure from parents and the Missouri Commission on Human Rights. The school served two mile-long blocks in the City of Kinloch. (Courtesy of the Ferguson-Florissant School District.)

Residents of Vernon School Neighborhood

---- Do you want a first class education for your children?????

---- Is Vernon School a necessary evil?????

---- How can we best approach resolving the problems which now face us?????

---- What are the real issues?????

LET'S GET TOGETHER AND TALK ABOUT THESE THINGS ON TUESDAY,

DECEMBER 28, 1965 at 8 P.M., AT THE VERNON SCHOOL BUILDING.

Sincerely,

Arthur Johnson, Chairman

Julia Boyd, Secretary

VERNON SCHOOL PARENTS FOR AAA EDUCATION

WHATEVER YOUR VIEWS MAY BE, WE WELCOME YOU TO COME AND EXPRESS THEM.

When the school closed, the students were assigned by grade level, which meant that families with children in different grades had kids in several schools. Ferguson-Florissant School District had asked the Kinloch School District to assume responsibility for the school, but its school board declined. (Courtesy of John A. Wright Sr.)

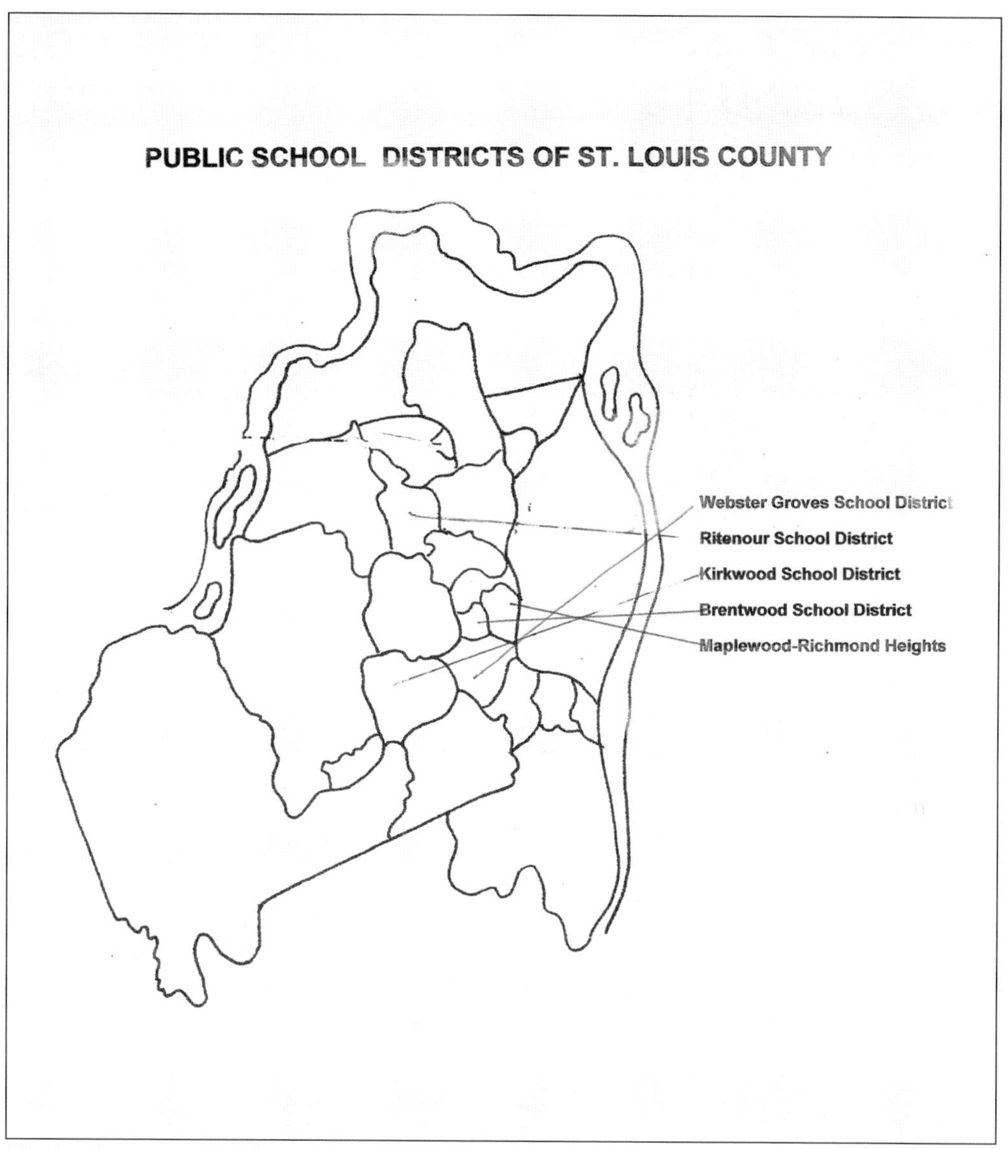

The last known recorded case in Missouri involving school desegregation before the 1954 *Brown* decision was *Arnold* v. *Kirkwood School District R7*. A black student applied to attend a white school in his district. The plaintiff based his case on the use of separate facilities. The case was denied and then went to the Supreme Court, where judgment was withheld until after the 1954 *Brown* decision. In 1973, letters were sent to the Webster Groves, Brentwood, Ritenour, Kirkwood, and Maplewood–Richmond Heights School Districts, which were still operating the all-black schools they had operated before 1954, from the Department of Health, Education and Welfare and the Office of Civil Rights requesting they develop a plan for the desegregation of their schools. (Courtesy of John A. Wright Sr.)

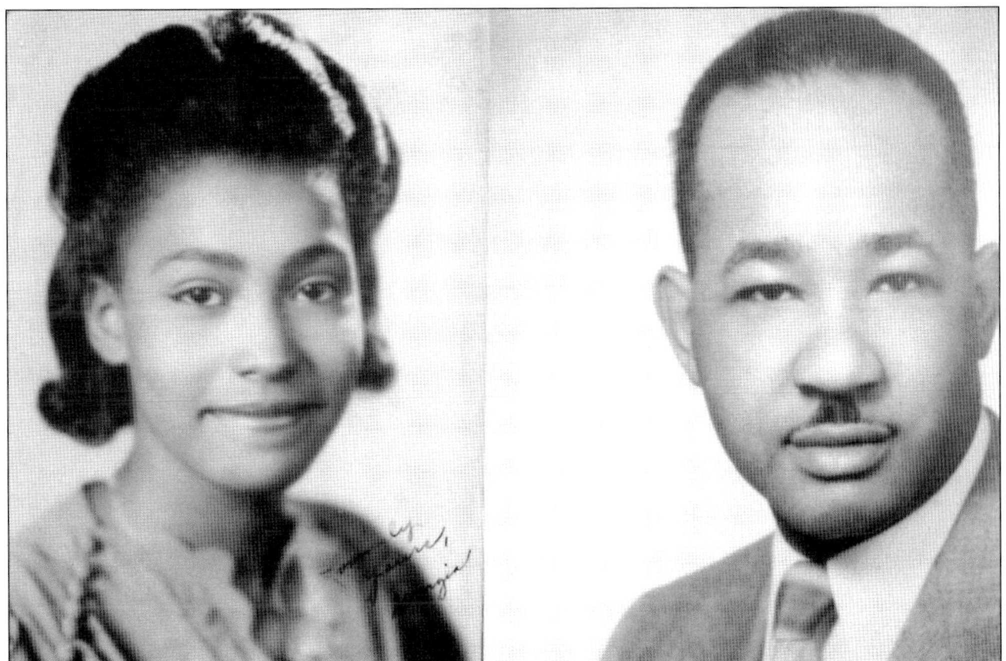

In 1945, Georgia and Thomas Rusan purchased two lots just north of the African American section of Richmond Heights, intending to build a new home. While putting the Rusans through many delays, the City of Richmond Heights failed a bond issue that would have replaced the site with a park and playground. In 1951, the city put another measure on the ballot, which also failed. (Courtesy of Georgia Rusan.)

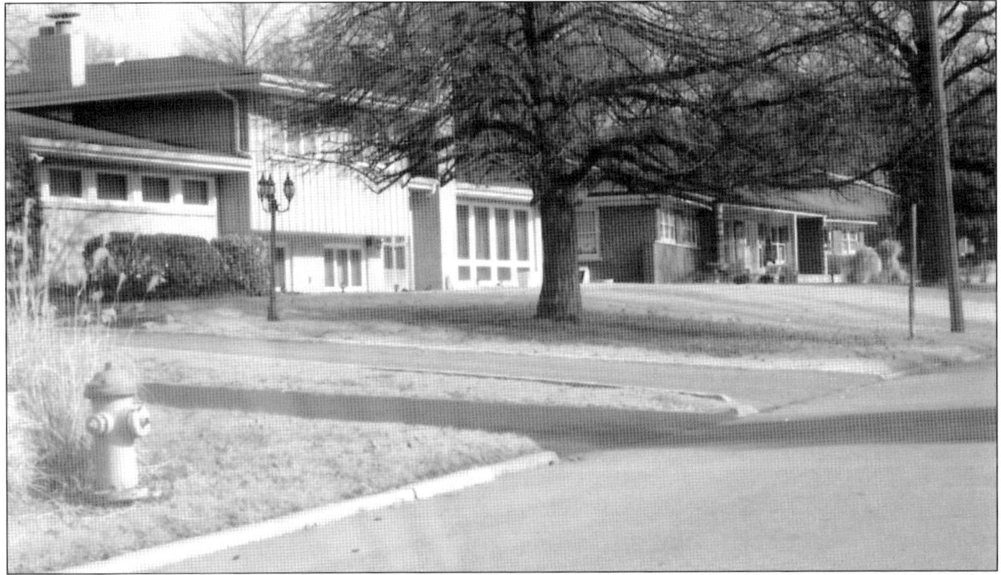

The Rusans' home was later taken by the highway department. They later purchased the land where the homes seen here now stand on Bennett Avenue to build a subdivision. They ran into many difficulties: white neighbors met to block construction, builders walked away, obtaining utilities was next to impossible, and some of the homes were vandalized during construction. By the early 1960s, Bennett Avenue was flourishing. (Photograph by John A. Wright Sr.)

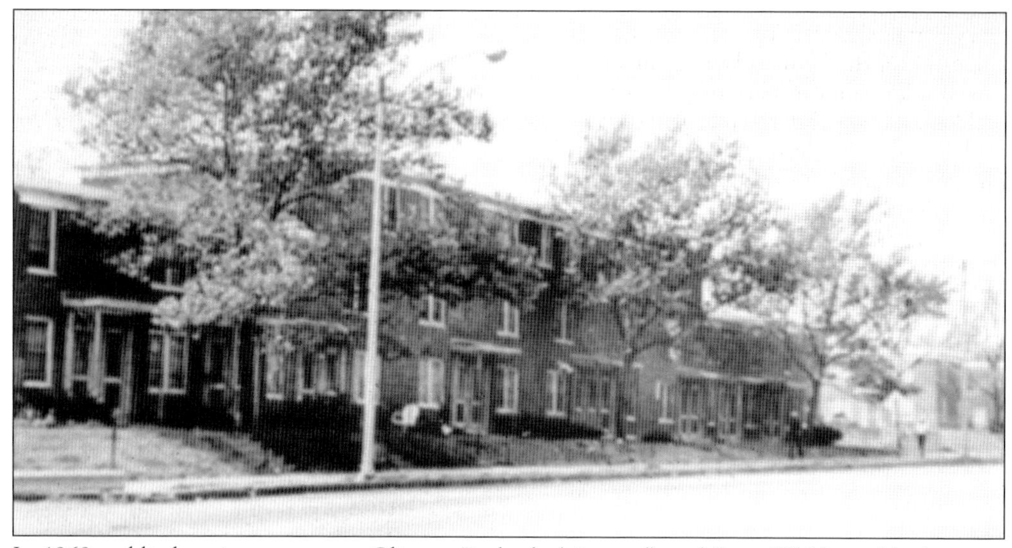

In 1969, public housing tenants at Clinton-Peabody (pictured) and Darst-Webbe public housing projects launched a rent strike that lasted nine months. The tenants were upset over high rent and poorly maintained units and refused to pay their rent. Some tenants were forced to pay over half their income for rent. (Courtesy of the St. Louis Mercantile Library, UMSL.)

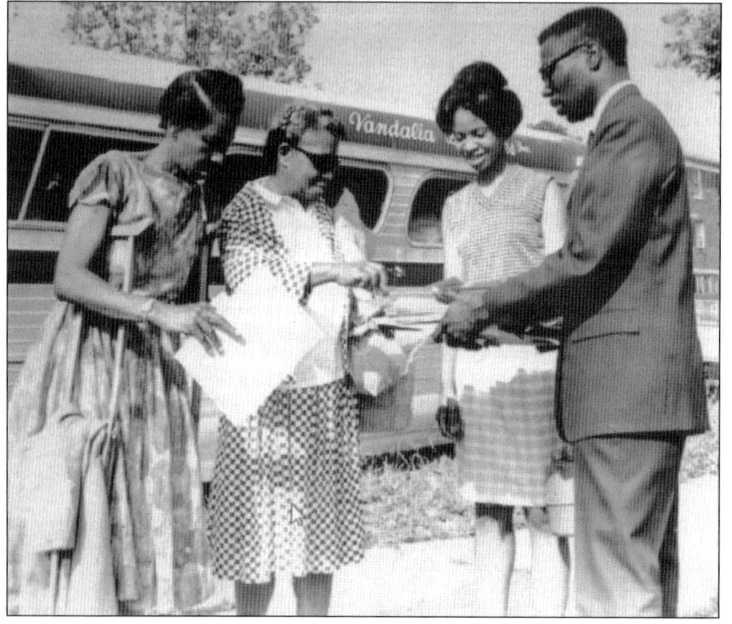

Pictured here is Rev. Buck Jones, one of the leaders of the rent strike, in conversation with some tenants over their objectives before boarding a bus to Jefferson City to meet with legislators. The St. Louis rent strike shaped federal legislation and helped make housing a central concern of the Black Freedom Movement. (Courtesy of the St. Louis Mercantile Library, UMSL.)

Ivory Perry, while working as a housing inspector for the Human Development Corporation, noticed recurring health problems among children and found they could be traced to lead paint. He began an intensive campaign to eliminate the threat of lead poisoning in the lives of St. Louis inner-city tenants. He was successful in getting an ordinance passed that forced landlords to remove lead-based paint. (Courtesy of the St. Louis Mercantile Library, UMSL.)

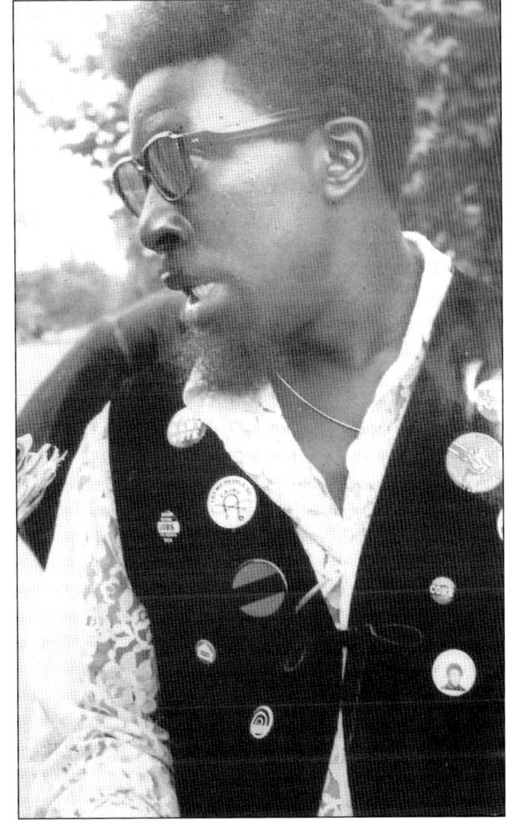

In 1956, Dr. H. Phillp Venable purchased land in Creve Coeur to build a home. Some white neighbors objected and worked to force him to sell. The city halted the construction and a three-and-a-half-year court battle ensued. The city seized the property through the courts and made a park. In 2019, the city apologized and renamed the park for Venable. (Courtesy of the City of Creve Coeur.)

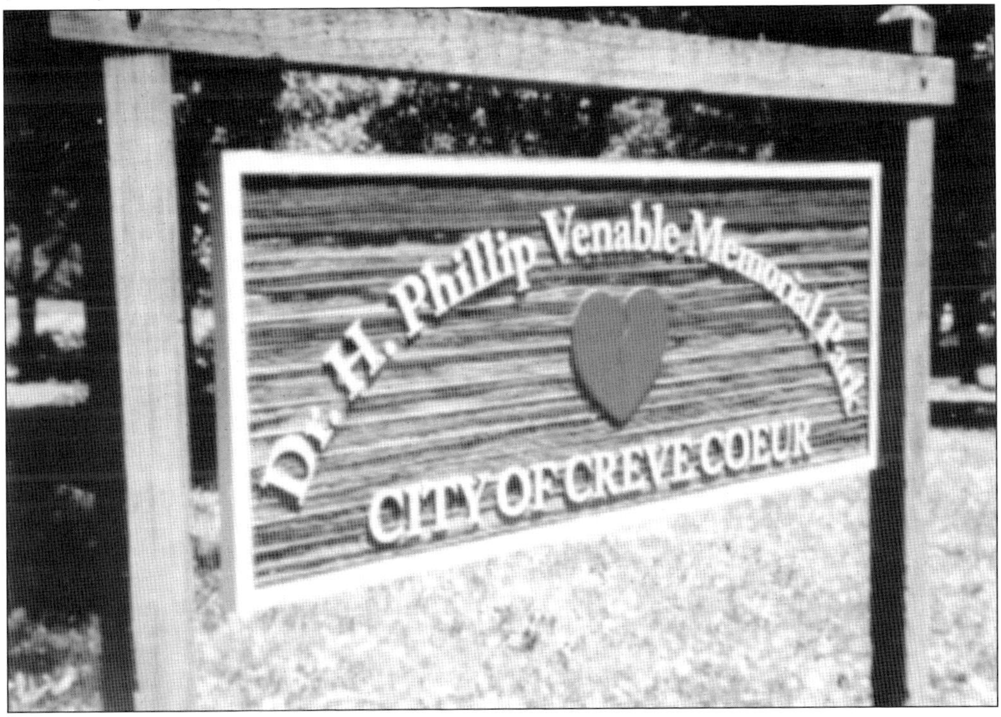

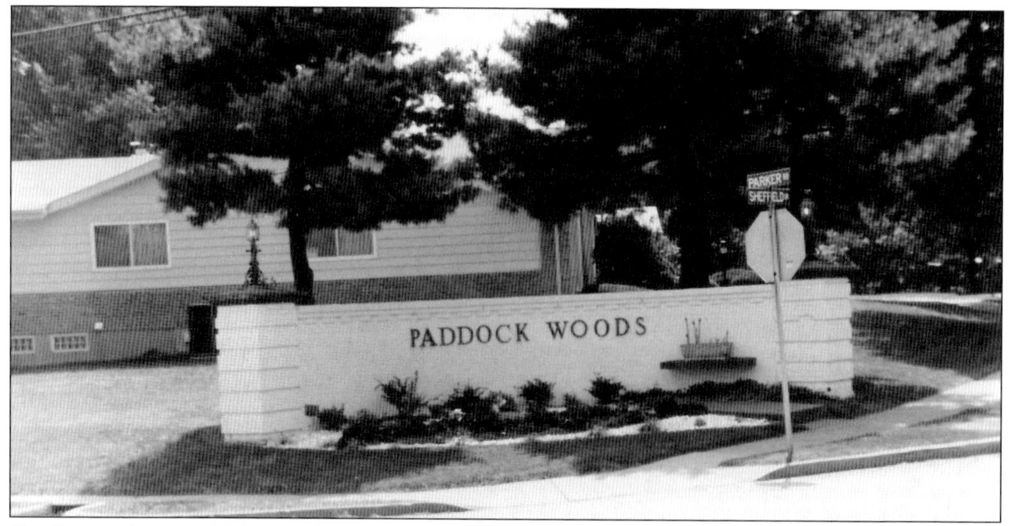

On September 2, 1965, Joseph Lee Jones filed suit in the US District Court against Alfred H. Mayer Company. They refused to sell him a home in Paddock Woods because he was black. His suit *Jones* v. *Alfred H. Mayer Co.* was dismissed both in district and appellate courts. On June 17, 1968, the US Supreme Court ruled 7-2 in Jones's favor. (Photograph by John A. Wright Sr.)

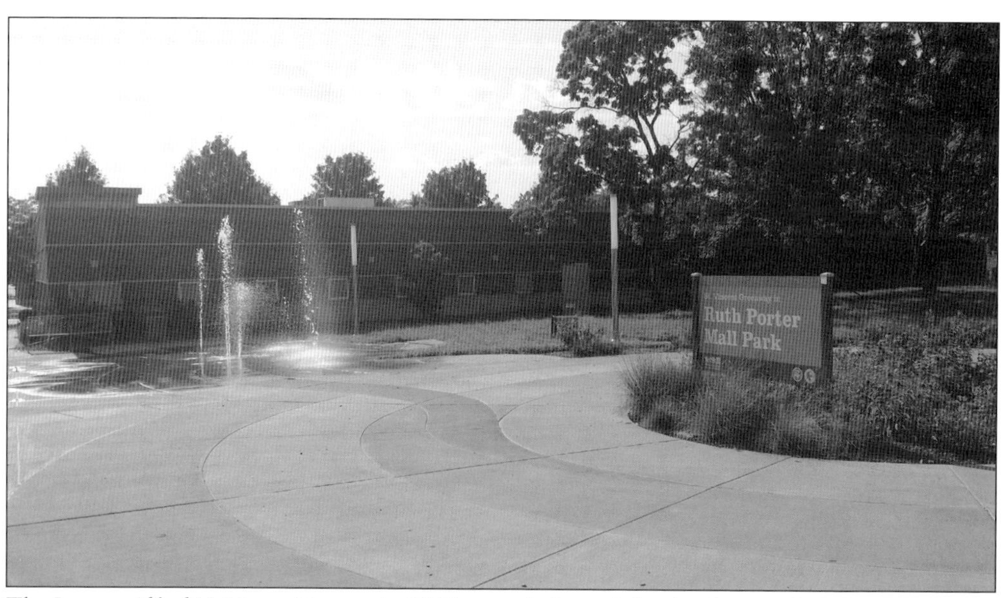

The *Jones* v. *Alfred H. Mayer Co.* case in 1968 was aided greatly by the Greater St. Louis Committee for Freedom of Residence founded by Ruth Porter in 1961 to break down housing restrictions and integrate housing in St. Louis. Ruth Porter is honored for her work with this park named for her at Delmar and DeBaliviere Avenues. (Photograph by Curtis Wright Sr.)

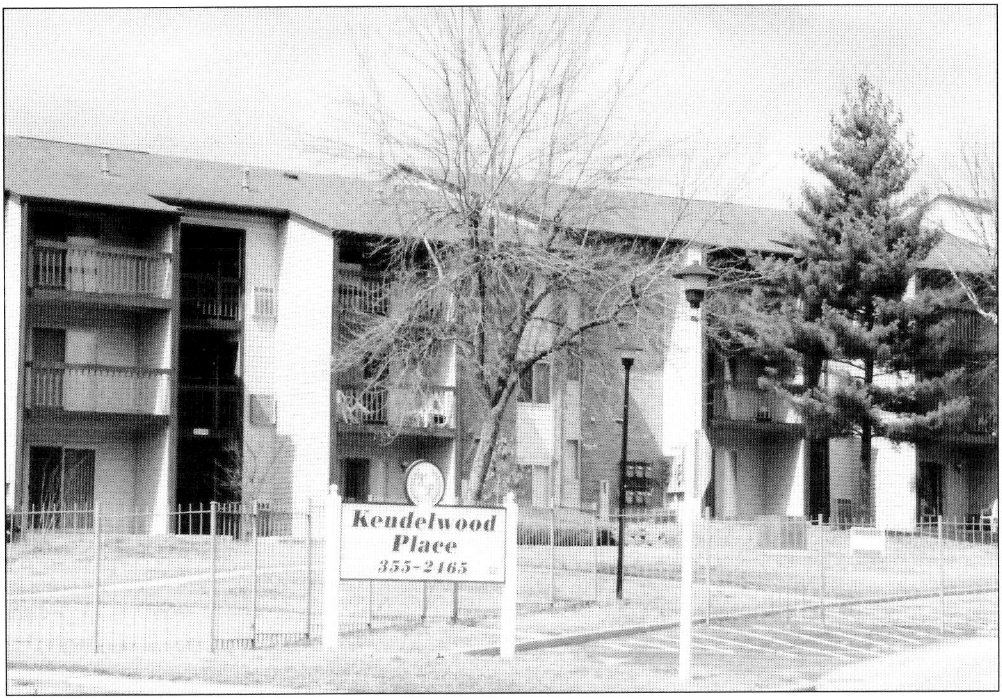

In 1970, the Inter-Religious Center for Urban Affairs proposed building a federally subsidized moderate-income and multiracial housing project on Parker and Jamestown Roads. The residents protested and incorporated, forming the City of Blackjack and passing a zoning code to block the project. The city lost in the courts and was forced to develop the housing units now known as the Kendelwood Apartments. (Photograph by John A. Wright Sr.)

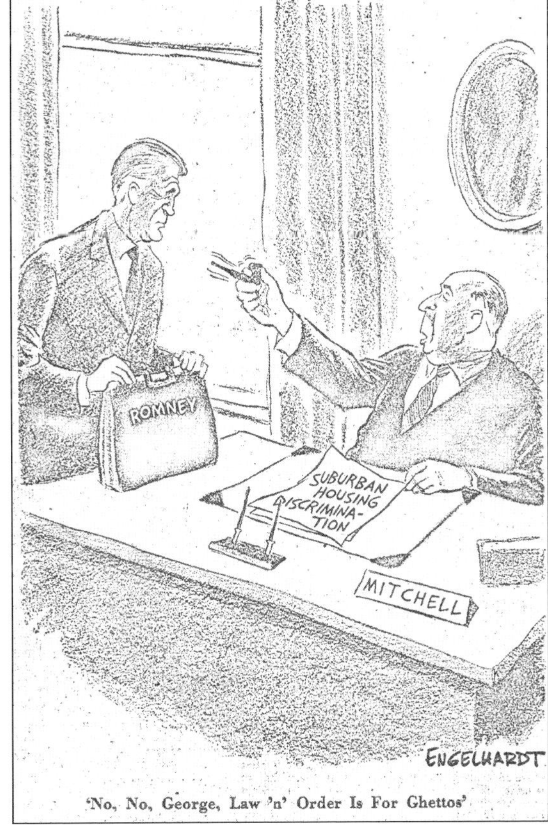

'No, No, George, Law 'n' Order Is For Ghettos'

It is reported that the Nixon administration did not want to get involved in the Blackjack suit at first but George Romney, secretary of housing and urban development, threatened to resign if the administration did not get involved. Nixon had initially opposed the Fair Housing legislation. Romney wanted to use his power to remake housing patterns. (Courtesy of John A. Wright)

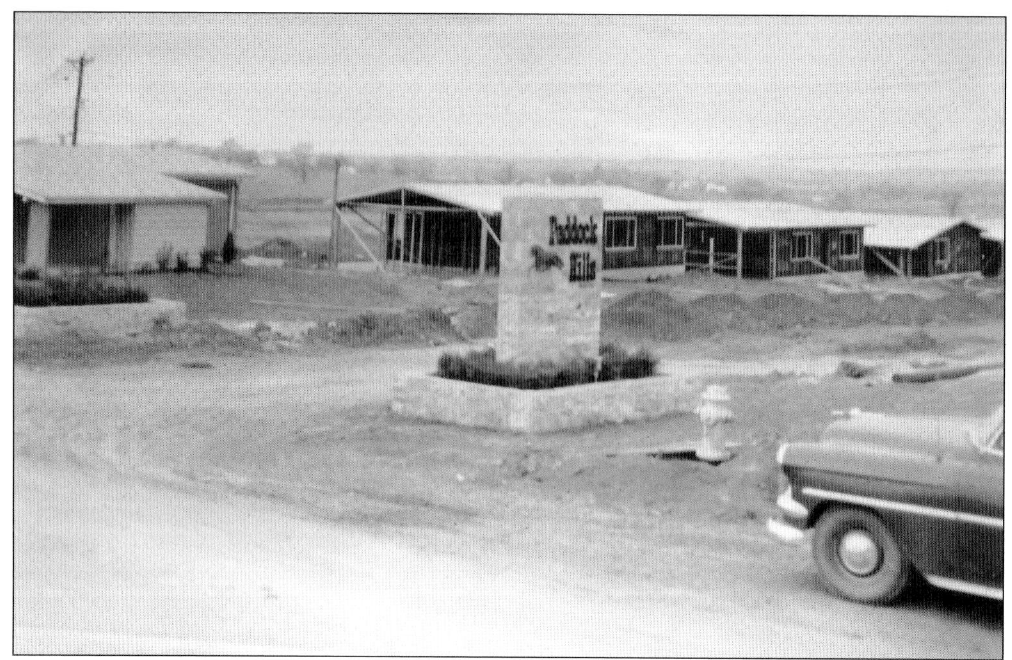

Housing options were a major issue during the last century, as they are today. Some relief came when whites began to leave the city for the county and new housing. According to Selwyn K. Troen and Glen E. Holt in their publication *St. Louis*, between 1960 and 1970, a net 34 percent of white city dwellers moved away from the City of St. Louis. (Courtesy of the St. Louis Mercantile Library, UMSL.)

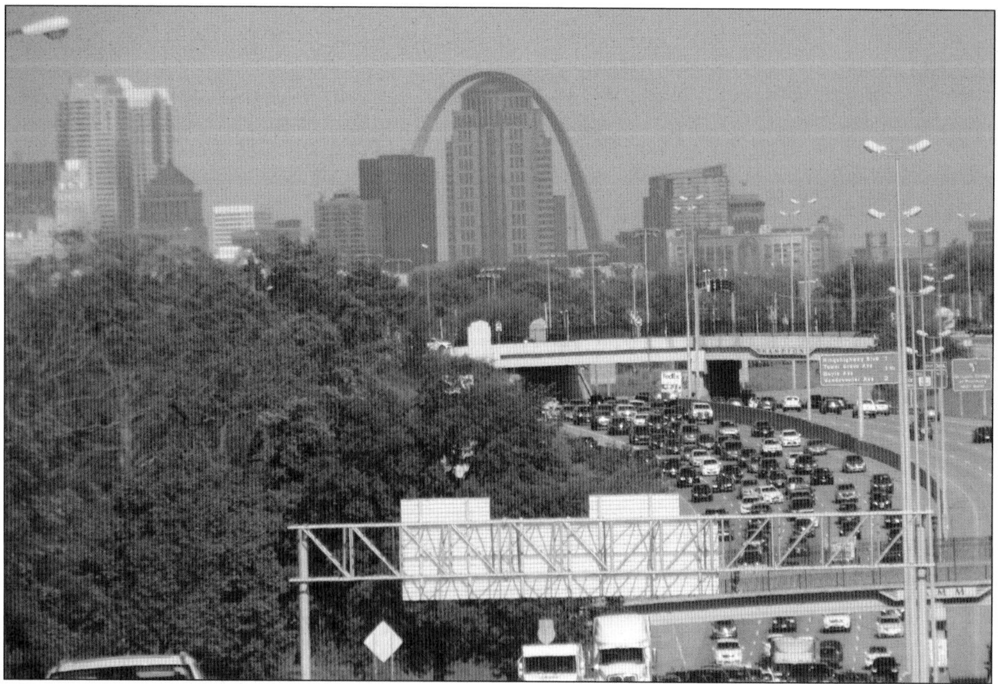

The construction of new highways also aided in the movement of whites away from the city to the suburbs. (Photograph by John A. Wright Jr.)

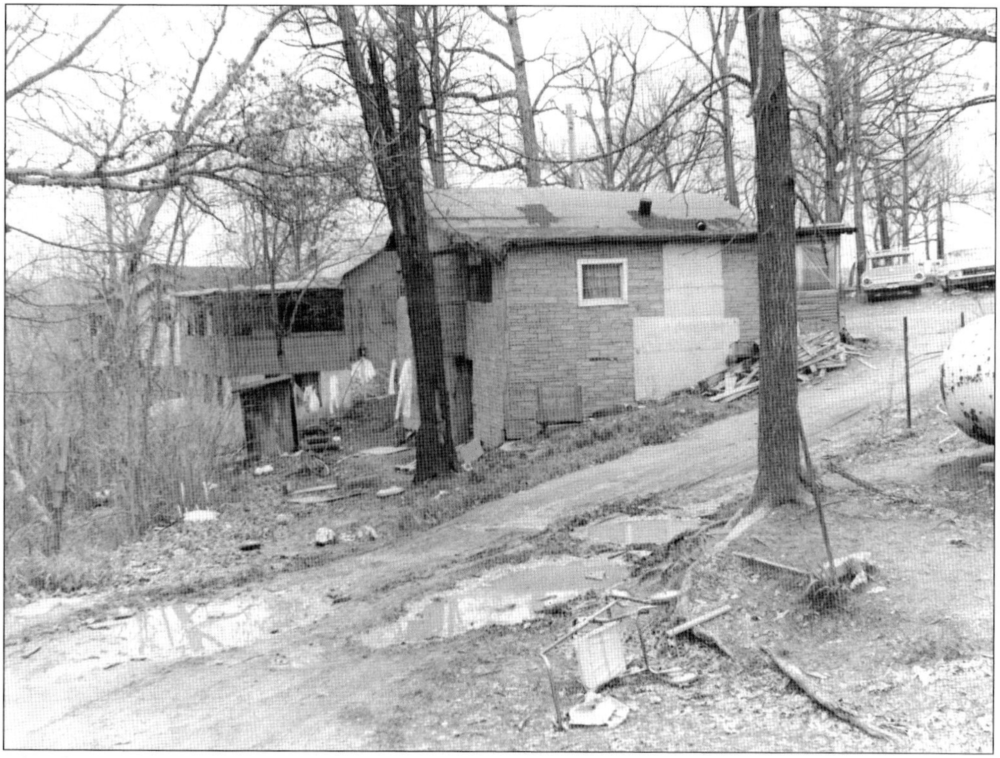

The destruction of some neighborhoods, even with good intent, can be difficult if not planned well. When unincorporated Meacham Park was annexed to the City of Kirkwood, some poor housing stock was taken out and replaced with new housing and commercial development. A misunderstanding developed between a resident and the City of Kirkwood that led to the killing of six city employees and the wounding of the mayor. The resident felt the city did not follow through on its promises, leading to the destruction of his business. (Both, courtesy of John A. Wright Sr.)

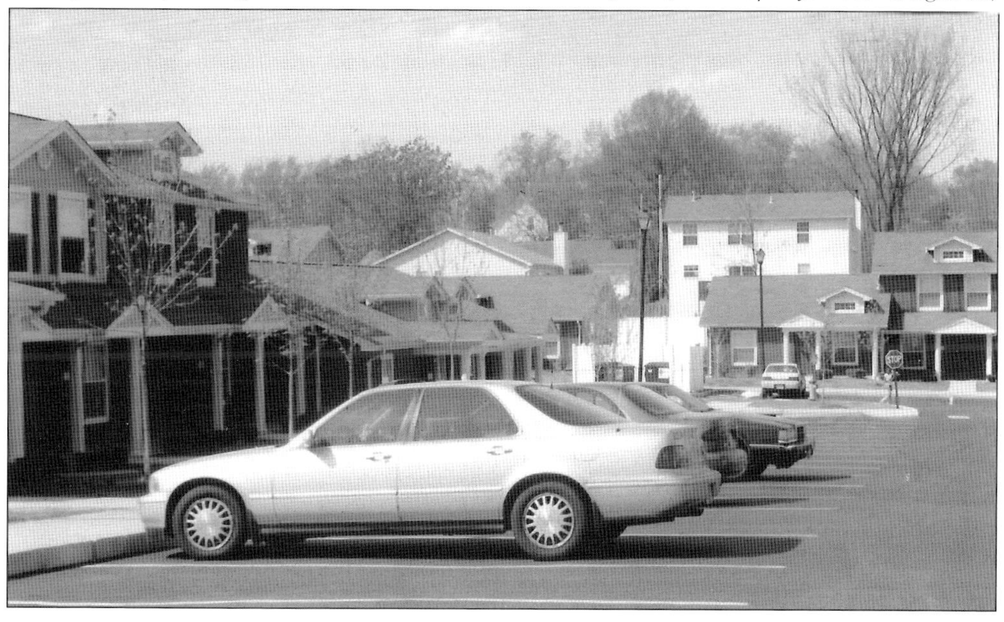

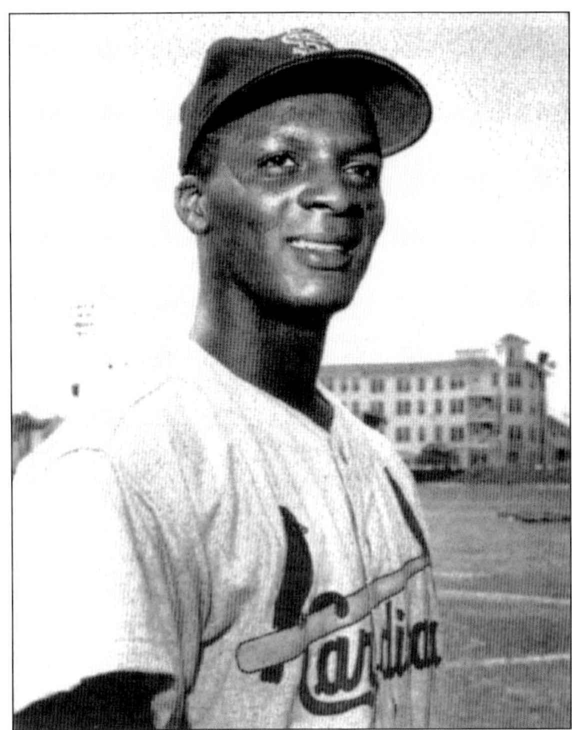

Former St. Louis Cardinal Curt Flood forever changed Major League Baseball when he challenged the league owners' ability to trade players to other teams. Flood demanded his rights, refusing to be traded. He took his case to the Supreme Court, where he lost. However, his case led to solidarity among players, who fought the reserve clause and won free agency. (Courtesy of the St. Louis Mercantile Library, UMSL.)

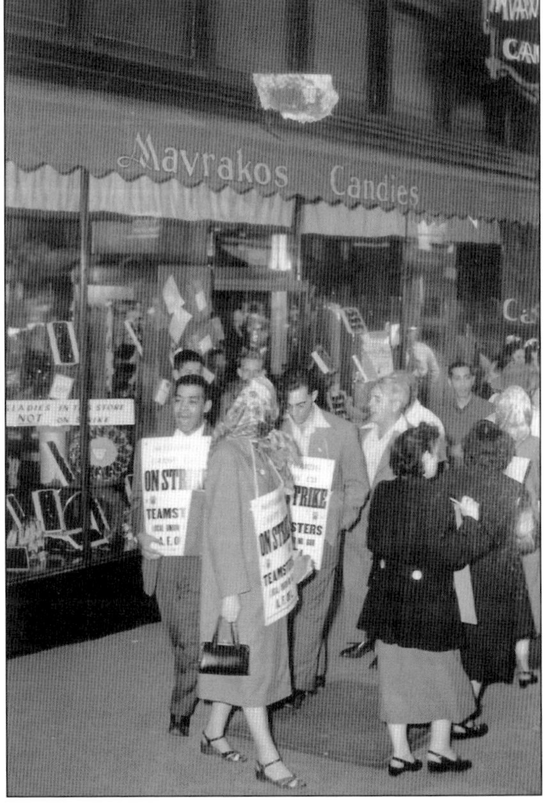

In 1961, after many failed attempts, the St. Louis Board of Aldermen passed a public accommodations ordinance by a vote of 24 to 2. All city-owned facilities were now open. The years of picketing for jobs and public accommodations were beginning to pay off. (Courtesy of the Western Manuscript Collection, UMSL.)

Ernest Calloway was one of the leaders in the civil rights movement in the 1950s and 1960s. In 1955, he was elected president of the local chapter of the NAACP. Under his leadership, membership grew from 2,000 to 8,000. He was successful in gaining increased employment in taxi services, department stores, the Coca-Cola Company, and Southwestern Bell. (Courtesy of the St. Louis Mercantile Library, UMSL.)

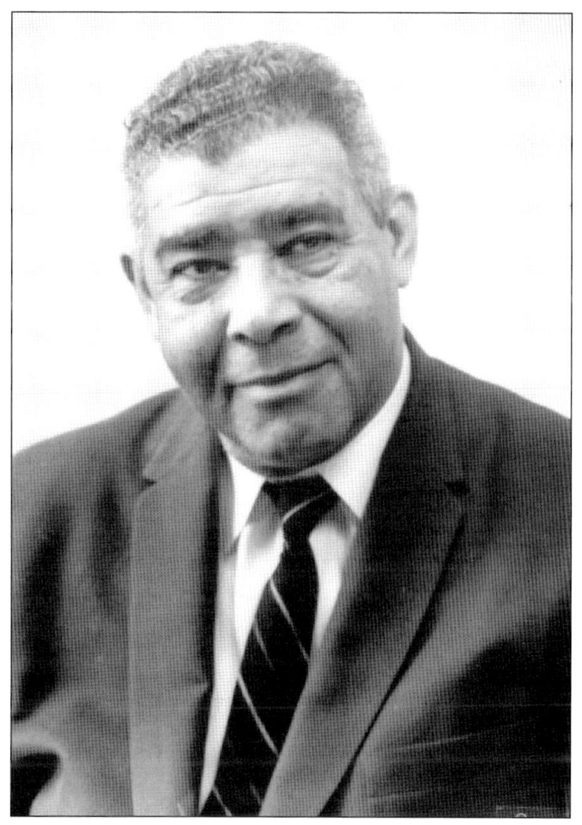

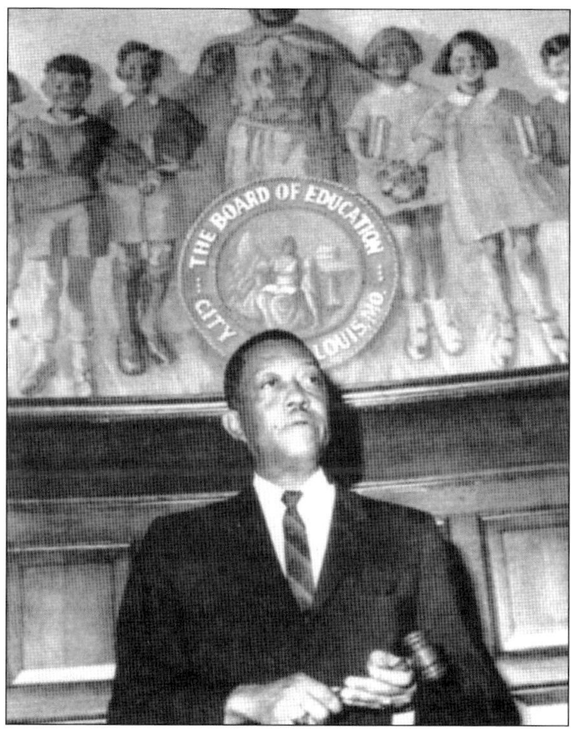

In 1959, Rev. John Hicks became the first African American to be elected to a citywide office when he won a seat on the St. Louis School Board. Ernest Calloway hoped that this step would not only allow for greater participation in education, but also act as a beacon to others to pursue public service. (Courtesy of the St. Louis Mercantile Library, UMSL.)

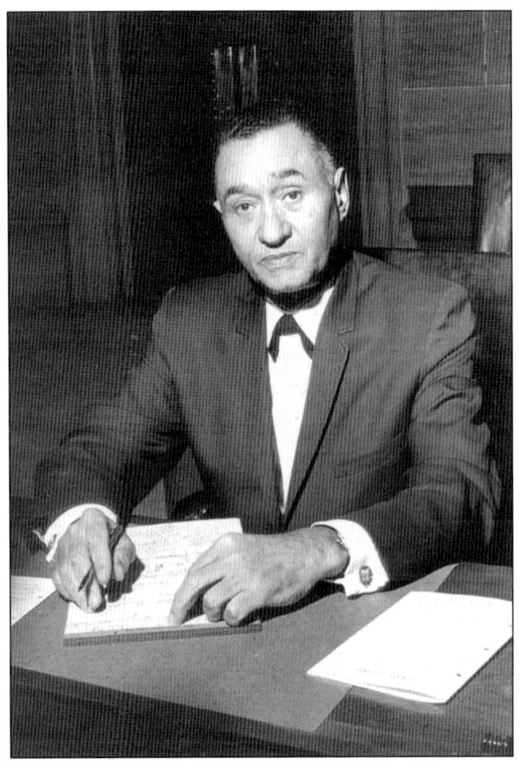

In 1960, with Ernest Calloway's help, Theodore McNeal became the first African American elected to serve in the Missouri Senate. Senator McNeal was active in union politics, having served on the staff of the Brotherhood of Sleeping Car Porters and Maids Union. He later served on the University of Missouri Board of Curators and was president of the board of St. Louis police commissioners. (Courtesy of Betty Wheeler.)

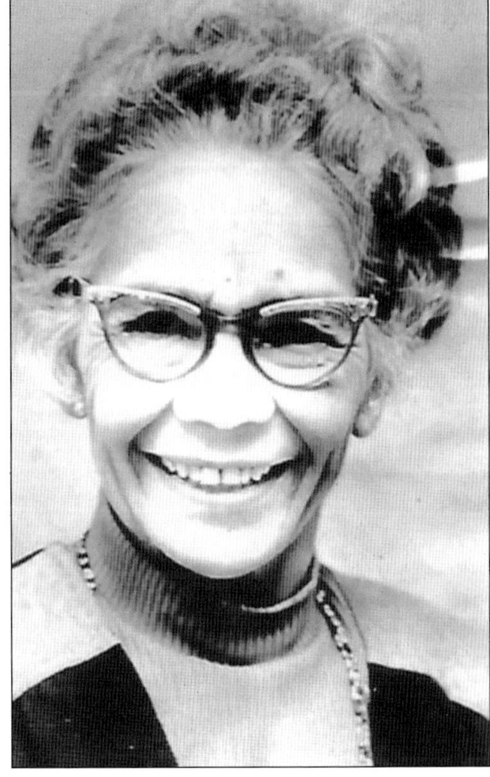

DeVerne Calloway, with the help of her husband serving as her campaign manager, became the first black woman to serve in the Missouri state legislature. Calloway was the first sponsor of favorable housing law. The DeVerne Lee Calloway Award recognizes outstanding female leaders in Missouri. She and her husband published the *Citizen Crusader*, which was later named the *New Citizen*. (Courtesy of the St. Louis Mercantile Library, UMSL.)

After the passage of the 1960 Voting Rights legislation, the National Urban League and the local Urban League planned massive voter registration activities. Pictured here are voter registration canvassers. (Courtesy of the Urban League of Metropolitan St. Louis.)

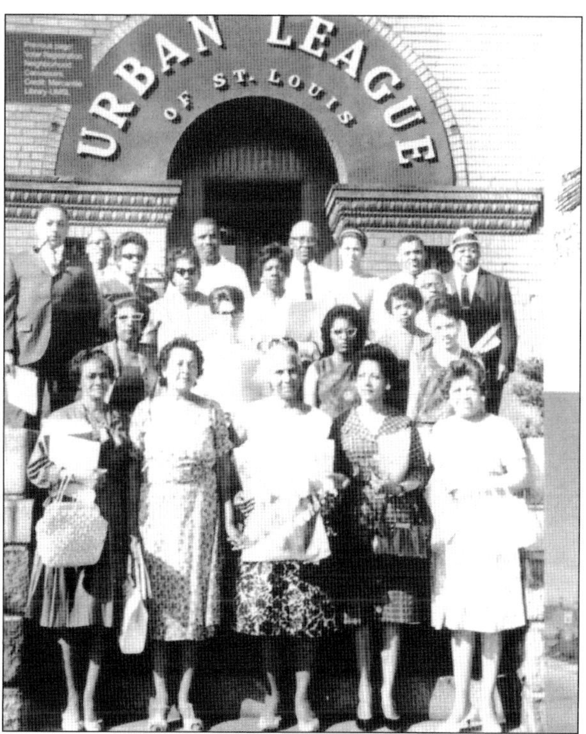

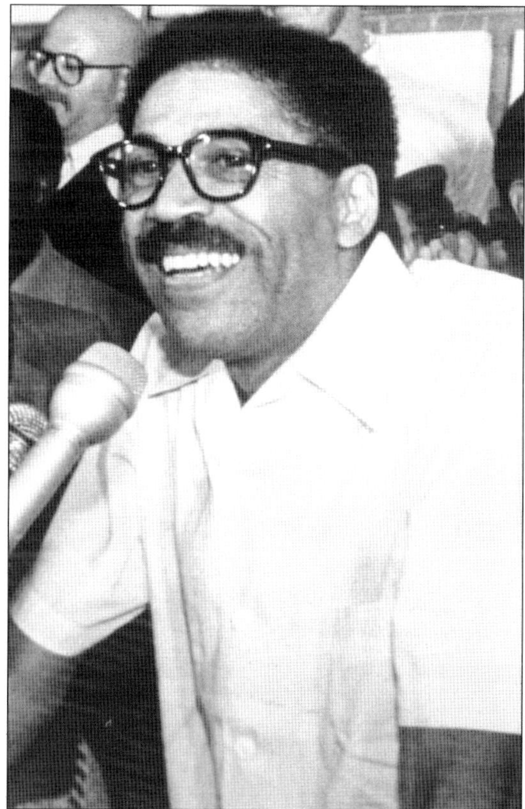

Thanks to strong voter registration and turnout, St. Louis was able to elect William L. Clay Sr. in 1968 as Missouri's first elected black to the US Congress. Earlier, he spent 111 days in jail for his participation in the Jefferson Bank demonstration to hire blacks. (Courtesy of the St. Louis Mercantile Library, UMSL.)

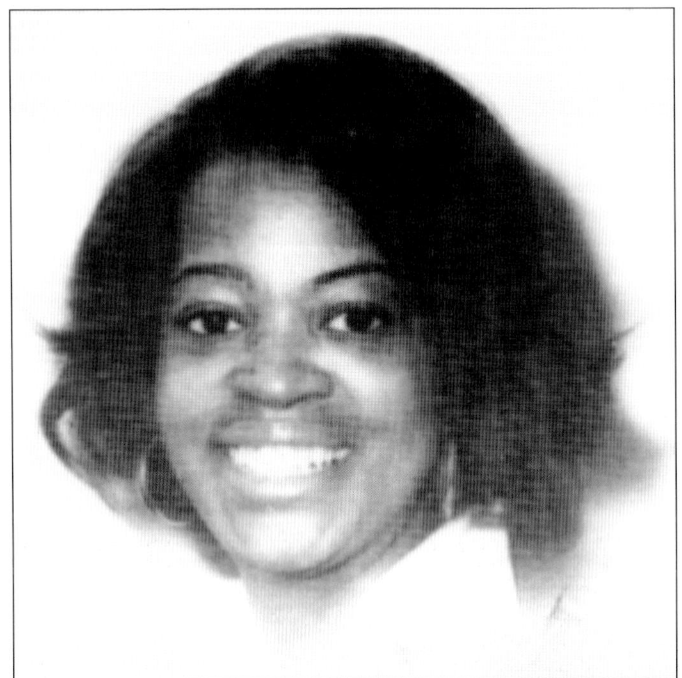

One of the actions that divided St. Louis politicians along racial lines in 1989 was the firing of Billie Boykins, St. Louis license collector. Boykins was the first black female elected to a citywide political office. The St. Louis Board of Aldermen voted 16-13, mostly along racial lines, to strip Boykins of her powers and the 50-odd patronage jobs she controlled. (Courtesy of the St. Louis Mercantile Library, UMSL.)

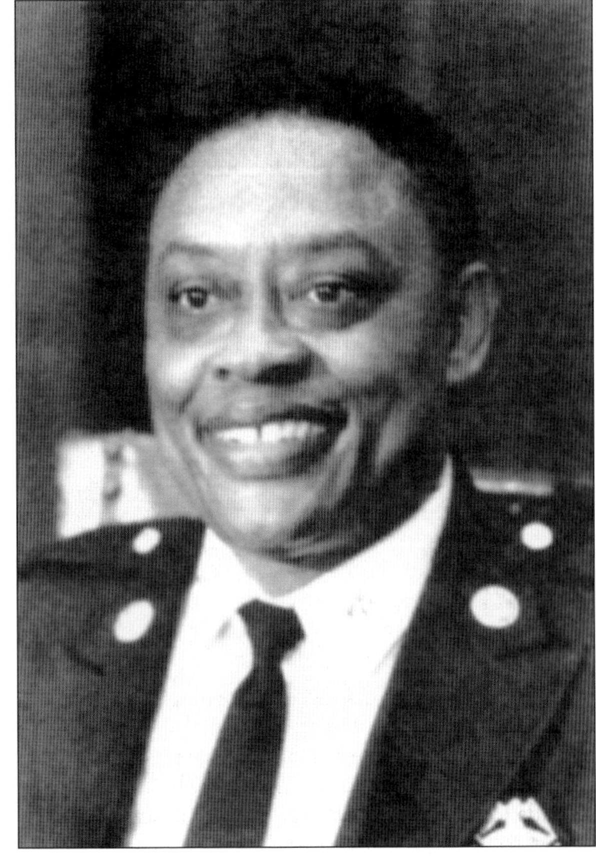

A 2001 event that drew a large protest from the black community was the demotion of Fire Chief Sherman George, the city's first black fire chief. George had been ordered to move on some promotions by the mayor, but he refused, stating that the tests they took did not measure the skills needed for the job. He took the case to court and lost. (Courtesy of the City of St. Louis.)

Six

THE CONTINUING JOURNEY

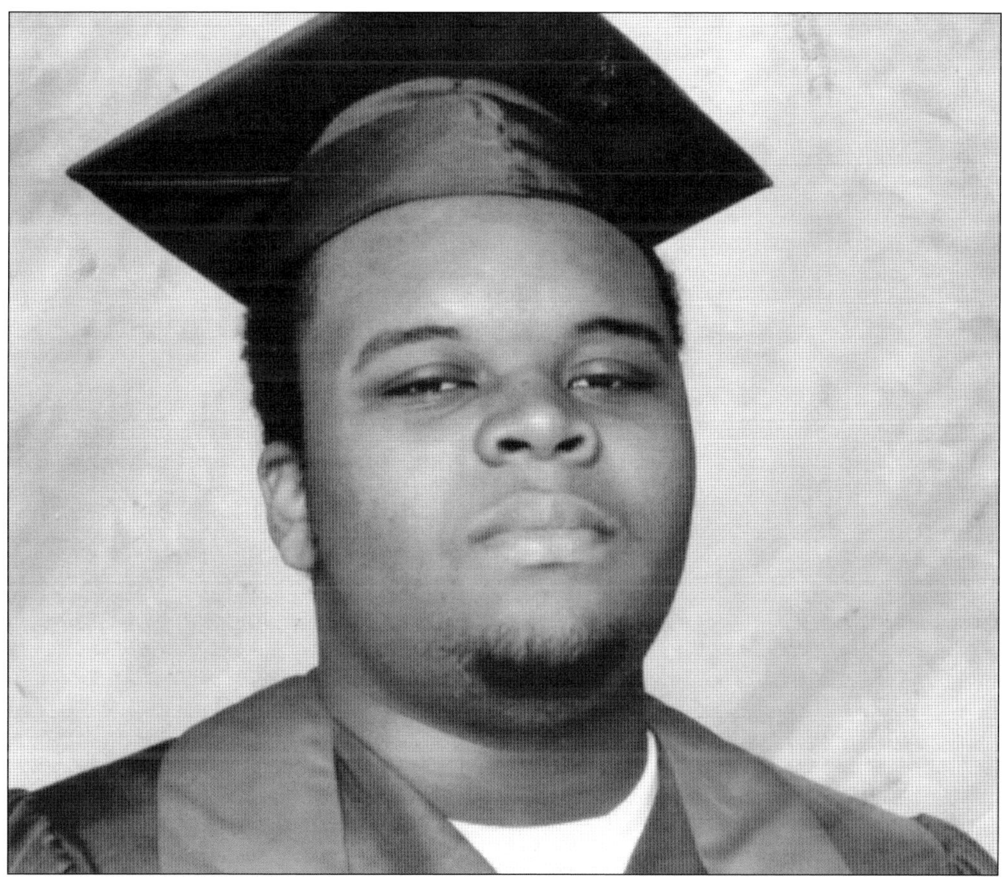

St. Louis was placed in the international spotlight with the killing of Michael Brown, an unarmed teenager, by a white Ferguson, Missouri, police officer in 2014. Brown's death helped spark an international outcry for changes in policing in African American communities. The mantra "Hands Up, Don't Shoot" was echoed around the country and was adopted by celebrities as a sign of solidarity for change. (Courtesy of the Normandy School District.)

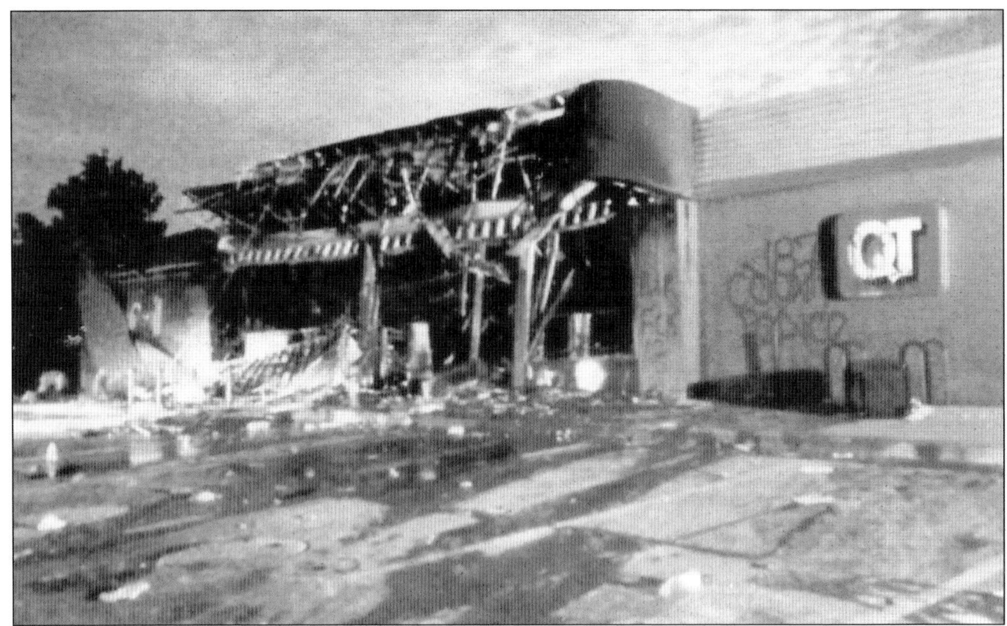

Michael Brown's death brought outrage in the community that ended in the destruction of property and a call for change in community policing. At the time, there were still lingering feelings from the police shootings of Keith Turner (1989), Earl Murray and Ronald Beasley (2000), Torrence Mull (2001), and Anthony Lamar Smith (2011). (Courtesy of the Urban League of Metropolitan St. Louis.)

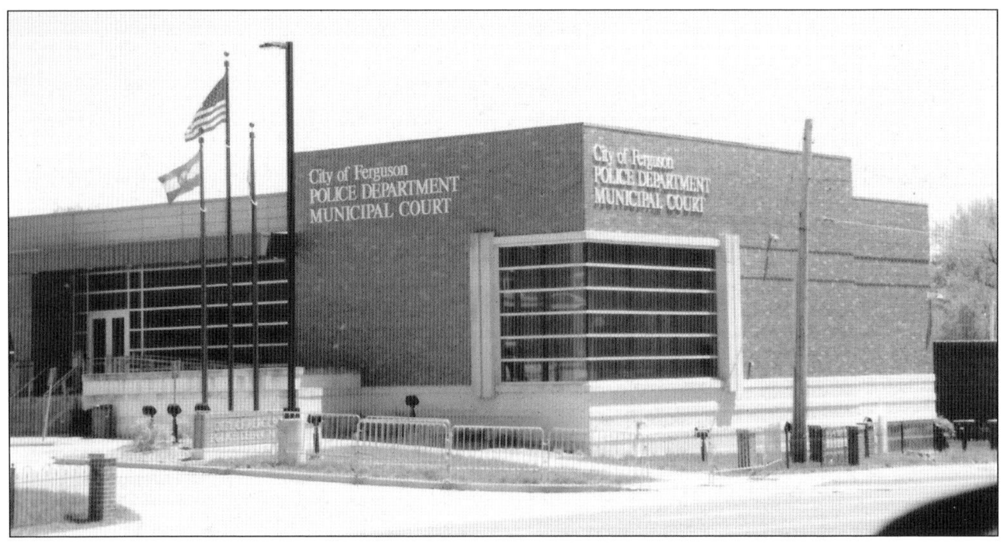

A close look at the Ferguson Police Department and other small north county communities found that their governments were operating off fines collected from those least able to pay. The operations were viewed as an ongoing pipeline to prison for the poor because of their inability to pay their fines. (Photograph by John A. Wright Sr.)

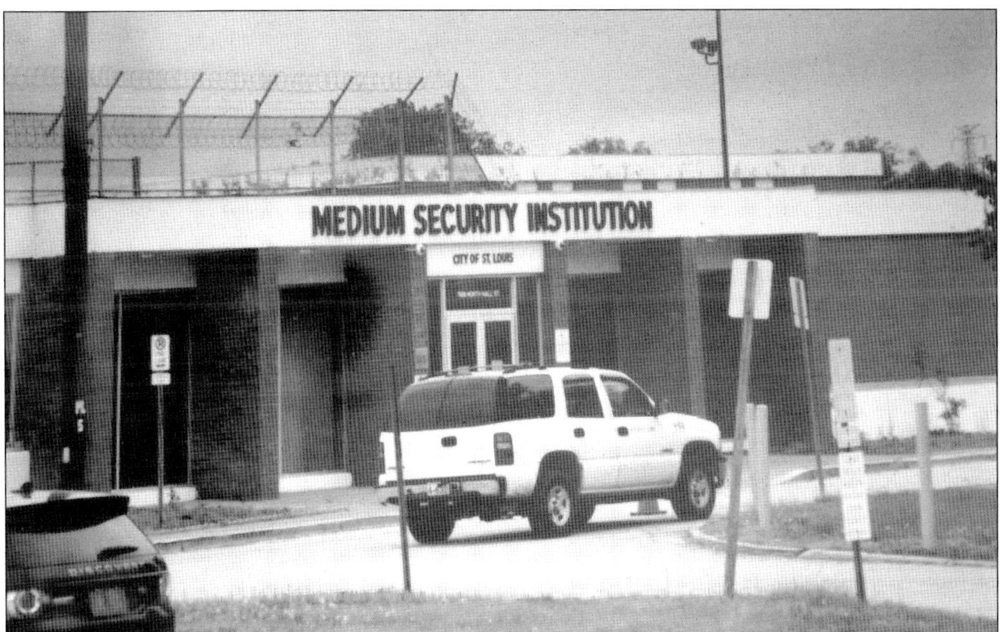

The Ferguson uprising led to a call for the closing of the St. Louis City Workhouse. Most of the inmates were there because of their inability to post bond, causing them to be detained until their court date. The Workhouse was defunded in the city's 2022 budget. (Photograph by John A. Wright Jr.)

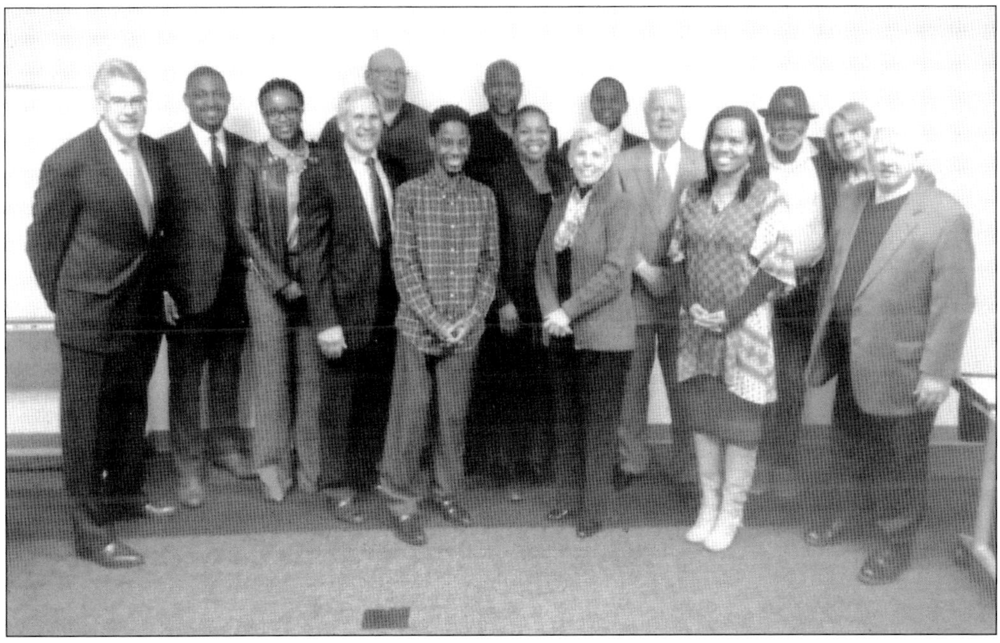
The death of Michael Brown Jr. came to symbolize racial strife and inequality in America. To assist in moving the area forward, the Missouri governor asked a group of regional leaders, the Ferguson Commission, pictured here, to study the situation and provide a path forward. (Courtesy of Shirley Brown.)

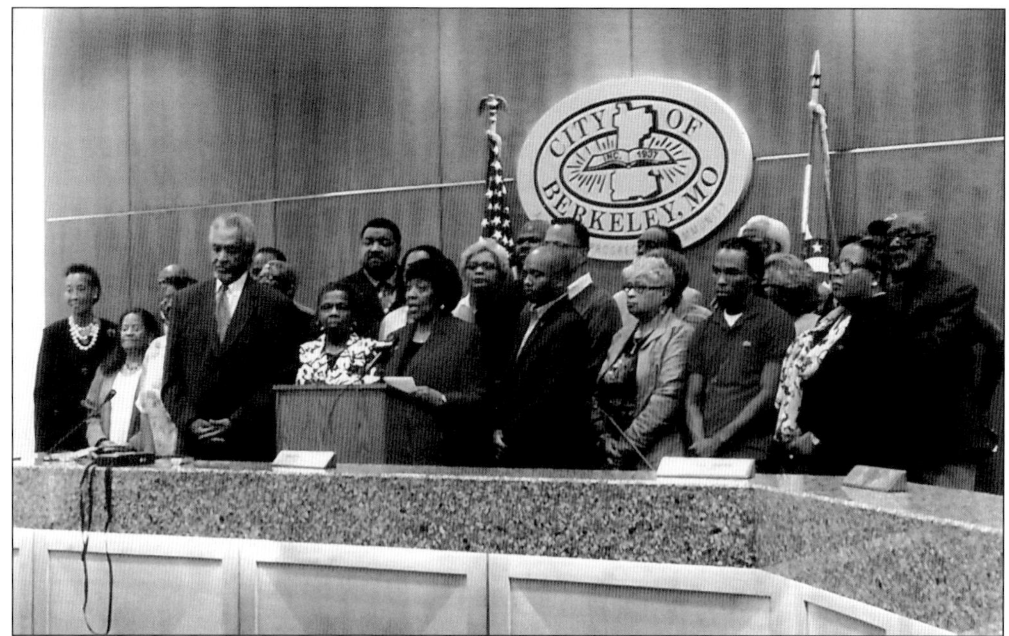

Pictured here are members of the Fannie Lou Hamer Coalition of St. Louis County composed of elected democratic officials whose members are unified in their shared civic interests to represent the community, uphold what is right and necessary, and build toward true representation in all areas of public life. (Courtesy of Hazel Erby.)

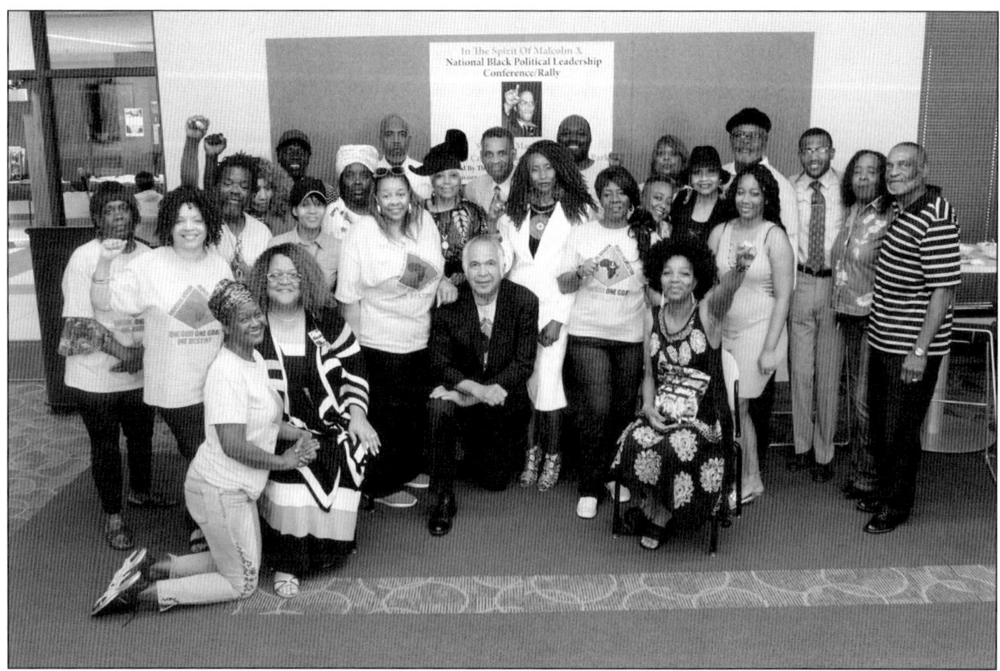

The Universal African Peoples Organization, pictured here, was one of the many organizations involved in the community efforts for unity after the killing of Michael Brown. They also provided food assistance during the COVID-19 pandemic. (Courtesy of Zaki Baruti.)

UNITED STATES DISTRICT COURT
EASTERN DISTRICT OF MISSOURI
EASTERN DIVISION

MISSOURI STATE CONFERENCE OF THE NATIONAL ASSOCIATION FOR THE ADVANCEMENT OF COLORED PEOPLE, et al.,	)	
Plaintiffs,	)	
vs.	)	Case No. 4:14 CV 2077 RWS
FERGUSON-FLORISSANT SCHOOL DISTRICT, et al.,	)	
Defendants.	)	

In 2018, the NAACP won its suit against the Ferguson-Florissant School District on the election of school board members. The district was part of a three-district merger, and its present system did not provide adequate representation for the minority community. The Supreme Court agreed with the lower court's decision that a change was needed in the election process. (Courtesy of Dr. Art McCoy.)

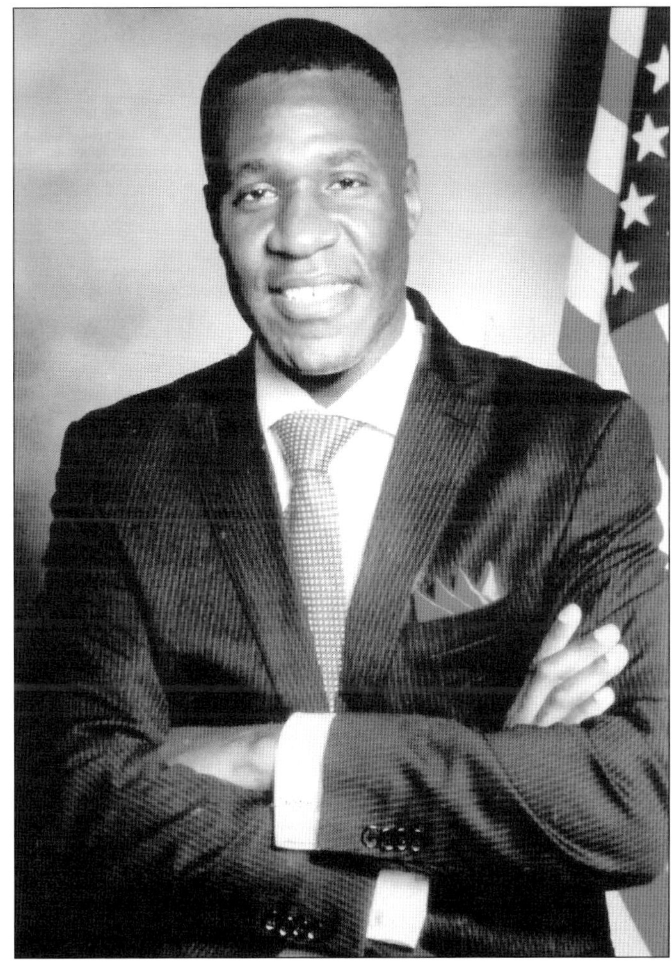

In 2014, the Ferguson-Florissant School District ran into conflicts with its first black superintendent, Dr. Art McCoy. He wanted to provide transportation to African American students from poor-performing districts under a plan authorized by the state, but the board objected. Earlier, the board ran into community objections over its desire to name a new school after a slave owner. (Courtesy of Dr. Art McCoy.)

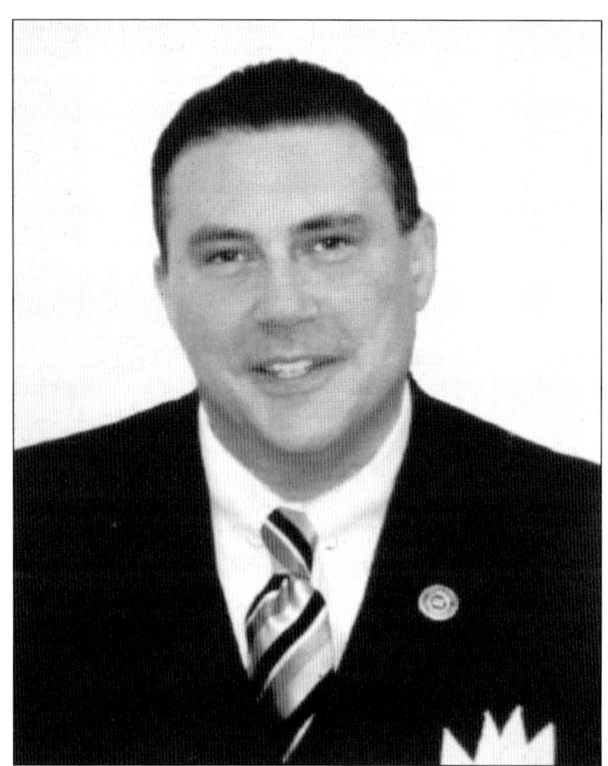

A great deal of credit goes to president and CEO Michael McMillan of the Urban League of Metropolitan St. Louis for program development after the Ferguson uprising. He was responsible for the Ferguson Empowerment Center and programs designed to address the many pressing needs of the community. (Courtesy of the Urban League of Metropolitan St. Louis.)

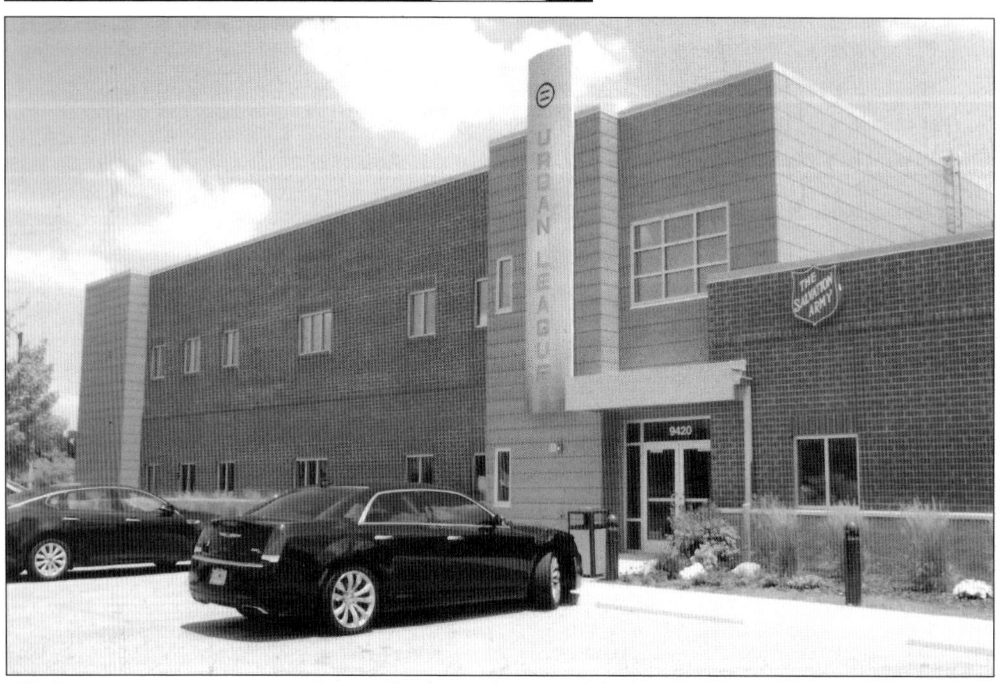

The Ferguson Empowerment Center, built on the site of the burned-out Quiktrip store, was the brainchild of Michael McMillan. It became the home of the Save Our Sons program, designed to help unemployed and underemployed African American men and others living in Ferguson and the surrounding communities. (Photograph by John A. Wright Sr.)

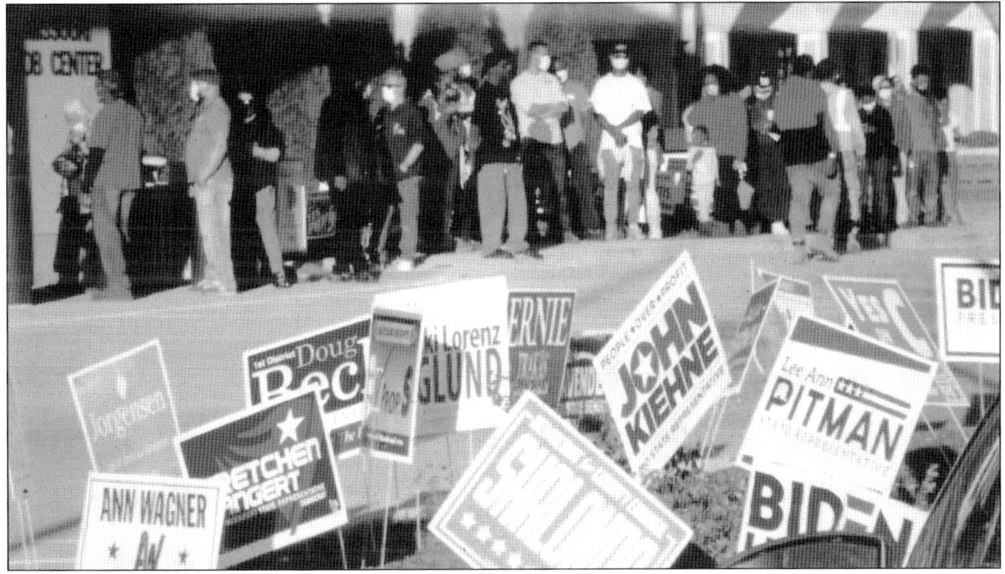

The killing of unarmed African Americans led to a call for more voter registration and voting across the country. A strong call for reform came after a judge acquitted Jason Shockey, a white police officer who shot a black man. Shockley said he thought the suspect was reaching for his gun; however, only Shockley's DNA was found on the gun. (Photograph by John A. Wright Jr.)

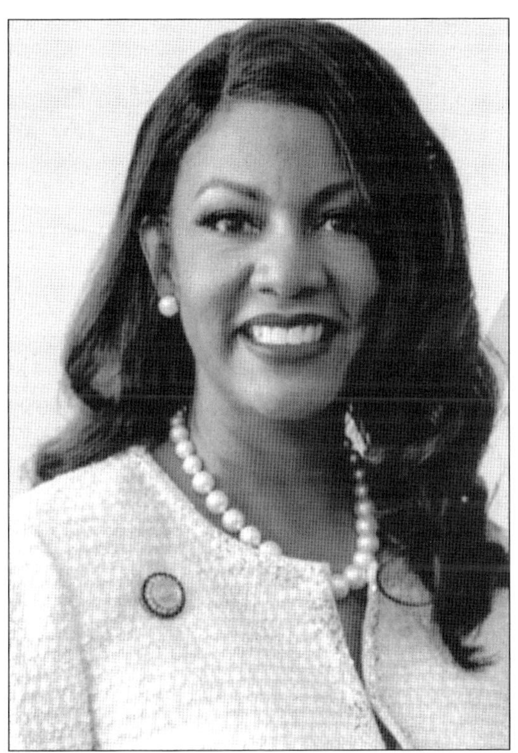

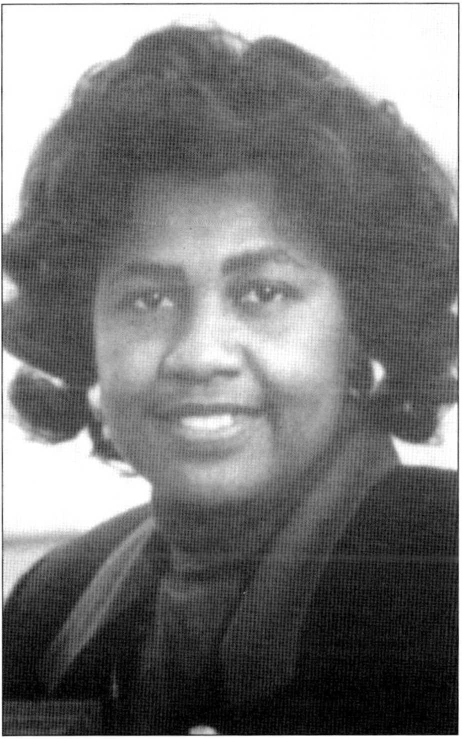

Because of strong voter turnout, St. Louis was able to elect its first black female mayor, Tishaura Jones (left), and reelect comptroller Darlene Green (right), as well as circuit attorney Kimberley Garner. (Left, courtesy of Tishaura Jones; right, courtesy of the City of St. Louis.)

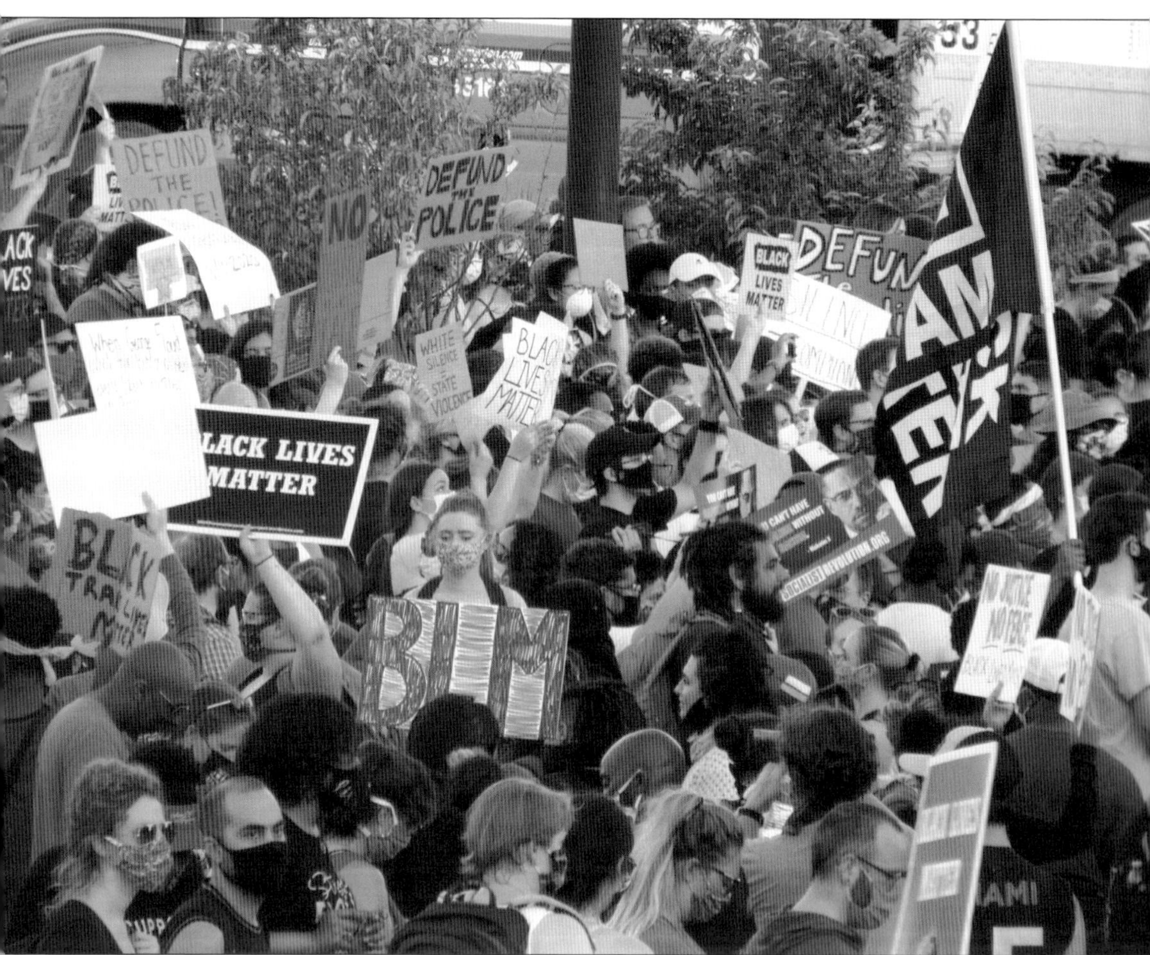

In 2021, as Missouri celebrates its 200th anniversary and reflects on the African American struggle over the same period, it is clear many barriers have come down. It can also be seen that many obstacles are remaining. Unarmed blacks are still being killed by police. There is still a need for equal justice, decent housing, quality health care, reduced unemployment, underemployment, quality education, and access to quality food. The destruction of black communities for commercial use in Clayton, Richmond Heights, Brentwood, Compton Hill, Kinloch, Robertson, sections of Meacham Park, Mill Creek, and southern Elmwood has taken its toll. The road to equal justice and access is a long journey and one that must and will be traveled with determination until victory is won. (Courtesy of John A. Wright Jr.)

INDEX

Discover Thousands of Local History Books Featuring Millions of Vintage Images

Arcadia Publishing, the leading local history publisher in the United States, is committed to making history accessible and meaningful through publishing books that celebrate and preserve the heritage of America's people and places.

Find more books like this at
www.arcadiapublishing.com

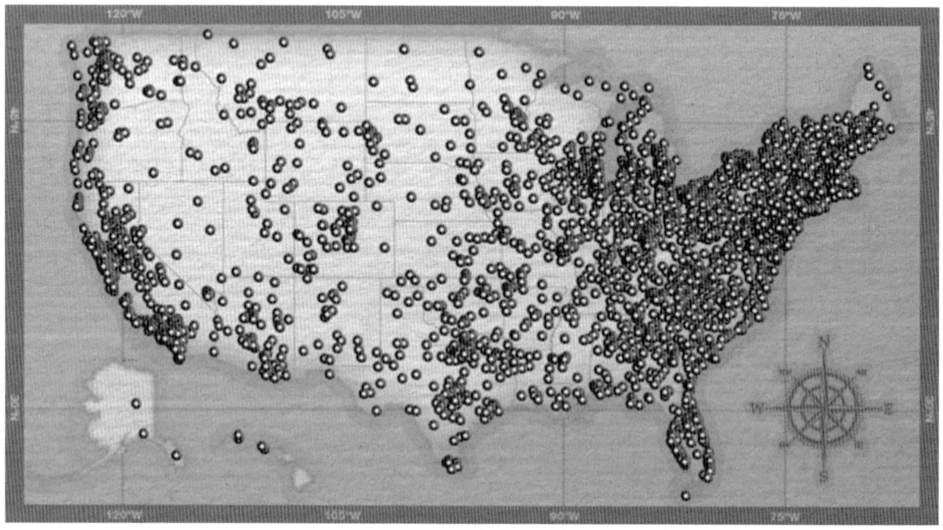

Search for your hometown history, your old stomping grounds, and even your favorite sports team.

Consistent with our mission to preserve history on a local level, this book was printed in South Carolina on American-made paper and manufactured entirely in the United States. Products carrying the accredited Forest Stewardship Council (FSC) label are printed on 100 percent FSC-certified paper.

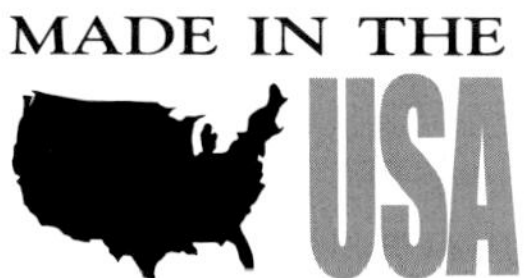